The Physics
and Astronomy
of Science Fiction

The Physics and Astronomy of Science Fiction

Understanding Interstellar Travel, Teleportation, Time Travel, Alien Life and Other Genre Fixtures

STEVEN D. BLOOM

McFarland & Company, Inc., Publishers
Jefferson, North Carolina

LIBRARY OF CONGRESS CATALOGUING-IN-PUBLICATION DATA

Names: Bloom, Steven D., 1965– author.
Title: The physics and astronomy of science fiction : understanding interstellar travel, teleportation, time travel, alien life and other genre fixtures / Steven D. Bloom.
Description: Jefferson, North Carolina : McFarland & Company, Inc., Publishers, 2016. | Includes bibliographical references and index.
Identifiers: LCCN 2016006850 | ISBN 9780786470532 (softcover : acid free paper) ∞
Subjects: LCSH: Science fiction—History and criticism. | Physics in literature. | Astronomy in literature. | Science fiction films—History and criticism. | Science fiction television programs—History and criticism. | Science in motion pictures.
Classification: LCC PN3433.6 .B58 2016 | DDC 809.3/8762—dc23
LC record available at http://lccn.loc.gov/2016006850

BRITISH LIBRARY CATALOGUING DATA ARE AVAILABLE

ISBN (print) 978-0-7864-7053-2
ISBN (ebook) 978-1-4766-2399-3

© 2016 Steven D. Bloom. All rights reserved

No part of this book may be reproduced or transmitted in any form or by any means, electronic or mechanical, including photocopying or recording, or by any information storage and retrieval system, without permission in writing from the publisher.

Front cover image © 2016 Sylphe-7/iStock

Printed in the United States of America

McFarland & Company, Inc., Publishers
  Box 611, Jefferson, North Carolina 28640
  www.mcfarlandpub.com

To my wife, Jennifer,
and our daughter, Aviva,
with love

Table of Contents

Preface   1

1. Introductory Physics   5
2. Introduction to Astronomy   25
3. The Physics of Space Travel   63
4. Universes, Dimensions and Space   99
5. Time Travel   121
6. Computers, Robots, Androids and Cyborgs   141
7. Teleportation and Replication   160
8. Weaponry   167
9. Extraterrestrial Life   180
10. Super-Human Powers   204

Chapter Notes   217
Bibliography   221
Index   229

Preface

Science fiction films, television, books and short stories have been popular for decades and have, since their onset, relied on science and technology for their core concepts. With rocketing to the stars, time travel, planet busting weapons and sentient robots, it's no wonder that they especially have relied on topics from physics and astronomy, and often from the cutting edge of these fields. Many fans have shown an interest in which concepts are possible (such as interstellar travel, time travel, teleportation or androids). In addition some fans have shown an interest in the basics, such as the background physics behind how a rocket works or how a star creates energy. Many books have been published on a select few of these topics (such as Michio Kaku's *Physics of the Impossible* and *Physics of the Future*), but usually only have a couple of specific examples from science fiction (often just from *Star Trek*). Several more comprehensive books have been published on these topics over the years. One of these is over 30 years old and needed serious updating in both the physics and the popular cultural references (Amit Goswami's *Cosmic Dancers*). An excellent recent book, especially for those with a solid introductory physics and mathematics background is Charles Adler's *Wizards, Aliens and Starships*. His discussion of the physics of flight and space travel is particularly extensive. However, he is not reserved in placing equations (including calculus) directly in the main text, so this may be a difficult text for the more casual reader. Another very recent offering, Barry Luokalla's *Exploring Science through Science Fiction*, is intended as a college textbook and is a little more general than what I have intended (touching on some other sciences, such as biology, which I only discuss minimally in this work).

So, where do I fit in to this picture? On July 20, 1969, on my fourth birthday, my parents unexpectedly placed my twin brother and me in front of our family television set, which at the time was a well-worn black and white model. Though, like many pre-school children, I didn't mind watching television, this was something other than what I was used to. We were watching a grainy transmission of something. I didn't quite understand what I was watching, but my mother did impart on me that this was a very important moment. I am sure that at the time I was more interested in birthday cake and what presents I had received (and, no doubt, being concerned that my brother didn't receive anything better than what I had gotten). However, I think a seed of an idea was definitely planted that day. It was shortly afterward that I began to read my older brother's copy of the *Golden Book of Science*. This book was filled with illustrations of bugs, plants, and even dinosaurs. However, I was most intrigued by the pictures of planets and galaxies. I began to understand at this time that astronomers were the people who spend their time observing these objects and drawing conclusions about them. I knew then that I wanted to be an astronomer.

From there, I went along the usual path for people interested in this field, studying a great deal of physics and mathematics, as well as astronomy, in high school, college and up to the point of receiving my Ph.D. in Astronomy in 1994. I was lucky to further work on my research during several postdoctoral appointments, but as excited as I was about some of my findings, especially during my time at NASA's Goddard Space Flight Center, I wanted to also spend some time teaching and directing students in research. Luckily, I was able to find my current job as a professor at Hampden-Sydney College. There I have been especially grateful to teach two interdisciplinary seminars, combining various topics with the physics of science fiction. The first of these was combined with philosophy and taught with Dr. Marc Hight and the second was combined with literature and taught with Dr. Steele Nowlin. Shortly after the first seminar concluded in 2003, I began to think about writing this book, but I did not think I had the time then to commit to it. I felt the same way after the second course was taught (coinciding with the birth of our daughter). Then after a visit by science fiction author and critic John Kenneth Muir to Hampden-Sydney I felt energized to begin this project.

I feel I need to say a little bit about what this book is meant to be. I hope to explain some complex topics that often appear in science fiction, while always referring to some of the examples from your favorite books, television, and film. If you are very familiar with physics and astronomy, you may be able to skip some of the first two chapters, or at least skim over the parts that are less familiar to you. It is certainly not meant to be an encyclopedia of science fiction, and not even a thorough listing of the science fiction that touches on the physics and astronomy mentioned in this book. It is also not meant to be a critical history of science fiction or any of the individual works touched upon, though I do make some critiques of my own throughout. So, though I hope I have presented many rich examples, I am sure I have inadvertently left out a number of excellent works. I also do not intend to pick apart your favorite movies or television shows. Every such television show or film was meant to be a creative and entertaining enterprise. In most cases, science was meant to take a back seat (at least in the end, no matter what the intentions) more or less from the beginning. I cannot fault writers and producers for that too much, since they can only create something that people will actually watch (or they will be unemployed), and sometimes that means making compromises.

In addition to the individuals already mentioned above, I'd especially like to thank my wife Jennifer for her support and our daughter Aviva for her infectious laughter filling our home. I am indebted to my parents and my brothers (and their families) for supporting my interests from a young age. Lastly, I'd like to thank all of my students, past and present, for helping me to understand how I can best explain complex topics.

Chapter 1

Introductory Physics

The discoveries in physics over the last millennium, and especially in the last 200 years or so make up a vast body of work, and certainly too much to cover in detail here; however, it is possible to give a sense of the some of the most important, critical themes of physics, as well as some of the most recent discoveries and their relevance to the rest of physics. Rather than give a crash course in all of physics, my intention is to bring up these important themes, and as I am going along, point to how they have been effectively used in science fiction.

Forces

Thought of in the simplest terms, a force is any "push" or "pull" on an object. But what causes a force? Are forces needed for motion? Though the nature of forces and motion has been studied since ancient times (Aristotle devoted much of his writings to discussing motion), true understanding of velocity, acceleration, force and their interrelationship was not understood well until Newton worked out the mathematics in detail. Newton devised his famous laws of motion in his 1687 work *Principia Mathematica* and was able to quantify forces with his second law that relates force, acceleration and mass. Furthermore, we will discover soon that since forces are needed to set objects in motion, the energy of motion will be intimately related to whatever forces initiated that motion. Firstly, Newton states that objects in motion will stay in motion unless acted upon by outside forces. Think about throwing a ball. The reason why the path starts to curve is that an outside force, gravity, is starting to act on it. If there had been no force of gravity at all, the ball would continue on its initial path forever. Also, if we think about driving a car on icy roads, the reason why the car has trouble stopping and turning is because the car's tires are experiencing a much lower outside force of friction than what the road under normal conditions would provide, which is usually depended upon to make these maneuvers. Thinking along these lines, the reason why you can sometimes come to a stop in your car when traveling on a long highway exit ramp, even without putting on the brakes (it's not advised to experiment with this) is because you have experienced enough of the outside force of friction on the car's tires. In addition, Newton said that an object at rest will stay at rest unless moved by an outside force. This makes sense, since there is no reason for anything to move unless something is pushing or pulling it. Therefore, a coffee cup on your desktop will likely sit there eternally unless a coffee drinker disturbs its slumber. Likewise, an object in the middle of interstellar space will stay put unless something collides with it, or the gravity of another object affects its trajectory. Newton's Third Law states that for every action there is an equal and opposite reaction. An excellent case of this of this law is a rocket. The hot gases get pushed out the back at high speed, and the rocket gets propelled forward at a high speed. In fact, as we discuss in Chapter 3, most of our concepts for rockets, even those proposed for the far future are based on this principle, and are called *reaction rockets*. A hunter would experience a similar effect when feeling recoil of a gun that has just been fired. Likewise a skateboarder will experience this when he uses one foot to push off from the ground in order to start going forward. In the 2014 science fiction film *Gravity*, one of the astronauts is trying to get closer to a space station where she can find a rescue capsule that will potentially get her back to Earth. By this point, she no longer has an active jet-pack, but she realizes that a fire extinguisher will crudely do the same job. In this case, the gases from the extinguisher act in the same way a rocket would, so if she can aim the nozzle in a direction opposite to where she wants to be, it can get her to where she wants to go. The film also shows correctly that there will be some complications. For instance, if she is tumbling a bit and the nozzle is wobbling, it gets difficult to aim as well as you'd like. However, an extinguisher is unlikely to give her a speed much more than several meters per second before the gases run out. So, if time is of the essence, this technique may not be effective if the target is much more than 100 meters away. However, if you have time, and good aim, it could work. You'll want to remember this for the next time you're stranded during a spacewalk. Unfortunately, as Daniel Overbye points out some of the detailed orbital mechanics is contrived. At one point they are trying to get from the Hubble Space Telescope to the International Space Station. These are in drastically different orbits and cannot be accessed with a space shuttle or similar vehicle by turning on the thrusters and hopping over (Overbye, "Astronaut and Writer at the Movies" 2013). Isaac Asimov actually had a character pull off a very similar maneuver about 60 years earlier. In his *Lucky Starr and the Pirates of the Asteroids*, Lucky is at one point ejected into space. He realizes that he will eventually die if he just sits out in space and lets his oxygen run out. So, instead, he decides to vent his oxygen supply, using it much the same way as we described above for the fire extinguisher. This pushes him back toward the ship with just enough oxygen to survive.

Fundamental Forces of Nature

Though any physics text will discuss many types of forces (air drag, buoyancy, friction, etc.) all forces fundamentally boil down to being interactions among submicroscopic particles (either individually or in aggregate), and these particles can only interact via four forces (or maybe a fifth force which we will contemplate later). On the largest scales, we have gravity, the interaction between any two or more objects of any mass. Going back to the 16th and 17th centuries, both Galileo and Kepler, who were contemporaries and in contact with one another, made some headway in understanding gravitational interaction, without ever putting a label on the interactions they studied. Galileo conducted many experiments, and understood that objects accelerate towards the Earth at the same rate, regardless of mass, a fact that would help Newton draw up a general theory of gravity. Though the story regarding Galileo dropping balls from the top of the Tower of Pisa is likely apocryphal, he did indeed roll objects down inclined planes to garner similar information, thus inspiring 400 years of admittedly dull introductory physics textbook problems involving inclined planes. In addition, Kepler, using details of geometry, accurately described the orbits of planets and the connection to them orbiting the Sun (recall that this was not yet an "obvious" fact about the eponymous Solar System). However, it was really Newton, as part of his general codification of forces, who really explained gravity in detail. Actually, gravity acts on all distance scales among objects of any mass, and is always attractive, but as we see in the chapter endnotes, for, say, two people who are standing one meter apart, the force of gravity is about one billion times weaker than the force of the Earth acting on one of these people (keeping them grounded, so to speak).[1] Therefore, we know that for typical everyday objects in our experience, gravity (aside from the Earth's gravity) will not play a role. However, on much larger scales (say, about the size of our Solar System and larger) gravity can be responsible for tremendous releases of energy, such as when matter falls on to a black hole. In addition, gravity has a critical role in the life cycle of all stars, as well as the overall fate of the Universe. The forces of electricity and magnetism work on smaller scales, but can be quite strong on these scales. The smallest subatomic particles can be positively charged, negatively charged or neutral. Opposites will attract, like charges will repel, and neutrals will not have any electric force. Like gravity, electrical forces drop off as the square of the distance (so, for instance, an electron and a proton have an attractive force that is more than 10^{38} times greater than gravity at a separation of about one millionth of a meter). Separately, physicists began to understand magnetism in 19th century. At first, this certainly seemed to be a separate matter from electricity, though the magnetic force also drops off with the square of the distance. At first, there would seem to be no connection between the magnetic properties of lodestone, the Earth as a whole, and the attraction or repulsion of charged materials. However, it was soon realized experimentally and put into a theoretical framework by James Maxwell that electric fields changing with time could create magnetic fields and vice-versa. With these conclusions, in the 1850s we had our first unification of fundamental forces, that is, the realization that though these forces acts as separate agents, they are two sides to a similar process and are ultimately connected. On smaller scales we still experience the nuclear forces, both the weak and strong forces. The weak force was realized when it was observed that unstable nuclei were releasing electrons and also alpha particles (helium nuclei). There had to be a force responsible for releasing these particles, eventually called the weak force due to its magnitude being weaker than electricity and magnetism. In the 1970s it was theorized by Weinberg and Salam that the weak force could be unified with electro-magnetism so long as the weak force had an associated field called a *gauge field*, similar to the way electro-magnetic forces interact with particles in a field. This gauge field is then mediated by particles interacting in a field (the W and Z); however, unlike with electricity and magnetism, these particles have significant mass, whereas the electromagnetic fields are mediated by massless photons (and likewise it's thought that gravity is mediated by massless graviton). In the usual theoretical framework for other fields, fields are governed by a symmetry that is mediated by massless particles. For the weak gauge fields, this problem of particles with mass is resolved with the concept of symmetry breaking. That is, symmetry would have to hold for all forces in order for them to be all mediated by massless particles. However, at some point in the evolution of the early Universe, this symmetry was broken, and some forces are mediated by particles with high mass. The presence of a Higgs field is responsible for this symmetry breaking that not only endows the W and Z particles with mass but all particles with mass (Randall, *Knocking at Heaven's Door* 2011). Fortunately, one ramification of the presence of the Higgs field is the prediction of the massive Higgs boson, which has just now possibly been detected (and won Higgs and Englert the 2013 Nobel Prize in Physics), giving yet more credence to the Standard Model, regardless of some of its deficiencies. Why we would have this symmetry breaking (and thus particles with mass, and why they have the specific masses they do) is still an open question in the Standard Model of particles physics and the unification of forces. Parts of this theoretical framework were confirmed by the detection of the W and Z particles starting in 1973, winning Weinberg, Salaam and Glashow the Nobel Prize in 1979. In addition, it was known for at least a decade prior that a much stronger force had to be the glue that keeps nuclei together, both responsible for keeping neutrons and protons together in a nucleus and for keeping together the constituent quarks that make up neutrons and protons individually. The concept of gauge fields that developed to unify the electro-weak forces could potentially be used to unify quantum chromodynamics (the strong force as applied to quarks) with the electro-weak force. This theoretical framework of a super-symmetric force calls for a unification of all forces at immense energies, essentially the kind that never could be achieved by man. Fortunately though, these theories made other predictions including the decay of protons. Though the decay time of a proton is immense (that is, many times longer than the known lifetime of the Universe), we know that the Universe has approximately 10^{80} protons so the chances of seeing any decay, if they really do decay, is possible. To date though, nobody has seen clear signs of proton decay, thus dealing a blow to the first super-symmetric theories. However, without a single theoretical framework or any experimental confirmation of this unification, some competing theories, such as string theory, have developed. So, though to a large extent, these forces have been unified, there is still the missing piece of the strong force and gravity remaining completely elusive, and much thought has been put into why that would be (Davies 1984).

Conservation of Energy

Perhaps the most important aspect of physics is the conservation laws. These laws dictate which physical quantities cannot increase or decrease over time for a closed system (say, a group of colliding objects): they must stay constant. One of the most important of these principles is the conservation of energy. That is to say, that energy cannot appear from nowhere (though people may claim they have invented a perpetual motion machine, it's always going to be impossible because it will always violate conservation of energy). The kinetic energy (energy of motion) of an object had to have originally come from some form of potential energy. We can think of potential energy as a form of stored energy an object has (Silver 1998). A book sitting on the edge of a table has stored energy related to the force of gravity from Earth acting on it. Another form of potential energy can come from chemical or nuclear bonds between subatomic particles. If an object (such as the book on the table) "loses" energy, it must go somewhere else, either as kinetic energy of the other object, or sound energy, radiation, etc. For instance, a falling ball starts its path with no kinetic energy. All of its energy at the top of its path is potential energy (the energy associated with being in the gravitational field of the Earth). At the bottom of its path, just before hitting the ground, all of the ball's energy is in the form of kinetic energy. An example we often see in science fiction is an asteroid collision with the Earth. At its farthest point from Earth (and probably the Sun as well), the velocity of the asteroid is relatively small, and more of the energy is in the form of potential energy. By the time the asteroid comes through our atmosphere, most of this energy has been transformed into kinetic energy, and then eventually, as the asteroid will heat up from friction in the atmosphere, and then finally explode on impact (releasing thermal energy, sound energy, etc.).

In the 1970s British science fiction series *Space: 1999*, the Moon is shot out of Earth orbit by a nuclear explosion on the far side of the Moon. At the basic level of energy conservation laws, this seems possible. That is, a large amount of explosive nuclear energy is converted to the kinetic energy of the Moon. In reality though, as Isaac Asimov pointed out in his *New York Times* op-ed piece regarding the television series (Muir, *Exploring Space: 1999* 1997), the amount of energy needed to get the Moon to escape Earth orbit would be about the same as the amount of energy it takes to break the Moon apart! Therefore, if you try to get the Moon to escape Earth's orbit, you will probably need to explode the Moon. Furthermore, the magnitude of energy needed to do this is far more than what you would get from conventional nuclear explosions.[2] As is stated in the endnotes, it's not trivial to blow up the Moon, and much more difficult to blow up the Earth. Therefore, though it makes for an interesting Superman origin story when the planet Krypton explodes, it can't be natural instability that would lead to this level of energetics. Very similar scenarios play out in the *Lost in Space* episode "Blast off into Space" and *Space: 1999* episode "The Metamorph." Interestingly, in an earlier Gerry Anderson production, the "Doomed Planet" episode of *Fireball XL5*, they get this concept right. The characters correctly state that if one planet (B) crashes into another (A) and is big enough to destroy Planet A, then Planet A's moon will be expelled into space. Apparently, Anderson and his crew recalled the theme, but not the science. A similar problem arises when considering moving the Earth from its present orbit to one that is significantly closer or further from the Sun, as in the *Twilight Zone* episode "Midnight Sun" and the film *The Day the Earth Caught Fire*. The amount of energy needed to do this would certainly destroy all life on Earth, but would also come close to completely destroying the Earth.

We will see this come up as a common theme throughout this book: Where's the energy? Whether its space travel or time travel or giant planet busting lasers, we will often need tremendous amounts of energy, and the challenge will be in figuring out where to get that energy (a problem often ignored throughout science fiction).

Conservation of Momentum

Another critical conservation law is that of conservation of momentum. Conservation of momentum will manifest itself, for instance, during all collisions. Say we have a car traveling north on the highway, and another car traveling south. If they hit, then what direction will the cars then move in? The simplest analysis shows that the combined cars would then travel in the direction of the car that has the highest combined speed and mass. That is, it is not sufficient for the car to be either heavier or faster, but the product of mass and speed must be higher. There can be more complications, such as the objects not hitting head on (at an angle), or objects breaking apart upon colliding. Another manifestation of this is the conservation of angular momentum. Any object that is changing its rotation or revolution with respect to some given point possesses some angular momentum. Note that this isn't necessarily an object that we normally think of as rotating, but could be as simple as a wrench being turned. When we say that this property is conserved we mean that so long as the object or group of objects being observed does not lose mass, then the total angular momentum of the system must be the same sometime later as it is when we first consider it. This principle explains why a large slowly rotating gas cloud can condense into a much smaller quickly rotating star. This is analogous to an ice skater spinning, and then in order to speed up the rotation, she pulls in her arms. As more of the mass gets distributed closer to the center, the object will speed up. In addition, we can explain in this how gases can start at great distances from a black hole, and swirl inward, dissipating energy all along the path. Also, as stars evolve, their cores become more and more concentrated. The outer layers of the star are lost in the final stages of the stars nuclear burning stage. What's left is a rapidly rotating star, where the core used to be.

Thermodynamics

During the 19th century it became clear that understanding the macroscopic properties of gases in particular would lead to great strides in both practical (and revolutionary) applications such as engines (steam engines first, then internal combustion engines) and understanding the theory of energy. Clearly, as some empirical evidence emerged, the scientists involved (though many were not academics) in these endeavors, such as Sadi Carnot and Lord Kelvin (William Thomson), began to develop and document relationships and laws. These discoveries led to thermodynamics becoming solidified as a valid and separate branch of physics.

The first law of thermodynamics essentially restates the conservation of energy, but it's important to understand that it was not at all a "given" assumption that this would be so. It was perhaps expected, but had to be verified by experiment, and furthermore, developed in the theories of thermodynamics. One of the great triumphs of physics is that wherever investigated, conservation of energy holds, though it has been criticized by a small minority (Sheldrake 2012). In the terminology of thermodynamics this law is usually cast in terms of the total work extracted from any system must be equal to the heat flow from hot to cold. That is, we can't get any extra work that is unaccounted for by heat flow (Kakalios 2005).

However, as Kakalios states, if the first law were it, then we could turn all heat energy into work. The second law puts further restrictions on energy conservation. The second law formally expressed states that entropy can only increase or stay the same for a closed system. First we have to get at the heart of what entropy really is. This law underwent significant evolution as it went from an empirical description of macroscopic observations to something much more specific and theoretical involving statistical mechanics and atomic theory. In interpreting Carnot's early observations of the inherent inefficiency of heat engines, Rudolf Clausius realized that there was a law of nature lurking underneath: that heat only flowed from a hotter body to a colder one, and not vice versa (Carroll, *From Eternity to Here* 2013). Clausius reached this conclusion by realizing that all heat engines give off some waste heat while doing work and thus there are no perfect heat engines that convert heat directly into work. This makes the process of the engine cycle irreversible. It turns out that precisely this law can be re-expressed in terms of a new quantity, entropy. Entropy in this sense was defined in terms of macroscopic observations that correspond to properties of the system (heat and temperature). This was a great triumph, but perhaps an even greater one was that of Boltzmann. He was able to find the equivalent between these macroscopic properties and the microscopic properties of the atom. Furthermore, he concluded that it wasn't necessary to find the exact properties of every atom in a gas. It was possible to generalize based on statistics. Essentially, entropy is a direct indicator of how many states are available to a system (all of the atoms, etc.), and is more loosely referred to as a measure of "disorder." This explains, for instance, why it's much easier, for instance, to smash a glass and have the glass stay broken, rather than seeing many objects, once smashed, evolve back to being the original integrated state. Or, why we do not see eggs getting unbroken and making their way back into whole shells. In each of these instances, there are more "states" available, and thus higher disorder, for the broken objects. Isaac Asimov's short story, "The Last Question" beautifully demonstrates the Second Law of Thermodynamics on the scale of the entire Universe. In the story, many different generations, one after the other, ask the ultimate computer of their day (Multivac) whether or not there is any way to escape the second law and avoid the increase of entropy and the "heat death" (Tipler 1994) of the Universe ("heat death" refers to an early theory of entropy which supposes that the entire Universe would eventually reach a state at which no further energy could extracted for any processes, including life). For billions of years, when the question was posed to the computer, it would answer that it just didn't have enough information to answer the question. Eventually, after all mankind (or the creatures that evolved from them) had died off, the computer was left to itself. Feeling the need to finally demonstrate the answer to the ultimate question, the computer restarted the Universe with a new Big Bang! Entropy is also a major theme interwoven in Tom Stoppard's play *Arcadia*. Featured in the play is a child prodigy, Thomasina, who realized well before the full theory was devised, that the rules of entropy will lead to the winding down of the Universe. The ultimate winding and grinding down of everything is also addressed in Phillip K. Dick's *Do Androids Dream of Electric Sheep?* (upon which the 1982 film *Blade Runner* was based). This is most colorfully exemplified by the rundown apartment complexes filled with "kipple": the special word reserved for ground down bits of junk. As one character described to another, "Kipple is useless objects, like junk mail or match folders after you use the last match or gum wrappers or yesterday's homepage. When nobody's around, kipple reproduces itself.... There's the First Law of Kipple. Kipple drives out non-kipple ... the entire universe is moving towards a final state of total, absolute kipplization" (Clute and Nichols 1995). Though, precisely speaking, this isn't the Second Law of Thermodynamics, it does share some of the futility of the heat death.

Additionally, a so-called "zeroth" law has been added to define temperature and the essential properties of a body that relate to temperature. Simply summarized, the law states that if one system is in thermal equilibrium with two others, then the others are in equilibrium with each other. This evolved into a definition of temperature, since it was soon realized that if these systems were in equilibrium, they could be defined by a unique quantity, which we characterize as temperature. This also allows us to reliably measure temperature, since temperature is effectively measured by putting one substance into contact with another (Schroeder 2000). However, there are some who feel that this is just an extension of the Second Law, and should not be afforded the status of a law in and of itself.

Another achievement of thermodynamics is the development of equations of state. Essentially that means we can relate temperature of a gas (and some liquids and solids) to measured pressure, temperature, density. The way in which these parameters relate can depend dramatically on the conditions. For instance, in a gas under normal conditions increasing the pressure will drive up the density and temperature as well. Likewise, we could purposefully change temperature, and expect to see changes in the other parameters. However, as we'll see later, for the sorts of conditions we'll see on the surface of a white dwarf star, an increase in temperature will not lead to an expansion, and the gas will continue to just rapidly increase its temperature until the gas can initiate nuclear reactions, and start a thermonuclear runaway (essentially, an explosion or bomb). Also, equations of state can change if we increase speed of atoms to close to the speed of light.

Relativity

Though we usually associate the word "relativity" with Einstein, the concept was not new with him. Three hundred years prior, Galileo had seen the need to consistently calculate the velocities of objects by taking into account all relative motion of the object and an observer. However, the need for a new relativity theory grew out of the development of electrodynamics of the 19th century. This theory among many other accomplishments, accounts for the propagation of light, but in this theory as originally conceived, light needs a medium in which to travel. This medium was referred to as "the ether" and was thought to be pervasive, whether the light was traveling through the vacuum of space or here on Earth. However, it was soon realized that if light were traveling through this ether, then your apparent measurement of the velocity of light would depend on what direction you were moving in relative to this ether. The most famous of the experiments to make an attempt to measure this effect was conducted by Michelson and Morley and they measured no effect, and thus, the conclusion had to be that there was no ether and that light had a fixed speed. This might seem like just a curiosity, but has some stunning ramifications (Hawking 1999). One ramification is that distances will seem shorter for objects traveling near to the speed of light (referred to as Lorentz contraction, after Lorentz, who first hypothesized this effect, even before Einstein devised a new and thorough theory of relativity). In addition, time will appear to pass more slowly for anyone or anything traveling close to the speed of light. This effect has actually been measured. One example is the decay of muons entering the atmosphere. Without time dilation, the expected decay of these muons is so short we'd only be able to detect their existence in the uppermost regions of the atmosphere. However, we are able to detect them at much lower altitudes. This is consistent with these particles moving at speeds near to the speed of light. From the particle's point of view, they are decaying in the time frame we'd see the decay in if they were stationary. However, a stationary observer would see these particles decaying over a much longer time period, thus giving them enough time to reach lower altitudes. As we'll see in future chapters, this last effect may have profound impact on future space travel if we ever reach near-light speeds.

Generally speaking, if physicists had never been able to examine objects at very high speeds (close to the speed of light) or in strong gravitational fields, our view of mechanics now would be pretty close to what it was from the time of Newton until the early 20th century. However, as experiments began to measure particles moving at high speeds, we began to realize that there were discrepancies. Einstein accounted for these discrepancies by realizing that if the speed of light were a fixed speed limit for all matter, then the rules for how we calculate velocities, distances, and time must change. At first this does not sound very dramatic, but it has some astounding consequences. For instance, time passes much more slowly for those traveling near to the speed of light. You could travel to the nearest star, Alpha Centauri, at close to the speed of light (say, about 90%), and get there, and then return, in about 10 years total. In this same time about 23 years would have passed here on Earth, and possibly your loved ones would no longer even be living.[3] This effect has even been experimentally confirmed, both on elementary particles such as muons, and GPS satellites orbiting the Earth.

At this time, Einstein and others also found Newton's theory of gravitation to be perplexing. Most notably, if the Sun were to be removed from our Solar System, Newton's theory surmises that the planets would notice that effect instantaneously. This is glaringly different from electromagnetic fields. The next step came in the form of General Relativity, which boldly stated mathematically that the geometry of space and time (usually referred to as space-time) is completely dictated by the distribution of mass that is present, and vice versa (that is, if you knew in advance what geometry you wanted, that would dictate what kind of mass distribution you need). The theory makes some very specific predictions that have important differences from the theories of Newton. For instance, a small deviation of the orbit of Mercury is predicted by this theory. In addition, light rays passing close enough to the Sun should be deflected by the Sun's gravity. This second prediction was confirmed by Arthur Eddington during a solar eclipse in 1919, and made Einstein into a celebrity. The curvature of space-time has potentially more profound implications. For instance, as we will see later in Chapter 5, some solutions of the relativistic equations lead to distributions of matter that allow time travel into the past (Hartle 2003).

Nuclear Reactions

As early as 1903 it was realized by Ernest Rutherford that the energy released in the radioactive decay of some elements, such as radium, was up to one million times more than the energies of a typical chemical reaction (Reed 2011). Soon after the development of the special theory of relativity, a more detailed theoretical explanation showed that large amounts of energy could be released by breaking up the nuclei of atoms into smaller, less massive atoms or by fusing them from smaller atoms into larger ones. An example of fission is the breakup of uranium-235 when bombarded by a neutron (for uranium, it will only work for this particular isotope) into xenon and strontium. The difference in binding energy of the original atom and the product elements accounts for the released energy and neutrons. Also, in this type of reaction, the neutron by-products can then bombard other U-235 atoms and lead to a chain reaction. In Chapter 2 we will see how fusion reactions are relevant to energy generation in stars. In Chapter 3 we will see how both fission and fusion technology may be applicable to powering a future spacecraft to the stars. Finally, in Chapter 8, we will see how this knowledge has been applied to development of weapons.

In addition to these aforementioned applications, there are some very practical reasons for studying sustained nuclear fusion reactions. As with the core of the Sun, we could potentially fuse atoms here on Earth if we could heat plasma to many millions of degrees. However, unlike the Sun we would not fuse hydrogen into helium (the cross-section for these reactions is low, and thus would be too inefficient for energy generation purposes). That is, it is the intention to fuse two forms of heavy hydrogen, deuterium and tritium, either through the fusion of deuterium with deuterium, or deuterium with tritium. Deuterium has one proton and one neutron and tritium has one proton and two neutrons. Unlike fission reactions, there wouldn't be radioactive by-products. Therefore, we could have a safe source of energy. However, unlike the Sun, we don't have the ability to confine the plasma by means of gravity. Therefore, we need some other way to contain the plasma, and from the beginning of such experiments, this has been accomplished with magnetic fields. However, for many years, it was difficult to understand how plasmas were behaving under such circumstances. For instance, charged ions would drift out of the magnetic field, due to collisions with other particles, but often at a rate higher than what had been predicted by accepted theory. In the early days after World War II, both the Americans and British were working on separate versions of a prototype fusion reactor. One of the most promising methods for containing a plasma, and perhaps, ultimately, sustained nuclear fusion is the tokamak, first designed by Andrei Sakharov (who at the time was also involved in building powerful nuclear weapons for the Soviet Union) in the 1950s. The idea was to confine a plasma by sending it around a magnetic field in a doughnut shaped tube (a torus). A second magnetic field would be applied to help keep the plasma from drifting up against the outer wall of the torus.

There have been many avenues of research in this area for almost seven decades; however, no reactor has really been able to sustain a reaction for more than a fraction of a second and only some reactors have hit the breakeven point, and then only intermittently. Nonetheless, because of the potential payoff, research continues in this area, with most bets being placed on the International Thermonuclear Experimental Reactor (ITER) (Clery 2013). ITER was first conceived in the 1980s in the aftermath of Mikhail Gorbachev becoming leader of the Soviet Union and becoming supportive of collaborative scientific efforts with the U.S., Europe and Japan. High projected costs and disagreements over both the primary focus of ITER (physics research in fusion vs. engineering related to future power plants) and whether a reactor of that size could even be stable led to many delays and the temporary withdrawal of the U.S. Even though construction has begun in France (starting in 2013), the first fusion experiments many not occur for over a decade (Gibbs 2014).

Another approach has been used at the National Ignition Facility (NIF). Here, deuterium and tritium are placed in a small capsule. A set of highly energetic lasers are then aimed at the capsule. Here, UV laser light is converted to X-rays; the elements inside the capsule are both highly compressed and brought up to an extremely high temperature to allow for fusion. Although they have officially ended their quest for sustained fusion using this method, NIF is still working on this method and testing its viability. They now conclude that they will likely need a more powerful laser to reach ignition. However, realizing that such equipment will likely not get funding in the near future, they are looking at other aspects of experimental design that could improve performance (Kramer, "Taking the Next Steps in Fusion Ignition Quest" 2015).

For a brief moment in 1989, it looked as if there might be success with cold fusion when Pons and Flieschmann released their results. Their experiment entailed putting deuterium in a small tabletop cell with one palladium and one platinum electrode. The cell seemingly produced considerably more heat than expected from a typical chemical reaction. They thus concluded that the cell was producing energy from fusion reactions, probably from deuterium being concentrated at the palladium electrode. They also detected neutrons, a by-product of fusion. However, shortly thereafter, with deep criticism and inability to either replicate the results or explain the original results with a consistent theory, cold fusion was mostly abandoned (Clery 2013).

Quantum Mechanics

In parallel to the development of relativity came the revolution of quantum mechanics. Just as relativity changed our notions of the Universe in the realms of high speeds and strong gravity, quantum mechanics changed our way of thinking on atomic size scales. The first dramatic discoveries were related to the quantization of light. That is, it was shown theoretically and experimentally that light can sometimes be treated as a particle with a very specific associated energy. This was first realized by Max Planck in his solution to a theoretical problem related to black-body radiation. A black body is an object that perfectly absorbs all incident radiation and then, if in thermal equilibrium with its surroundings, re-radiates it. The theory being considered at the time actually predicted that a black body should emit an infinite amount of radiation, which had to be false, since no finite object could do this. The possibility of photons, light described as discrete bundles with very specific characteristic energies, turns out to be critical to the theoretical solution of this problem, which then allows for finite amounts of radiation. The solution also relates to the interpretation of atomic spectra, which had been observed from terrestrial and stellar sources since the early 19th century. It became clear that atoms were releasing light only at very specific wavelengths. The next step came with Rutherford's discovery of the atomic nucleus (mentioned above), which allowed for more accurate modeling of the atom. The aforementioned spectra can be explained if the structure of the atom is such that light can only be emitted at very discrete wavelengths. This structure was originally explained by Neils Bohr in terms of electrons in atoms moving between specific energy levels that correspond to orbits around a proton. In this process, a photon would be released with energy equal to the difference between the energy levels. Though Bohr orbits soon were realized to be too simplistic, they did allow for progress in understanding both the atom and atomic spectra (Caroll and Ostlie 2007). Intricately related to the particle properties of light was the explanation of the photoelectric effect, first observed by Hertz in the 1880s. This curious effect shows that changing the intensity of ultraviolet radiation shining on a metal did not increase the number of electrons ejected from the surface of the metal. However, changing the frequency (or equivalently, the energy) of this ultraviolet light could change the electron flow dramatically. Einstein (who won the Nobel Prize for his role in this discovery, and not relativity) was able to explain this in terms of the conservation of energy, and the emerging quantum theory. Below a certain frequency of light, the photons do not have enough energy to eject electrons; however, above that frequency, they do, implying that light has a characteristic frequency and associated energy, and is thus quantized.

Another important development was the theory of wave properties of particles. Though we have already seen that light has particle properties (in addition to its well understood wave properties), it was less evident, and took longer, for physicists to realize this duality for particles. De Broglie hypothesized that a particle would have a characteristic wavelength related to its momentum and energy, in the same way light would. This was only experimentally determined to be the case several years later, separately by Clinton Davisson and George Thomson, when electrons were discovered to diffract in ways very similar to light rather than pass through slits in the way expected for much larger particles. However, if a particle has a wavelength, then there stands to be a deeper explanation of the cause of the wave. A more complete model came when Schroedinger developed the theoretical underpinnings of quantum mechanics. In this model, the paths of the electrons in the atom are determined probabilistically. That is, electrons didn't have a specific location, such as a well-defined orbit, but rather, a probability of being in a certain location. The interpretation of Schroedinger's equations can be understood in light of the wave-particle duality. Just as sometimes light acts as a wave, and other times a particle, the same can be true of all matter. That is, what we normally think of as particles can also exhibit wave properties. These waves are directly related to the probability of being in a particular location (Beiser 2003).

But perhaps most shocking is the overall interpretation of quantum mechanics, which has always been controversial due to its lack of footing in common experience. The most common interpretation since the dawn of formal quantum mechanics has been the formal probabilistic one adopted by Neils Bohr, and dubbed the Copenhagen interpretation. The primary finding of quantum mechanics is that the microscopic world, meaning at the level of the atom, is described probabilistically and not deterministically. That is to say, that unlike macroscopic objects such as baseballs, we cannot perfectly describe the path of an individual electron that is part of an atom, without knowing some key variables (such as how much time has passed, and what is the initial velocity). Rather, we can only say that with some probability that is determined theoretically, that an electron that is part of, say, a hydrogen atom can be in a particular spot at a particular time. You might cleverly object and say, "If I didn't study baseballs in enough detail, I'd think their paths were probabilistic and not deterministic. But if I study the problem in more detail, I will notice that where the ball eventually lands depends on some very well defined variables. So, perhaps, if we all study electrons and atoms more, we will be able to find out what these variables are determine their paths more precisely." If you thought this, then you are in good company, because Einstein had this view. In fact, even until the 1980s this traditional probabilistic view (with no hidden variables) hadn't been completely confirmed. We won't get into the details of all of the experiments, but suffice it to say that the fundamentals of quantum theory have been backed up by many experiments. However, there have always been some difficulties with this interpretation. In this particular interpretation, a particle's overall state can be represented by a sum of probabilities of being in one particular state (that could represent energy, or some other property). However, once such a particle is actually observed, it must only be in one particular state (the one it is measured to be in). The traditional view calls this "collapse of the wave function," but the only way we can really think of this is to say that before a particle is measured, it really is said to be in a mixture of states and only can be described as being in one particular state once observed. Though counterintuitive, it does not make sense to ask "which is really the state before it's observed?" The answer within this interpretation is that there is no one "real" state. It is really in the mixture of states. An excellent adoption of this trope into science fiction is in Greg Egan's 1992 novel *Quarrantine*. In this book, the theory maintained is that human consciousness itself is what collapses the wave function. Though it makes for a very interesting read, this theory is not taken very seriously by practitioners of quantum mechanics.

In the early days of quantum mechanics Albert Einstein posed a number of thought experiments to Neils Bohr that was meant as challenges to the theory. In turn, each of these challenges was disposed of, though sometimes subtly. One of the toughest challenges was that of the famous Einstein, Podalsky, and Rosen (EPR) thought experiment (named for the authors of a journal article on this topic written by these three scientists). EPR proposes that you start an experiment with two particles that are connected through their momenta and distance from each other. This can be the case for electron/positron pairs created from high-energy photons. For such particles, if you know the momentum of one particle, then you automatically know the momentum of the other. If you know the distance one has traveled from the starting point, then you automatically know the distance that the other has traveled. These particles are said to be entangled since this relationship between them is true no matter how distant they are from each other. This kind of entanglement was bothersome to Einstein and his collaborators, mainly because it implied that one particle could "communicate" what its state was to the other particle no matter the distance between them, in direct violation of relativity and the speed of light as the ultimate speed limit. Einstein considered this to be proof that there must be "hidden" variables at play. That is, that quantum mechanics isn't probabilistic as it seems, that there must be some sort of variable that pre-determined the momentum of both of these particles. Theoretical progress by Bohm and then Bell led to the rejection of "hidden variables," and thus, almost complete acceptance of quantum mechanics. In fact, Bell proposed specific measurements (referred to later as Bell state measurements) that could be made that would indicate a difference between particles governed by quantum theory or those governed by hidden variables (or at least, variables in addition to quantum theory as it stood at the time). For instance, if we have two photons, A and B, we can measure a three-dimensional property such as the spin. If we measure the spin of A along one direction, say the horizontal direction, which we'll call the X direction, then because of entanglement, we will also immediately know about the × spin of B, but not the spin component in the other directions. The same would apply if we measured the along the vertical direction, which we will call y, first. As a result, if we measured many spins of many entangled pairs, we should find a stronger correlation between the spin components of A and B than if quantum theory was incorrect. As alluded above, these measurements were finally conducted by Aspect in the 1980s, and confirmed in various manners since, closing the book (for most!) on the hidden variable question. We'll see the potential for exploiting entanglement and Bell state measurements both when we discuss quantum computing and teleportation in future chapters (Darling 2005).

Subatomic Particles

The internal structure of the atom began to be seriously studied at the turn of the 20th century. Ernest Rutherford discovered via experiment that the atom had a concentrated nucleus, and much of its structure was actually empty space. In the decades immediately following, it was discovered that the nucleus was further made of either protons and, in most cases, also neutrons (depending on the element involved). Most of the progress in understanding the substructure of the atom then came in the 1960s after the discovery of quarks, theorized by Murray Gell-Mann to be the building blocks of protons and neutrons. However, there has been a bit of a battle over the theoretical framework. The primary overarching model for particle physics which we have previously discussed in terms of fundamental forces, used to explain the existence of all the particles we know of, is the Standard Model. The standard model explains (almost!) all particles as being in three categories: light particles, leptons, which include, among other particles, electrons and neutrinos (there are a total of six types of leptons), heavy particles, hadrons, which are all made of combinations of six possible quarks. In addition, there are particles that mediate forces, including the perhaps recently discovered Higgs boson. The Standard Model has generally succeeded; however, there are still some significant difficulties. One of these is the so-called "hierarchy problem." That is, estimates of what we might expect particle masses to be based on first principles end up being up to ten quadrillion times greater than what we actually observe to be the highest particle masses. So, either our estimates are well off from what a complete theory of quantum gravity would give or some unknown process is suppressing the masses (Carroll, *The Particle at the End of the Universe* 2012). The upper bound estimate discussed above is defined as the Planck mass, and is about 2×10^{-8} kg. Though this seems like a very small number (about the mass of a small insect or that of about 100,000 interstellar dust grains), it's considerably more massive than the most massive subatomic particles discovered as yet. Similarly, we can determine the Planck scale length, and like the Planck mass, is derived from fundamental constants and is about 10^{-35} meters, much smaller than any length scale within an atomic nucleus. Another ramification of these considerations is that the gravitational constant that determines the strength of all gravitational interactions is inversely proportional to the square of the Planck mass. So, if the real observed "floor" to subatomic masses is much smaller, it implies that the strength of gravity, theoretically speaking, should be stronger than we observed it to be.

Similarly, we misestimate how much energy we see in empty space (this energy isn't from any other source, it is "vacuum energy") if we use our best determinations from quantum gravity theory. We only observe a fairly small energy density (and even this was just observed in the last 15 years or so), many orders of magnitude smaller than predicted. Together, these misestimates would suggest that we are in need of a more complete theory, whether that be the theory of quantum gravity, or a theory for subatomic particles.

However, as discussed previously, failure to have a grand unified theory has led to alternate explanations for particle physics, such as string theory. This theory was first developed in the 1980s as a potential theory that would unify all forces. In this theory, instead of particles being represented as points in space, they are treated as vibrations on string (and, here, as Sean Carroll points out, asking what the string is made of is more or less the same question as asking what the "point" is made of for point-like particles). However, string theory has its own deficiencies. For the most part, this theory has been developed due to its overarching mathematical approach to explaining the elementary particles and forces we observe. However, string theory has had even more trouble than the Standard Model in explaining the exact values of particles' masses, and the relative strengths of fundamental forces. In particular, it can't make unique predictions about what particles we should be able to observe at accessible energies while making further predictions at energies we will probably never be able to access. In addition, string theory has long since grown into a grander M-theory, which among other things, hypothesizes multiple spatial dimensions which we will discuss at length in Chapter 4. We have yet attained an overarching model that's entirely satisfying (Randall, *Knocking at Heaven's Door* 2011).

Chaos and Fractals

It turns out that not all deterministic systems (such as those governed by the equations of mechanics or thermodynamics) are predictable. In the late 19th century, the French mathematician Henri Poincare realized that weather seemed to be unreliably unpredictable even though the relevant parameters should be able to determine the future fairly well (Silver 1998). In the modern era, the mathematician Edward Lorenz realized that in predicting weather through computer simulations, he'd often get widely diverging results depending on very small changes in initial conditions for the model. It was soon realized that his conclusion applied to many physical systems, and this led to the field of chaos. Chaos in physics refers to dynamical systems that, as discussed above for the example of weather, can have wildly different final results even if initial inputs are similar, but still differing by a small amount. In this way such systems lose their predictability (Gleick 1987). One relatively simple example from the study of mechanics is the double pendulum. In this system, one pendulum is connected to the end of another pendulum (that is allowed to swing in two dimensions from, say, the ceiling) (Taylor 2005). Depending on the initial conditions, the motion can be quite different. More complicated systems include the orbits of asteroids and comets (Lecar et al. 2001). In addition, it has long been thought that theory of chaos can, in certain circumstances, be applied to the financial markets (Weatherall 2013), thus making them somewhat more predictable than previously thought (and thus also more profitable).

Fractals are systems that can be described by a fractional dimension that often differs from the geometric dimension of the system. These systems are self-similar (Vicsek 1989) meaning that the small-scale structure is identical to the large-scale structure. An often stated early discovered example of this is the coastline of England (and of course other coastlines). If we look at the overall structure of the coastline on scales of hundreds of miles, this looks very much like the coastline on much smaller scales (just a few miles). In this case, "fractional dimension" means that the area defined by the coastline segments put together is not proportional to an integral power of the chosen length scale of the coastline, as would be the case for the relationship between the area of a circle and the radius of the circle. Instead, the "power" is a fraction. Furthermore, it was thought for a time that the Universe itself might have fractal structure. In this model, galaxies form into clusters, clusters form super-clusters, and so on, eventually including the largest possible scales of the Universe. However, the most recent observations show that this "clustering hierarchy" breaks down on the largest scales (Peebles 1993). Fractals are also relevant to everyday engineering applications such as the study of structure of alloys and the use of water pumping to force petroleum through wells (Vicsek 1989).

A great example of how chaos and fractals are used in science fiction is Jeffrey Carver's Chaos Chronicles trilogy, especially *Strange Attractors* (the title itself taken from the terminology of chaos theory). The text features

Shadow People, who are said to be fractal beings. Recently, elsewhere in popular culture, a reference is made to the fractal nature of snowflakes in the lyrics of the song "Let It Go" from the 2013 Disney film *Frozen*.

It turns out that we can describe dynamical systems in terms of specific points or areas of a space defined by important variables. In physics, this can be as simple as a point in space that tends to be approached by swinging pendulum losing energy. In finance this can be key index values, such as that of the S&P 500. This approached region is called an attractor. For chaotic systems, this attractor can shift. When this shift can be described by fractals, then the attractor is called a strange attractor though not all strange attractors are in chaotic systems (Silver 1998).

Are the Constants of Nature Constant?

In *Science Set Free*, Rupert Sheldrake asks whether it is possible that some of the constants of nature are not truly constant. He shows that over time, even measurements of the gravitational constant, G, have shown a difference of a little over one percent. While this is not necessarily evidence of variability, it does open up the possibility that the nature of some of the fundamental forces, such as gravity, are changing. This concept does pop up in science fiction. We see this early in the "Gravity Zero" episode of *Science Fiction Theater*. Here a physicist was able to effectively reduce the value of "G" leading to breakthroughs in rocket technology. In the *Star Trek: The Next Generation* (*ST:TNG*) episode "Deja Q," when presented with the problem of a moon being knocked out of its orbit, possibly by a passing black hole, Q suggests rather casually, "Simple. Change the gravitational constant of the Universe."

A few years into the mission of the interplanetary probe Pioneer 10, the satellite's precise position and velocity could not be properly predicted by the expected trajectory of the spacecraft based on gravitational interactions and radiation from the Sun. Since Pioneer 11 saw a similar drift, it was determined that this was not just a one-time interaction with some other small body, but a real effect that these probes were encountering as they went into the outer Solar System (Tyson 2012). At first it was thought that perhaps there needed to be some sort of modification to the theory of gravity (perhaps including variability of the gravitational constant), but it turns out that in this case, the anomaly can probably best explained by differences in how the spacecrafts were heated as they were facing the Sun or then turned away from it. The dramatic differences in how the spacecrafts then radiate this energy back into space can affect the velocity of the probes, and thus explain the anomaly. Sheldrake also opens up the possibility that the speed of light and the fine structure constant may be changing (Sheldrake 2012).

Chapter 2

Introduction to Astronomy

Since the days of Jules Verne, recent astronomical discoveries were being absorbed into science fiction (Clute and Nichols 1995). As we did in the first chapter, it will be necessary, before we get to examples from science fiction that touch on the forefront of astronomy today, to discuss some of the basics, from how we know what we know, to the current state of astronomical observations from the Solar System out to the most distant reaches of the Universe. Before we get to the cutting edge observations, let's look at how science fiction approaches basic astronomical observations.

Astronomical Phenomena

In our everyday lives we are constantly experiencing astronomical phenomena. For instance, we often realize that we can only see certain phases of the Moon at particular times of day, that eclipses only occur rarely, and that seasons vary during the year, and in an opposite manner, depending on whether you live in the Northern or Southern Hemisphere. Let's tackle phases of the Moon first. The precise phase we seem will be dependent on the relative positions of the Earth, Moon, and Sun as the Moon travels in its orbit around the Earth. We can, for instance, only see the full Moon when the Moon is in the part of its orbit that keeps it opposite from the Sun, and thus getting one face fully lit from our perspective. Unfortunately, some great works get this wrong. For instance, *Space: 1999* always showed the Moon in full phase, even though the premise of the show was the Moon was cast adrift in the Galaxy, so only rarely having a source of light to keep it in a full phase. In this instance, the Moon should almost always be seen as completely dark, unless it is passing near or in orbit of another star.

People often wonder why eclipses do not occur during every lunar cycle. Most diagrams in astronomy textbooks make it look like the Moon should block out the Sun fairly often. However, the main flaw in these diagrams is that they are only in two dimensions. That is, in three dimensions, the Moon will most often be somewhat misaligned with the Earth and Sun. Solar eclipses can only occur when the path of the Moon around the Earth happens to take it in to a position in the sky where it would cross over the disk of the Sun. Furthermore, these events can only be seen from limited points on the Earth. The Isaac Asimov short story (and then later, an expanded novel with Robert Silverberg) *Nightfall* dealt with a society that was deeply mystified and flummoxed by darkness, including solar eclipses, due to being in a multiple star system. Because of their rare nature (the scientist protagonist in the story theorizes that the eclipses occur every 2,000 or so years), most people became panicked and riotous when they occur. Though some scientists tried to explain the phenomenon and calm the people, these efforts were mostly in vain and society was left in ruins by the end of the story.

A common misconception is that the changing seasons are related to the shape of the orbit of the Earth around the Sun. That is, its elliptical orbit takes it closer to the Sun at times, making it warmer, and farther from the Sun at other times, making it cooler. Such an interpretation is probably exacerbated by seeing such planets in science fiction. In *Lost in Space* ("The Hungry Sea"), the Robinsons first land on Preplannis, a planet that has a highly elongated orbit that leads to scorching hot temperatures followed by freezes. In *Doctor Who* ("The Ribos Operation"), the planet Ribos has long periods (32 years each) of cold and heat due to its elongated orbit. However, there are a number of problems with this interpretation when applied to the Earth. First of all, the seasons are opposite from each other in the Northern and Southern hemispheres, which would be very perplexing if the temperature was mainly dictated by distance from the Sun. Related to this issue, the Earth would only be closest to the Sun during the summer for one hemisphere. The explanation for the seasons is solved when we realize that the tilt of the axis of the Earth with respect to the orbit can change the amount of light we receive as we go around in our orbit about the Sun.

Though we historically have kept up with the positions of stars by assigning them constellations, we note particularly that constellations only relate to apparent position in the sky, and not actual position in space. Therefore, for instance, it's common for stars in the same constellation to be at very different distances from Earth. This reality is often ignored in science fiction. For instance, *Star Trek* often refers to Orion traders and Orion "green slave women" first introduced in the "Menagerie" episode of the original series and continued into later series such as *Star Trek: Enterprise* (*ST:E*). Perhaps this is just shorthand for a particular star system in Orion, but it gives the impression that these folks come from anywhere at all in the constellation Orion. An additional problem is that the constellations will only look as they do from the perspective of the Solar System. If we go to another location in the Galaxy, the same set of stars may not appear as a discernable constellation at all. The visible constellations from another star system may include stars that are barely visible from Earth or not visible at all, depending on how far away they are. There was also a bit of confusion over naming conventions of stars in particular constellations. In particular, the brightest stars in a constellation are designated by the Greek letters, with alpha indicating the brightest, beta the second brightest, and so on until the 22nd letter, omega. Starting with the 23rd brightest star, stars are given numerical designations. So, for instance, 51 Pegasi refers to the 51st brightest star in the constellation Pegasus. In the *Lost in Space* episode "Welcome Stranger," Jimmy Hapgood states that he was once caught in "the Epsilon orbit." Will asks, "Epsilon Indi?" to which Hapgood replies, "No, Eridani." All of this seems to put the emphasis on "Epislon," when all that means is that it's the fourth brightest star in whatever constellation it happens to be located it in (and irrelevant once someone gets deep into the Galaxy away from Earth, since both the constellations and the brightness of any stars in them would be significantly different). However, both are stars that are relatively close to the Earth, and have been discussed as star systems to explore in the distant future.

There's No Fire in Space: Clearing Up Misconceptions

Many people know that it is impossible to have fire in space due to the lack of oxygen, yet television and film producers and writers have continued for decades to add in this feature. The most common reason given is that audiences expect explosions with fire and noise to go along with their explosions, even if they are in orbit of the Earth (as in *Armageddon*) on the surface of the Moon (as in *UFO*, *Space: 1999* or *Moon*) or in deep space in (far too many to mention!). Some films further confuse matters by directly tying absence of air to absence of gravity. For instance, in *The Doomsday Machine* (mentioned in Chapter 3) when the ship loses air in one section, the two crew members who were in that compartment exposed to space suddenly rise up from the floor, implying that gravity has been lost. Though it might be far-fetched explaining how they had Earth-like gravity in the first place (see Chapter 3), there certainly wouldn't be a direct connection between loss of air and loss of gravity. It's understandable that people would make this connection, since generally speaking, where there is weak gravity, there is also little air. It's interesting to note that certain films that (correctly) emphasized the absence of these features (such as *2001: A Space Odyssey* and *Gravity*) gained by getting it right. However, it's still rare to adhere to such production values, and I have the feeling that as long as we have an *Enterprise*, we will see and hear it explode in space (or explode other things in space).

Confusing Measurements

There has also been some confusion in proper use of units of measure. For instance, in the *Lost in Space* episode "Sky Pirate," when it's discovered that Alonzo Tucker's spaceship has a faster-than-light drive, he's asked, "What's your speed in parsecs?" Since parsecs are a unit of distance, the question (which refers to a speed) doesn't make much sense, though we can surmise that John Robinson meant to ask Tucker about his speed in parsecs per second, or some other unit of time. Practically the same error was made a decade later in *Star Wars* when Han Solo, remarking on his ship the *Millennium Falcon*, brags, "It's the ship that made the Kessel Run in less than twelve parsecs." Also, in the *Lost in Space* episode "Return from Outer Space," Will Robinson states that a light year is equal to 19,150,000 miles (too small by a factor of 300,000 or so) and that Alpha Centauri is 5.3 light years from Earth (off by about one light year). Though, in a later second season episode ("Wild Adventure"), Will may have gotten things right. What appears to be shortly after the emergency takeoff they made in the previous episode ("Blast off into Space"), Will surmises that they must be traveling "near the speed of light" and thus have already traveled "a million miles or more." The ship's navigator, Don West, confirms Will's musings. In actuality, assuming that getting up to such high velocities is possible (we discuss that more in Chapter 3), the ship would be able to travel one million miles in just a few seconds (depending on exactly what speed they were at and how long it took to get to that speed). In any case, it seems like a reasonable calculation (one of the few from that show!), since Will is probably making his comments soon after their launch. However, there is one catch. It's unlikely that most people would be able to take accelerations much greater than about 100 meters/sec. With that acceleration, it would take a bit more than a month to get close to the speed of light. Though the beginning of this episode and end of the previous don't rule this out, it seems more likely that they are implying that a much shorter amount of time has passed since launch.

The Origins of the Universe

Now it's probably best to start with the beginning. Not so much the beginning of astronomy (which is the traditional way of teaching astronomy at the college level), but with the beginning of the Universe.

The accepted model of the Universe is that it is approximately 14.5 billion years old and in a state of expansion from a beginning which has been labeled the "Big Bang." We will get to the exact nature of this expansion in a moment, but conceptually speaking, these conclusions are based on two major discoveries of the 20th century. The first of these was the discovery by Vesto Slipher, and then expanded upon by Edwin Hubble, that galaxies move at higher velocities from us as we go to larger distances. This was interpreted to mean that at some point in the distant past, these galaxies would have been much closer together, and perhaps not even formed as galaxies yet. It's important to note that in this model, observers in any galaxy would see a similar effect. That is to say, we do not have a special place in the Universe. Galaxies aren't just moving away from us, but all galaxies are moving away from each other. By examining the details of the expansion closely, we can effectively run the clock backwards to see when this initial explosion occurred, and thus determine an age of the Universe. There have been many modifications of Hubble's initial study due to improvements in the observations themselves, but the fundamental model is the same. The second major discovery was that of the cosmic microwave background radiation in the 1960s. This was seen as direct evidence for a "hot big bang" in which a very hot initial Universe was cooling down to just several degrees, and then emitting microwaves (via black body radiation discussed in Chapter 1) from everywhere in the Universe. Until this point, many physicists still supported the notion of a Steady State Universe (an infinite Universe with no definite starting time). The interpretation of these results also required the assumptions that the Universe is homogeneous (uniform) and isotropic (same in all directions). Though this is expected to work for a general interpretation, we do know that at some point, at some level, these assumptions would have to break down, since an evenly spread out Universe eventually formed into a lumpy Universe with galaxies (according to recent modeling, probably after about one billion years).

Dark Energy

Over the years, some problems developed with both of these major discoveries. One of these problems was in determining whether the expansion rate stays the same over time, slows down, or speeds up. The necessary measurements just weren't accurate enough for decades. Interestingly, it was thought that the Hubble Space Telescope (HST) would solve this problem soon after its 1990 launch, but due to some initial issues with the HST mirror and some positive developments with ground based astronomy, the problem was solved, with some astonishment, in the late 1990s, by Saul Perlmutter, Adam Reiss, Brian Schmidt and their collaborators (the latter two were from a group competing with Perlmutter's, often fighting over who should be getting proper credit for their discoveries) and would later win a Nobel Prize for their work (in general, cosmology has very much interested the Nobel committee). By observing a particular type of supernova, called Type Ia (we will see another type of supernova discussed later), that was both expected to have the same luminosity (the astronomer's term for power) anywhere it occurred in the Universe and the ability to be seen over immense distances, it could be used as a very precise standard candle for calculating distances to galaxies. More precisely speaking, we infer its luminosity from the way in which the supernova explosion dims over time. It turns out that the shape of the graph of how the brightness dims over time is very precisely correlated to the luminosity of the explosion. This particular type of stellar explosion is caused when temperature inside white dwarf stars sharply increase due to matter accreting from another star in a binary system. In such a system, nuclear reactions can go out of control in the white dwarf, and the star will be completely obliterated. Once we determine the luminosity of the explosion (and by extension, distance to the galaxies in which they reside) we can then determine the velocities of the same galaxies that harbored the supernovae, and determine the Hubble constant (Panek 2011). These precise observations reveal that the expansion of the Universe is accelerating over time. That is, as we progress further forward in time from the Big Bang, the expansion of the Universe is increasing at a greater rate. These observations were questioned for some time, even among the various team members. They needed to double check whether the light curves (the graphs of brightness versus time discussed above) of Type Ia supernovae really were always effective as standard candles. Perhaps some light curves were not as well correlated with luminosity as others? Perhaps supernovae at great distances were different than the ones we see in nearby galaxies? Furthermore, some thought there could still be effects due to dust that had not yet been taken into account. However, all of these effects have been analyzed in the intervening years, and in applying them to the data, none leads to any significant deviation from the original results (Nicolson 2007).

When we bring up acceleration, our mind immediately turns to a force (thinking of Newton's Second Law). To this day (the discovery was made in 1997), we do not know what this force is and it has just been given the name "Dark Energy." We will also soon see that the most recent observations of the cosmic microwave background also support a Dark Energy scenario. Understanding the cause is certainly one of the biggest open questions in all of astrophysics and perhaps to all of physics in general, since it might have further implications for the (lack of) unification of all forces. One of the best candidates so far for an underlying cause is vacuum energy. According to one expression of Heisenberg's Uncertainty Principle, over small enough intervals of time, significant amounts of energy (that is, the energy associated with a particle) can pop in and out of existence. In a typical lab at room temperature, this effect may be of no consequence, but over the entire Universe, this can be significant. One nagging problem is that theoretical considerations indicate that the vacuum density should be considerably higher than it is (a factor of 10^{120}) and without adequate explanation of the discrepancy, the search continues for viable theoretical alternatives. One such alternative is "quintessence." Though the precise nature of quintessence is also not very well understood, it could be used to describe energy density associated with a field that will evolve in a way that is consistent with observations, but does not require such a high discrepancy between theoretical prediction and observation (Nicolson 2007).

However, even with dark energy taken into account, the Universe still appears to be in an overall state that is just between expanding forever and closing in on itself. Such a Universe is described as being "flat," since the overall density of matter and energy leads to a flat Euclidian geometry of space within the framework of general relativity discussed in Chapter 1. This in itself is seen as problematic, since it's expected that marginally open Universes will become more and more open with time, and the same with marginally closed Universes. Therefore, we must conclude that the Universe is and probably always has been very nearly flat. After we've considered some other difficulties we will come back to one of the most important theoretical developments of the 20th century, cosmic inflation, which led to a much more palatable interpretation of these results. One word of caution here is that most of the matter and energy accounted for here is in the form of either dark matter or dark energy, and physicists are still not particularly sure about what either one are.

Cosmic Inflation

A second problem with cosmological observations developed with interpreting the cosmic microwave background (CMB). As the situation stood until the last decade of the 20th century, measurements of the CMB were just too smooth to be consistent with theoretical expectations even after the much-awaited results of the COBE microwave satellite came out in the early 1990s. Due to quantum fluctuations in the early Universe just after the Big Bang, we'd expect these fluctuations to carry out to the present day. Even if there were an evening out of these fluctuations at a local level, the Universe would have expanded much too quickly for this evening out to be signaled to other parts of the Universe. Theoretical developments from as early as 1980 could partly explain these results. In 1980, Alan Guth proposed cosmic inflation of the early Universe. During that early period, the Universe would have expanded very rapidly for a very brief period of time (that is to say, a factor of at least 10^{27} by volume in 10^{-32} seconds, an unfathomably small time period). Most notably, this theory can account for small initial fluctuations being spread out into the current Universe. Another consequence of this theory is that the average density of the Universe will be close to the critical density needed to keep the Universe flat. However, a problem arises. If we take stock of all matter we can detect via any kind of radiation, we come up far short of critical density. Astronomers have tried to solve this problem by introducing the possibility of "dark matter," that is forms of matter that do not radiate but interact with normal matter in other ways. We will discuss the history of this problem in the next section, but various problems arise. That is, even when dark matter is taken into account, we cannot achieve critical density in a way that is consistent with other observations. It turns out that the answer comes in accepting "dark energy" seen before, since critical density takes into account all forms of mass and energy. Once we take this step and apply it to the most recent microwave data taken with WMAP since 2005, we can consistently accept the inflationary model, and explain both observations of supernovas in distant galaxies as well as the CMB in terms of dark energy.

However, though inflation has always been very promising because it helps with smoothness, flatness as well as some other problems we have not discussed here, it calls upon a rudimentary theory of quantum gravity. Another important consequence is that inflation allows for a Universe to be created essentially from nothing. That is, quantum fluctuations in a vacuum can create an ultra-tiny Universe which inflates into the Universe we know. For sure, there is still no well devised theory of quantum gravity, so at best these are self-consistent assumptions that seem to lead to theory agreeing with observation. It's probably ultimately still dissatisfying for those who want to know the answer to the question of what caused the Big Bang. At some point, science simply can't answer those questions. That is the best we can do for now.

Dark Matter

In 1932, Dutch astronomer Jan Oort (perhaps one of the most accomplished astronomers of his time, eventually discovering the origin of comets and developing radio astronomy) first observed that the speed of stars in the disk of our Galaxy seemed to indicate that there was much more mass than could be accounted for by observed stars. Though this particular result was later seen to be faulty, the general conclusion was later seen to have merit:

our Galaxy has more mass than what is luminous in the forms of stars or other radiating matter (such as gas clouds giving off radio waves or dust that emits infrared radiation). Caltech astronomer Fritz Zwicky observed in the 1930s that as a whole, the galaxies of the Coma cluster appeared to be moving faster than what could be accounted for gravitationally from the total mass of galaxies that was then observed by conventional means in the cluster. Furthermore, these similar results were attained by other astronomers looking at other clusters such as Virgo (Freeman and McNamara 2006). This was the first hint that there was some other hidden form of matter, unseen by conventional telescopes (i.e., observing at visible wavelengths). It was later observed in more detail by Vera Rubin and Kent Ford in the 1970s that spiral galaxies have more mass than can be explained by the light that is emitted by stars, gas, dust or any other forms of normal matter. As hinted at by Oort, a similar effect has now been seen in our own Galaxy (Caroll and Ostlie 2007) and even galaxies much different morphologically than our own, such as ellipticals (Trimble 1987). Even very cold normal matter should be emitting some light. We infer the presence of this dark matter by the gravitational effect that it has on all other matter in whatever galaxy (if such dark matter did not exist, then the speed we measure for stars and gas in these galaxies would be much lower than what has been consistently observed for decades). Later, it was also observed that entire clusters of galaxies also have much more matter than can be inferred from the mass of the galaxies and intracluster gas. None of this however explains what dark matter actually is. There have been some competing theories, first generally falling into categories of baryonic (normal matter) and non-baryonic (either a neutrino or some other similar sort of particle that has not been discovered yet). Since we'd expect most normal matter to somehow radiate, any theory for baryonic matter would have to involve matter that just isn't emitting any detectable radiation due to its small size and very low temperature. Though acronymed MACHO for Massive Compact Halo Objects, the adjective "massive," in this case, is meant to be relative to the other options for dark matter, such as sub-atomic particles. The actual objects themselves can be much less massive than the Sun. There are now fairly tight limits of how much dark matter could be in such a conventional form. We can detect the presence of such matter via gravitational lensing. Einstein suggested that gravity's influence on light should act like a lens, deflecting its path. In the case of MACHO's potentially passing between us and a more distant star, the light from the star could bend into our line of sight in a way that would amplify the brightness of the star. The way in which the star's brightness would be amplified is different than variability that is inherent to the star, particularly in the way it would amplify similarly at every wavelength, so we should be able to pick out MACHO-related events from more prosaic variability. Though precise results differ, none have suggested that more than 20% of all dark matter can be baryonic (normal matter, from our perspective) and some suggest much less (Nicolson 2007). Therefore, we seek explanations that focus on the vast majority of the remaining matter, falling most generally into cold dark matter (CDM) and hot dark matter (HDM) particle theories, with "cold" and "hot" being shorthand for non-relativistic (slow, much less than the speed of light) and relativistic particles (fast, close to the speed of light). Computer simulations of how galaxies and clusters of galaxies would form show that HDM (neutrinos being an example) generally leads to much more massive clusters that then break down into smaller structures. Cold dark matter appears to be more consistent with how we expect galaxies and clusters of galaxies to have formed from the time of the Big Bang until now. Thus, the most accepted idea now is that dark matter is "cold" and falls into the category of weakly interacting massive particles (WIMP; this acronym actually came before MACHOs were so named. Of course then astronomers picked an acronym that would humorously contrast with WIMP). The "weakly interacting" was also intentionally picked because these particles are expected to feel the weak force and be similar to the W and Z particles that govern these forces (Carroll, *The Particle at the End of the Universe* 2012). If such WIMPs exist they might be observable in a couple of ways. They should probably be electrically neutral, since we know that charged particles tend to radiate in electromagnetic fields that permeate the Universe (Carroll, *The Particle at the End of the Universe* 2012). We see no such radiation, so they must be neutral, if they exist. They could be potentially observed in space, if like other particles, they are energetic enough to annihilate with each other. There are indeed some who have made some initial claims to have observed dark matter annihilation with the Fermi Gamma Ray Observatory, and in particular, corresponding to a heavy dark matter particle of about 130 GeV (Weniger 2012). Weniger and others are now calling on the Fermi team to potentially commit more time to observing these lines so that definitive results can be reached before the end of the life of the Fermi Observatory in 2016. Still others have observed similar such effects with the Alpha Magnetic Spectrometer (AMS) on board the International Space Station. The AMS detected an excess of positrons that may have a more prosaic explanation (i.e., origin from pulsars or other galactic objects) but could also be a by-product of dark matter annihilation (Blau 2013). As of now, the precise origin of the positrons is unclear, but can be consistent with dark matter annihilation. Particularly interesting is that the positron excess is not directionally dependent (anisotropic), as we'd expect from relatively nearby galactic objects, but not expect from dark matter that would be all around us. However, because our galaxy's magnetic field tends to deflect the paths of charged particles, even positrons coming from particular places in space can look as if they have an isotropic origin. In addition, the Italian

PAMELA satellite showed similar excess positron results. It may also be possible to observe by-products of such types of dark matter (called axions) with the Large Hadron Collider (Carroll, *The Particle at the End of the Universe* 2012) due to interactions with a Higgs-like particle (which we already know exists) if the proposed particles are not too massive (Randall, *Knocking at Heaven's Door* 2011). In S.W. Ahmed's novel *Dark Matter*, it turns out that dark matter is actually just normal matter (planets with civilizations and such) protected by a special field that has continued to be a mystery to certain undeveloped civilizations such as ours. This would be a special version of the MACHO hypothesis.

Stellar Observations

In order to understand some critical problems in astronomy, such as the formation, evolution and death of stars, we have to understand how stars create their energy. However, to comprehend this, we first have to understand how we can observe stars in the first place. It will be productive to consider this from a historical perspective.

Not surprisingly, observations of stars began when humans could first see them. Modern observations actually began well before the invention of the telescope, as ancients realized that stars appeared to move diurnally as well as change positions throughout the year. Though these motions were often explained by models that ultimately turned out not to be correct, such as the epicycle model of Ptolemy. The ancient Greeks, starting with Hipparchus, ranked the brightness of stars and centuries later this morphed into the modern magnitude system (which Richter later also adopted for rating the energy released in earthquakes). Once we were able to determine the distances to stars, we would begin to get a picture of how much energy is emitted from stars.

One of the most important steps was getting a sense of the distance scale to stars. Obtaining these distances may seem esoteric, but it is actually the key to determining how much energy is actually being emitted by a particular star. We can think of this in the same way we might think about a light bulb. If a light bulb of a particular wattage is placed close to you it will appear to be very bright, but if placed much more distantly, it may look no brighter than a firefly. Also, assuming we did not know the wattage of the blub, we could calculate it by measuring the amount of light we receive at a given distance from the bulb. Once the amount of energy being emitted by stars was known to be similar to that emitted by the Sun, it was realized that there must be a similar underlying process for creating energy in these objects. At first, it was hypothesized that energy could be emitted as an object gravitationally contracts. As the object collapses, energy is released, and potentially radiated away. Kelvin was among the first to calculate how long such a process could keep a star alive, and it would be in the tens of millions of years for a solar-type star. At about this time, biologists were beginning to realize that the Earth was likely to be much older than this, and therefore a contradiction existed between biologists and theoretical physicists. The solution to the problem came with the advent of Einstein's Theory of Relativity. Once the equivalence of mass and energy was realized, the detailed theory of nuclear energy production was worked out.

Another breakthrough came in understanding the spectra of stars. As discussed in Chapter 1, in the late 1800s it was discovered by Max Planck that any hot object would emit radiation across the electromagnetic spectrum. That is, even something that is clearly giving off visible light would also be emitting some amount of low energy light that we would now call radio waves, but also emit high-energy radiation such as X-rays and gamma rays. However, the amount of radiation being given off at a particular wavelength would be related to temperature of the object. Cooler objects (hundreds of degrees and cooler) will give off infrared radiation and radio waves, while extremely hot objects (millions of degrees) would emit more X-rays and gamma rays. Additionally, since we can split up the incoming white light of a star into its component parts, that is, light from all colors of the rainbow, we can observe light emitted in the form of spectral lines. That is, light emitted at very precise wavelengths based on the energy transitions electrons undergo within an atom. A second important effect to take into account is the Doppler Effect. In this effect, light waves emitted by a moving source (including spectral lines) are shifted into the blue end of the spectrum if the source is moving toward us, and the light waves are shifted into the red part of the spectrum if the source is moving away from us (Caroll and Ostlie 2007).

Star Formation

An equally important question to work out was how stars formed in the first place. When it was realized that the interstellar medium was full of hydrogen gas, often in expansive regions around hot stars that contained thousands of solar masses worth of hydrogen, the connection between this gas and the possible formation of the stars it surrounded was made. Also, we certainly see that stars exist, and that we see the cores of molecular clouds collapsing, which has been taken to be evidence of stars collapsing from large gas clouds into concentrated objects. In addition, James Jeans showed theoretically that gas clouds have a critical radius, below which they would collapse due to their own gravity. It turns out that for typical gas cloud densities, this radius is a little less than one light year, and then the implied mass would be about the mass of the Sun (that is, a typical stellar mass). Though Jeans made a number of assumptions that likely do not strictly hold (no magnetic field, no rotation), this was still taken as a major theoretical development that supported the notion that stars collapse from these larger observed gas clouds. Furthermore, including these details does not change the most significant conclusions by much (Draine 2011). However, a number of processes in the interstellar medium should act to resist star formation. Even in extremely cold space (not more than about 10 degrees above "absolute zero"), molecules will possess some motion. The consequence of this random motion is that the gas in these large clouds will tend to drift apart, thus disintegrating the cloud over the lifetime of the Galaxy. Also, any charged particles in these clouds will tend to follow the magnetic field lines of the Galaxy (which most likely will be in a direction that is not the inflow direction of the collapsing cloud), also adding to motion that works against star formation, i.e., the collapse of the cloud into smaller clumps (Shu, Adams and Lizano 1987). In addition, rotation of clouds will act against their collapse. Yet they do collapse to form stars, so something has to happen. Currently we think that this something is shock waves in the interstellar medium which act to break apart a molecular cloud into bits that can more easily collapse. Two primary causes of shock waves may be supernova explosions from the death of massive stars and winds from massive stars. However, this seems tautological, in that we are saying that we need stars to create stars! This might be acceptable for the second generation of stars and beyond, but clearly the first generation of stars needs something else (Seeds 2005).

After initial collapse, we expect this collapse to continue for anywhere between 100,000 and 10 million years depending on the mass of the collapsing object. The most massive objects will collapse faster and the least massive objects will take longer to form into a star.

How Stars Work

Stars work by generating nuclear energy. However, the nuclei of atoms can only collide and fuse if the temperatures are many millions of degrees in the core of the star. How does it get that hot? At every point in the star, the star must have a balance between gas pressure and the force of gravity (from the star itself) so that it neither expands into nothingness nor collapses in on itself. For this to happen, the star must be relatively cool (though still hot by human terms) near the surface, so that the gas pressure does not push away the small amount of mass near the surface. But in the center of the star, the temperatures must be very high so that the resulting gas pressure can act against the immense gravitational forces from the entire mass of the star above. Once the center of the star is this hot, it will be adequately hot for nuclei of atoms (in the case of the Sun, hydrogen) to fuse together and release energy in the process (as discussed in Chapter 1). During this fusion process, the total amount of mass in the end is less than what we begin with. This missing mass is converted to energy, considering Einstein's famous $E=mc^2$ equation. Though the amount of energy drawn from one reaction is tiny, there are so many reactions going on in the core of the Sun at any one time that it adds up to an enormous amount of energy (4×10^{26} joules/sec as opposed to the 100 joules/sec you'd expect from an incandescent light bulb).

Stellar Evolution: Supernovas, Pulsars and Black Holes

All stars must evolve as they begin to deplete their supply of hydrogen. However, for the least massive stars, this will only happen very slowly, and there may be almost no noticeable evolution over the history of the Universe. For intermediate mass stars such as the Sun, we will definitely notice effects of evolution, especially over billions of years. After the Sun burns hydrogen to helium for billions of years, the helium core that's left contracts to a very dense state. This core cannot effectively heat up as a normal gas would, and so pressure tends to build up outwards in the surrounding layers of hydrogen. This will lead to the Sun swelling to a size that will take it out to the orbit of Mars as it becomes a red giant star, and then later lose its outer layers to become a white dwarf (the remaining core of the former red giant). Though these outer layers leave the red giant at a rate of a few miles per second, this event is just a whisper. The most dramatic evolution will occur for the most massive of the stars. These stars will undergo nuclear burning all the way to iron, in various stages, each one lasting for a shorter time than the previous, and with the last burning stage of silicon to iron only lasting about two days! (Caroll and Ostlie 2007). The star can't burn heavier elements since all reactions involving the burning of iron will actually lose energy instead of gaining it. At this point, the star must collapse (with no outward pressure to hold up all of that mass). How then does a collapse lead to an explosion? The infalling material will tend to rebound from the denser core, eventually sending a strong pressure wave (a shock wave) outward, causing the explosion (in addition, vast energy production in the form of neutrinos invigorates the shock from below, keeping it from stalling). This particular type of stellar explosion is referred to as a Type II supernova. There are other types of supernovas

(Type I) as well that involve the explosion of stars in a binary system that we already discussed in reference to the discovery of dark energy. We know that a few supernovas (some likely Type I, and others, Type II) occurred in our Galaxy in the previous two millennia, as we can observe the rapid expansion of the remaining gas, and match to the location in the sky of spectacular stellar events that were recorded by the Chinese (one as early as 185 AD) and for some events, also recorded by European astronomers such as Kepler and Tycho. Some of these were even observed during the daytime and would have been bright enough to cast a shadow at night (Marschall 1988). Curiously, no such events have occurred in our part of the Galaxy in the hundreds of years since the invention of the telescope, though there is some evidence that they have occurred in other far reaches of the Galaxy, obscured from view. Past supernovae should leave behind certain elements that won't be found elsewhere in space. In particular, the INTEGRAL satellite found traces of radioactive isotopes of aluminum that would indicate a supernova rate of about one every 50 years, which is much higher than directly observed visually from the Earth (Diehl et al. 2006).

The 1956 Arthur C. Clarke short story "The Star" dealt with the discovery of the remnants of a civilization that had been destroyed by the supernova of its parent star. Though many planets, or at least civilizations and their artifacts, would be destroyed in a supernova explosion, it is possible that some planets would be ejected from the stellar system entirely, and then wander around the Galaxy as a rogue planet. Though such planets would be interesting, they would be difficult to visit, as they would be extremely cold and have no light to speak of. In the end of the Clarke story, it is determined that this supernova, as viewed from Earth, was likely to have been the star of Bethlehem (though it's now more widely accepted that this was more likely to have been a rare conjunction of Mars, Jupiter and Saturn in 7 BC—the contradictory nature of the date nomenclature not withstanding). In the *Doctor Who* serial, "The Three Doctors," it is revealed that Omega, the first Time Lord, was able to power time-travel by causing a star to become a supernova. Supernovas are the most energetic single time events in the Universe and can generate as much as 10^{43} joules. As we will learn later, if time travel is even possible, it will probably require extreme amounts of energy. Thus, it's right-headed to think that we might want to funnel energy from a supernova in order to be able to travel in time. However, causing such an event to happen is another step even beyond this. In the *Lost in Space* episode "The Condemned of Space," the *Jupiter 2* encounters a supernova; however, this is depicted as a series of loud explosions that shake up the ship a bit, but then are a little too easily escaped. Unfortunately, in reality, if the ship had been close enough to be shaken up by the shock wave, then, even assuming that they could survive such a thing, it probably would have been close enough to have received deadly doses of radiation. Though there are actually two different films with the title *Supernova* (a third exists, but has no connection to astrophysics), one was made for television, stars Luke Perry, and is actually about an extremely destructive solar flare. The other film stars James Spader and was about a fictional "nine-dimensional matter" that interacts with a blue giant star to cause a supernova.

In addition, there is another class of stellar explosion called "nova" which are often confused with supernovas, especially in science fiction. A nova starts in a system with a compact binary (two stars in close proximity). One star is a normal star, and the other is a white dwarf. In a close system, the matter from the normal star will accrete onto the white dwarf by first forming a disk of matter that spirals onto the white dwarf (Patterson 1984). This additional matter will increase the surface temperature of the white dwarf, bringing it to the ignition point of hydrogen, causing an explosion on the surface, visible as the nova (Kay et al. 2013). For instance, the reference to the star Beta Niobe "going nova" in the *Star Trek: The Original Series* (*ST:TOS*) episode "All Our Yesterdays" probably was meant to be a supernova (and is most often interpreted that way by fans). In the *Outer Limits* (reboot) episode "Inconstant Moon" (and the Larry Niven story on which it's based) it is said that the Sun might be "going nova." This would be a surprising reference made by an astrophysicist, since neither a nova nor supernova is possible for the Sun (as it turns out, that wasn't the case. The Sun was just experiencing a historically bright flare). In the *Lost in Space* episode "Welcome Stranger," the space cowboy character Jim Hapgood (Warren Oates), as he's leaving the Robinsons' planet on his private rocket, says, "There's a nova coming in! It's all purple, silver and gold! Look at it go, boy!" At this point we see a meteor-like object whizzing in front of the spacecraft against the background stars, suggesting that the "nova" is a moving object. In the *ST:TNG* episode "The Inner Light," the *Enterprise* encounters a mysterious probe that seems to take over Captain Picard. We learn later that this probe was part of last-ditch effort of the planet Kataan to preserve what was left of their civilization as their Sun was about to "go nova." In this case it would seem that neither a supernova or nova are very likely, since the time from birth to supernova phase of a massive star would not leave enough time for evolution of intelligent life as we know it. A nova would expose any planets to intense radiation before any nova explosion. However, perhaps Kataan could have been the outpost of a previously evolved civilization. No doubt part of the confusion over novae and supernovas arises because some of the original science fiction stories that explored these possibilities were published before supernovae were determined to be a separate class of objects with different physical causes and much greater intrinsic power. Early science fiction would have just used the term "nova" in the same way that Tycho Brahe had hundreds of years

2. Introduction to Astronomy

before to describe any "new star" that appeared in the sky (all of which were realized later to be different types of stellar explosions).

As a result of so-called core collapse supernovae (Type II), the remaining core will be a neutron star. The matter in the stars has the same density as an atomic nucleus, which would be about the density you'd get by stuffing a moderate sized asteroid into a packing crate! The novels of Robert Forward (*Dragon's Egg* and *Starquake*) focus on a bizarre species, the Cheela, which can maintain a civilization on the surface of such a star. The conditions would be extreme, to say the least, with surface temperatures in the thousands and gravity billions of times stronger than on the Earth. Forward portrays the Cheela as essentially two-dimensional amoeba-like creatures, flattened out by the star's gravity. Nothing on the star's surface can be greater than about two inches tall, including all plants and animals. The environment is also too hot for normal biological chemistry to work so all life is just built on compacted nuclei of atoms.

Furthermore, neutron stars can rotate rapidly and generate extremely strong magnetic fields. These magnetic fields can trap and accelerate charged particles. Together, the rotation, and the concentration of accelerating particles create a beacon that can be observed if the beacon is fortuitously rotating through our line of sight, in some cases many times in one second. Such neutron star beacons are called pulsars. In the *ST:TNG* episode "We'll Always Have Paris," a rogue scientist is conducting time experiments in the environment of a pulsar. Though the time distortions depicted in this episode would likely take considerably more energy that even a pulsar could provide, it is right to think that the strong gravity near the surface of the neutron star would distort time, as we discussed in Chapter 1.

The most massive of stars can then collapse further, and in fact collapse to such high densities that even light cannot escape from its surface, thus earning the famous moniker "black hole." In fact the physics of such objects calls for a collapse to a single point in space (called a singularity, and possessing no extent in space at all). Whether singularities can really exist is the subject of some debate among astrophysicists; however, we do see in nature objects that seem to otherwise possess characteristics of black holes. Though black holes may indeed be singularities, each one has a characteristic radius that acts as a "point of no return." If one passes beyond this point, there is no turning back, and you are forever trapped by the black hole. We should note that this does not necessarily mean that you are instantaneously "sucked in" to a black hole. You can be in this state of limbo for a long time, especially if you are nearing a very massive black hole that has a large characteristic radius that puts you far enough way that you will not immediately be affected. However, for stellar mass black holes, you will likely get into problems even before this point. Black holes have been the subject of episodic science fiction, and in the early days, couldn't really settle on what they should be called, though the term "black hole" was coined by John Wheeler in 1967, and used in scientific literature shortly thereafter. For instance, in the *ST:TOS* episode "Tomorrow Is Yesterday" (aired in 1968), the term "black star" is used, and then a few years later in *Space: 1999*, we see an episode entitled "Black Sun" (aired in 1975), about a journey into a black hole (and the same term, "black sun," is also used in later episodes of that show). We'll explore here and elsewhere how these shows use black holes, and how accurate these depictions are likely to be. Black holes are often used as devices for time travel, or space travel across large distances (as a wormhole). The reality is that even if certain versions of black holes were to allow for it, any astronaut and his ship would be torn by the extreme tidal forces experienced when approaching the black hole (this is depicted reasonably, at least the first time the black hole is encountered, in "Black Sun"). In the "Black Hole" episode of the animated series *Ren & Stimpy*, both Ren and Stimpy experience the strong tidal forces when approaching the black hole. However, from there on in, presumably after crossing the event horizon, they begin to experience some surreal effects, such as seeing floating cooked turkeys in the sky. More recently and more seriously, the film *Interstellar* has the protagonist, an astronaut named Cooper, purposely flying directly towards a black hole. He also has some very bizarre experiences, apparently after crossing the event horizon, which we will discuss more in the chapters on extra dimensions (Chapter 4) and time travel (Chapter 5). As in "Black Sun," we can't know exactly what happens at this point, it seems more likely that they would be instantly killed.

Black holes need not just result from evolution of massive stars. In fact, we believe that supermassive black holes may exist in the center of every galaxy. Decades of observations indicate that in the center of our Galaxy resides a 2×10^6 solar mass (this number can vary by a factor of two in the literature) black hole (Melia and Falcke 2001) and in other galaxies can easily be 10^8 solar masses (Caroll and Ostlie 2007) and the most massive black hole of this type can be about 10^{10} solar masses or even greater in some galaxies, such as NGC 4889 and NGC 3842 (Overbye, "Astronomers Find Biggest Black Holes Yet" 2011). Hydrogen gas falling on to a supermassive black hole is now known to be the fuel source for active galaxies. Interestingly, we know that the rate of gas falling onto our galaxy's central black hole is tiny. It has been recently proposed that magnetic fields from a nearby pulsar are disrupting flow onto this black hole, thus possibly suppressing the radiation we'd expect from a massive black hole (Schwarzschild, "A Pulsar Reveals a Strong Magnetic Field Near Our Galaxy's Center" 2013).

Very small quantum black holes may also be possible, though these also do not result from star formation processes. It may be possible to infer their existence from results of the Large Hadron Collider. Most basically put, if we have a particle that has roughly the Planck mass, and an associated length scale that is approximately the Planck length (as discussed in Chapter 2) it can become a quantum black hole. However, at face value, it would be impossible with today's technology to detect such a black hole since the energies associated with the Planck mass are orders of magnitude greater than the upper bound of what the LHC can detect. However, as we discuss in Chapter 4 in more detail, this may be mitigated if large extra dimensions are possible. If there are large extra dimensions, it could mean that the Planck length is much larger than what we have been assuming for a Universe with three spatial dimensions. Current experimental limits on the size of extra dimensions suggest a Planck scale that is within reach of LHC (Dvali 2015).

Planet Formation and the Discovery of Exoplanets

As we have seen, early in a star's evolution it will begin to turn on its nuclear reactions. During this early phase, it's expected that planets would likely form from a disk of gas and dust that surrounds the nascent star. We know this phase is brief because we see these disks in molecular clouds with current star formation but not in clusters of very young stars such as the Pleiades (Armitage 2010). Another compelling fact is that the size of this disk is roughly the same scale as our Solar System, about 100 A.U. (excluding the much more distant Oort Cloud of comets) and shows evidence of dust grains mixed in with gas. In fact, circumstellar dust disks were first discovered around main sequence stars (Vega in particular) in 1983 using data from the infrared satellite, Infrared Astronomy Satellite or IRAS (B. Zuckerman 2001). We expect that all planets form by dust grains sticking together enough to eventually form what we think of now as small asteroids, essentially very large boulders. Once they get to be about 100 meters across, the growth slowed down, and the objects got bigger via infrequent chance collisions. Eventually, once the remaining objects were about ten times this size, gravity became important in attracting the objects to each other. At this point, the remaining planetesimals rapidly accreted to form much bigger planets (Armitage 2010). The general idea from here is that icy planetesimals (that would eventually become gas giants, such as Jupiter) could only form in the outer Solar System where the disk is cold. These could combine quickly and eventually also attract large amount of light gases such as hydrogen and helium. These notions of planetary accretion make it into the 1978 *Doctor Who* (with Tom Baker as the Doctor) episode "The Underworld." In this episode, the spaceship that the Doctor makes it on to gets stuck in a nebula that is beginning to form planets. They soon notice that a planet starts to form around the spaceship! In fact, another ship with which they were attempting a rendezvous had long ago turned into a full planet. Though we have already seen that a full planet can't really form in this way, it was a good attempt at showing how an artificial object could potentially morph into something more natural, such as a planet.

What happens next was a matter of little debate before 1995 because the end results we see in our own Solar System guided the models for planet formation. Our models regarding Earth-like planets forming from small rocky planetesimals and gas giants forming from icy planetesimals seemed to be consistent with our Solar System. However, we have known since 1995 from the discovery of planets around other stars, that these models may need some modification. We will first discuss how these planets have been detected (and how we might detect more in the future) and then discuss the implications of the results. We have multiple goals in our search for exoplanets. One goal is to see whether our observations of other star systems are consistent with our own Solar System or whether they demand another model for planet formation. Another goal is to see whether there are any exoplanets similar to Earth in mass, composition and conduciveness to life as we know it, or already show evidence for the existence of life. We can then extend these results to

An early Hubble Space Telescope image of Jupiter. Many of the detected exoplanets to date are thought to be gas giants similar to Jupiter. NASA (STSCI).

2. Introduction to Astronomy 45

see what the implications are for life (and possibly intelligent life) in the Universe.

Some early attempts to find exoplanets (mostly between 1944 and 1974) by Peter Van de Kamp of Swarthmore College either were shown to be in error or at best, never confirmed with progressively more modern techniques (Encrenaz 2013). He was using an astrometric method that had been used to discover stars orbiting in binary systems. This method essentially tracks the small changes in position of a star due to the tugging of a companion. Unfortunately, this method has proven to be too inaccurate for use in detecting planetary companions, though that situation may change with the next generation of astrometric space telescopes, such as the recently launched European satellite, Gaia. Interestingly, this was the technique used to find the planet that would destroy life on Earth in the film *When Worlds Collide* (Luokkala 2014).

For more than the first decade of planet discovery, most of the planets discussed above were discovered using Doppler spectroscopy (also called velocimetry). Interpreting the velocities using the Doppler Effect, we can see that recurrent blue shifting and red shifting in a periodic manner is expected to occur for a star moving in an orbit that is not inclined very much to our line of sight. Though we most often think of planets moving around a much more massive star, in actuality both planet and star are moving about a common center of mass. In most cases, the planets we are interested in are far too dim to observe directly, so we must focus on the parent star. We can see the light shifting into the blue or red by looking at specific spectral lines and watching them shift. The amount they shift is directly related to the orbital velocity, which will depend on the mass of the orbiting planet and its distance from the star. This motion can be complex if there are multiple planets orbiting the star, which we now have seen is often the case.

Another increasingly common way to detect planets, particularly since the advent of the Kepler mission (which has now probably come to an end) is the transit method. A special telescope onboard the spacecraft scans the sky, looking at thousands of Sun-like stars. This data is transmitted back to the ground, where computers can look at how the detected light of a particular star varies with time. If a significant dip in the light is seen, it may be due to an orbiting planet partly covering the disk of the star (in this way, it's very similar to an eclipse, though much less of the light is being blocked out.) The stars are then observed over and over, and if these transits repeat, then we know we have discovered a planet around the star. These dips in flux are often at the 1% level, which is why it was uncommon to observe this effect from the ground before the advent of the Kepler satellite. In some rare cases, we may be able to combine both the Doppler and transit methods. The advantage of that is that the Doppler method gets you information about the mass of the planet. The transit method gets you information on the diameter of the planet. Putting the two together, it is possible to determine the average density of the planet. Since gaseous planets will have a much lower density than rocky planets, we can use this information on density to gain information on the composition of the planet. The first such combined set of observations was made by David Charbonneau and others in 1999. This led to the determination of a planetary density to be about 0.3 gm cm^{-3}, which is more than a factor of two less than the density of Saturn, the lowest density planet in our Solar System. Clearly, this is a gaseous planet, and may even be "stretched out" by tidal forces, leading to the lower density (Encrenaz 2013). Some researchers have even gone beyond this to determine more about the atmosphere of terrestrial planets. That is, with the information from these observations, it might be possible to determine whether the depth of the atmosphere is small or large as compared to the radius of the planet (Cooper 2013). A planet that was truly analogous to Earth would have a relatively small atmospheric depth but also relatively high density due to the heavier gases, such as oxygen and nitrogen. Further in-depth studies such as those above have shown that in theory a variety of planetary types that we would not have expected just from observing our own Solar System could exist. For instance, there are planets rich in carbon that may be covered in oceans of hydrocarbons such as oil and there may also be iron rich planets and water worlds (Stevenson 2013). Later in this chapter we will discuss some of the odd planets in science fiction and consider whether they are really possible.

Additionally, in about two percent of cases we can detect some planets through gravitational micro-lensing of distant stars. It is possible for a foreground object to pass in front of a distant star. The gravity from the foreground object can act as a lens on the star, and one of the effects can be a significant brightening of the star. In the case of exoplanets, the foreground object is a planet (but the star will almost always have no relation to the planet. It's a much farther away star, most likely). The major disadvantages of this technique are that the statistics demand that we'd only discover several planets per year this way, and we have no way of targeting particular systems or even know the nature of the star system in which we find this planet. One great advantage is that is the only current method for getting information on very distant planets. Eventually, we may be able to determine whether the statistics on distant planets are similar to those for more close-by planets, and ultimately whether the distribution of planets is at all dependent on location within the Galaxy. In addition, this technique is much less sensitive to mass than other techniques, meaning it might eventually become the best method for discovering the bulk of low-mass planets. In about three percent of cases, light from a planet can be observed directly, but with today's technology, this will remain one of the less common ways to detect exoplanets as it is limited to detecting very large planets that are in far orbits around the parent star.

As of this writing, about 1,000 planets have been discovered, most being in orbits around Sun-like stars. Extrapolating from these results suggest that about seven percent of all stars undergoing normal nuclear burning possess planets including a number of red dwarf stars (J. A. Johnson 2014), further implying that there are tens of billions of planets in the Galaxy. In fact, there have already been some discoveries of planets around red dwarf stars. *The Outer Limits* episode "Wolf 359" suggests the possibility of life on a planet of a nearby red dwarf star (the basic facts given about this star's properties within the episode are correct). However, it's likely that any planet that is close enough to the red dwarf star for water to be mostly in liquid form on the surface would be tidally locked. That is, over time, the rotation rate of the planet matches its orbital period around the star, and as a result, one side of the planet is always facing the star. This can lead to rather extreme conditions on each side of the planet, and possible raging storms in the transition zones (Crowell 2007). We'll discuss conditions for life more in Chapter 9. The vast majority of the planets discovered are giant planets in close orbits around their parent star. With many being closer to their star than Mercury is to the Sun, they are appropriately referred to as "hot Jupiters." Interestingly, in one of Isaac Asimov's final novels, *Nemesis*, written in 1989, a few years before the initial planetary discoveries an alien intelligence was discovered on a giant planet, Megas, orbiting very close to its parent red dwarf star. Current techniques only allow us to detect planets down to about two times the mass of the Earth, but definitively detecting Earth-mass planets in Earth-like orbits may be a few years off. However, again extrapolating from the most recent observations, about 20 percent of all Sun-like stars have Earth-sized (if not completely Earth-like) planets in Earth-like orbits (Schwarzschild, "Earth-size Expolanets" 2014). It turns out that for some of these planets we can gain additional information on the nature of the atmosphere of the planets. It turns out that the gases in the atmospheres of gas giant planets will absorb light in a wavelength dependent manner. Therefore, the amount of light blocked during a transit should also be wavelength dependent. The exact nature of this dependence can then be used to determine which gases are in the atmosphere of a particular planet. We now know that "hot Jupiters" have carbon monoxide, water and methane in their atmospheres (Knutson 2013) as well as some with carbon dioxide (Encrenaz 2013). Furthermore, astronomers have been improving the Doppler method to at least be able to detect planets that have been called "extrasolar Neptunes" or "super-Earths" depending on what their ultimate composition turns out to be (Lovis et al. 2006). Certainly, at least some of these have a density that is far too low to be a terrestrial planet in the sense we mean for our own Solar System. They possibly have cores of water ice, or perhaps have rocky cores surrounded by hydrogen or helium atmosphere (Benneke and Seager 2013). In the future it might be possible to detect Earth-like planets around solar-type stars by using space-based infrared spectroscopy to detect evidence atmospheric water, carbon dioxide and ozone. In particular, presence of water and oxygen can be reasonably assumed to be correlated with presence of life, but that need not always be the case, and every case needs to be examined as extensively as possible. The infrared range for spectroscopy is preferable to the visible range in searching for relevant spectral lines, since at these wavelengths, the relative brightness of parent star and planet is not as dramatic. Though other direct detection methods are possible, such as using nulling interferometers, for now, these are only in planning stages. A nulling interferometer splits the light coming in from a bright star, sends it through an optical system of mirrors such that some of the light cancels itself out. This will allow astronomers to see dimmer sources such as planets that are closer to the bright star (Woolf and Angel 1998).

One of our primary conclusions from these results is that there are many gas giants in the inner part of star systems, in contrast with our own Solar System. Additionally, about 12 percent of such systems have multiple such planets. Taken together with our accepted theories of planet formation discussed above, there must have been a migration process by which giants in our solar system moved from where they formed to where they are now. In general, such migrations can occur by gravitational interaction with another planet, or, if it occurs early enough, there can be interaction between a planet and the gas or dust disk, causing the planet to spiral inward. Though this process was likely not relevant for our Solar System, it's clear that is must be relevant in a significant percentage of all of them (Encrenaz 2013).

We see potential exploration of these planets enter into science fiction recently, in the short stories such as "Choices" (about exploration of a planet in the Epsilon Eridani system) by Les Johnson and "A Country for Old Men" by Ben Bova (about exploration of the Gleise 851 system).

Planetary Interiors: Can We Reach the Core of the Earth?

Just as we have learned about the atmospheres and surfaces of planets, we have been learning more about the interiors of planets. In these cases the information is usually considerably more indirect. We have not yet drilled into the crust of any moon or planet (a little bit on some comets and asteroids), and on the Earth, have not successfully drilled past about 10 km straight down through the continental shelf. Considering that the center of the core of the Earth is over 6,000 km down from the surface, 10 km is not very impressive on the face of it. There are now efforts to drill even further down into the mantle from the ocean floor, where the crust is thinner. On the other hand, travel to the core of the Earth has been in science fiction lore since the time of Jules Verne's *Journey to the Center of the Earth* (1864). Though true to some of the theory of that particular time, this tale now shows its age, with the exploratory team meeting up with dinosaur-like creatures and not experiencing the sorts of temperatures (thousands of degrees) we know we'd experience as we go toward the core. There have been two more recent film adaptations. An even more modern version of this kind of story appears in "The Core." It may indeed be possible for a probe to plunge down through the molten parts of the mantle, potentially all the way down to the core. However, manning such a probe and keeping a cabin appropriately pressurized for people might be too difficult to manage.

Physics of Earthquakes

It's been known since the early 1900s that the continents of Earth are drifting. This was concluded from the noticeable way that some of the continents appear to fit together like puzzle pieces. Though the exact mechanics were not yet known, it certainly meant that large sections of the Earth's crust were malleable and a significant force was setting them in motion. As the observational evidence for drift came together the theories did as well, and it is now known that sections of crust (plates) are moving due to convection from the mantle below. Just as in a pot of boiling water, where less dense hotter liquid rises up, cools, then contracts and sinks, sections of the mantle will do the same. However, since the mantle is solid, convection can only occur very slowly. As plates move on top of the roiling mantle, much as objects move on a conveyor belt, the plates hit into each other, with great amounts of friction building up. The occasional release of this built-up energy can be felt as earthquakes (Kay et al. 2013). Earthquakes have been central to several films for four decades, including *Earthquake, 10.5,* and most recently *San Andreas* (really they all share the obvious plot element of massive destruction from some previously unexperienced earthquake, always in California.).

Terraforming

A common theme in science fiction is that if a planet isn't suitable for human living, then perhaps we can make it suitable (meaning, for now, more habitable by humans without cumbersome pressure suits and such). In fact some, such as Robert Zubrin, have suggested we could transform Mars with current technology into a more Earth-like planet if we needed to for colonization purposes (Zubrin 1996). There may be several ways to accomplish this, but one way of doing it is to melt the polar caps to release enough carbon dioxide into the atmosphere in order to both warm it and increase the air pressure. It may be possible to melt the caps by placing large mirrors in orbit (at least 10 square kilometers in area and hundreds of thousands of tons for even a single mylar mirror above the southern polar cap). Another method might be to have groups of initial colonists building factories to purposely create chlorofluorocarbons (CFCs) to warm the atmosphere (an intentional version of global warming seen on Earth). And although this would likely require the power levels of at least the level of one of the largest cities on Earth, at a cost of hundreds of billions of dollars, neither is beyond the realm of physical possibility, especially for decades in the future. A third method would be to have certain bacterial agents release the necessary amounts of carbon dioxide. The bottom line is that it could be good enough within 20 years. A more complicated matter might be getting enough oxygen into the atmosphere for it to be breathable without apparatus such as supplementary oxygen tanks (Zubrin 1996).

Before getting into such things too deeply, we must consider the ethical implications of completely transforming a planet, even if it is to our benefit. After all, we have many objections to testing animal subjects here on Earth, or in altering native habitats and generally polluting the atmosphere and water. On a much larger scale, it would certainly seem that terraforming of a planet could be at least as objectionable, or even more so. In addition, there could be some unintended consequences of such a stupendous undertaking.

The inevitable politics of colonization and the transition to terraforming are central to the Kim Stanley Robinson Mars trilogy, which includes *Red Mars*, *Green Mars*, and *Blue Mars*. In the *Space: 1999* episode "The Last Sunset" the inhabitants of the planet Ariel attempt to divert the Alphans from landing on their planet and possibly colonizing it by giving them the gift of breathable air, and essentially terraforming the Moon. Though it's plausible that the Moon could hold onto an atmosphere for a brief period (we discuss this in the chapter endnotes), the most implausible part of this episode is that an alien race is somehow delivering them atmosphere in small spacecraft, and then releasing it all at once onto the Moon. Such an atmosphere would have a mass of many quadrillions of kilograms, probably requiring at least trillions of small spacecraft to deliver it. *The Outer Limits* (reboot) episode "The Human Factor" starts during a mission to terraform Jupiter's moon, Ganymede. The challenge in this case would be in raising the temperature enough to make the moon habitable, though this might be possible by purposely inducing a greenhouse effect.

Lessons from Planets: Global Warming and Climate Change

The potential warming of the Earth over the last century (and especially over the last several decades) and related potential dramatic changes in climate have been a matter of political and social controversy. In a recent article, Paul Higgins discussed possible approaches to handling climate change such as how to mitigate the effects by reducing emissions, adapting to the changes, or introducing additional changes to counteract the original ones (Higgins 2014). Though the precise data and their interpretation have been subject to much discussion, there can be little doubt that the Earth's atmosphere has warmed by approximately 0.8 degrees C since 1880. However, though there seems to have been an acceleration of this warming more recently from the late 1980s until the late 1990s (Houghton 2005), and this trend appears to have dampened more recently to the effect of less than 0.1 degree C, though some have disputed this "hiatus" (Karl et al. 2015). We include some potential explanations for these changes below. In addition, there has been a significant melting of Greenland and Antarctic ice, leading to sea level rise and ocean warming (Stocker et al. 2013).

Perhaps igniting most of the controversy has been a matter of the cause of the warming. We know that the increase in temperature is correlated with the increase in carbon dioxide in our atmosphere that is coincident with the industrial revolution starting in the mid 1700s, but especially the 1800s. Other greenhouse gases also contribute significantly, such as methane (Stocker et al. 2013). However, there is also some evidence that at least some elements of climate change, particularly those related to the upper atmosphere, such as depletion of ozone, may be related to variability of the Sun's radiation at least as much as causes related to industry (Lean 1997). The contribution of solar variability to long-term temperature changes near the Earth's surface is much less certain (Lean 1997). Recent work by a team of European environmental scientists shows that severe winters in Europe over the last 325 years have not been correlated with sunspot minima (occurring on an 11-year cycle), as suggested previously by others (Oldenburgh et al. 2013). There has been some recent controversy over the results of Dr. Valentina Zharkova, who has suggested that future solar activity around the year 2030 may have some similarities to the Maunder Minimum of the late 1600s and early 1700s (Shepherd, Zharkov and Zharkova 2014). During that period, Europe and

North America experienced historically cold temperatures dubbed the "Little Ice Age." Zharkova has hypothesized that a new "Little Ice Age" may occur starting in 2030, when we might be going into another Maunder Minimum. This hypothesis has drawn much criticism from climatologists who are quick to point out that these findings negate the effects of anthropogenic global warming which were practically non-existent during the pre-industrial period of the first Maunder Minimum and are now dominant (Gamble 2015). In addition, work by Hansen and others at NASA supports the idea that there is definitely some anthropogenic global warming, but also other components (Schmunk 1997). Some research has shown a possible connection between cosmic ray flux (mostly from solar flares, but potentially also galactic) and cloud formation, especially close to the Earth's surface (Bago and Butler 2000). However, this process is not yet well understood. It may be that particles from the Sun have a more dramatic effect on water-dominated clouds close to the surface, rather than high-altitude clouds dominated by ice (Bago and Butler 2000). Some have even suggested that global warming could potentially be mitigated by seeding clouds and other such activity, but others have grave concerns over such activity, especially in terms of unintended consequences (Tsonis 2013). We already mentioned that global warming may be "slowing down" in the last decade. There have been several proposed causes, such as oceans taking most of the heat (which itself can cause habitat and weather problems) or perhaps, as mentioned previously, solar radiation may just be at a slightly lower point, and responsible for some of this "lost" atmospheric heat. In addition, some of the same pollution that adds greenhouse gases to the atmosphere can also add particulate pollution that can actually lead to cooling. In addition, volcanic eruptions can exacerbate this effect. A similar effect was seen just after the eruption of Mount Pinatubo in 1992 (Y.N. Staff 2013). As we'll see in a bit, at least one planet, Venus, did indeed experience a runaway greenhouse effect that had disastrous effects. So, even if there is a slowing of the warming of the Earth in the short term, it's unlikely that this means we have no chance of seeing more at a later time.

The 2004 film *The Day After Tomorrow* depicted a sudden global climate change in the form of sudden global cooling from super storms forming over the Atlantic and tornadoes in the West destroying Los Angeles. Though the time scales are way off (we couldn't get quite those extremes in such a short time), some of the individual threats, such as more frequent damaging storms like Hurricane Katrina (2005, especially in Louisiana and coastal Mississippi and Alabama) and Sandy (2012, especially in New York and New Jersey), could be realistic.

Other films, such as *Silent Running*, *Wall-E* and the "Journey to Where" episode of *Space: 1999*, show the general effects of pollution and mistreatment of the environment. In each, environmental disaster leads either to resettlement into domes on Earth, away from the dried-up countryside, or resettlement into space. In the Phillip K. Dick short story "Survey Team," a group of scientists on a future post-apocalyptic Earth explores Mars as an alternative place to live only to find that it had been trashed by its inhabitants to the point of being unlivable. Later the survey team finds out that the Martians left to settle Earth six thousand years prior. The clear implication is that humans were thus responsible for destroying two planets: first Mars, and then Earth.

It's particularly interesting to see in "Journey to Where" (where we see a glimpse of future Earth in the year 2120) that there are fully domed cities, now also up on huge platforms, up above a dried out countryside. We see similar landscapes on other planets in *Space: 1999* episodes, such as the planet Elna in "Devil's Planet" (though these domed structures may be buildings within a city, and not the full city itself) and also the domed cities of Zeno in "Missing Link." At this time (1976) the film version of *Logan's Run* also featured a domed city. This particular type of domed city is seen in science fiction as early as Asimov's 1954 novel *Caves of Steel* and in the subterranean cities of the 1958 J.T. McIntosh novel, *The Million Cities*, but likely became an even more popular device after the architect Buckminster Fuller proposed something similar to enclose parts of Manhattan to reduce pollution (Hatch 1974). He had another related suggestion to build floating airborne cities made of the same structure as geodesic domes, but in a spherical enclosed structure. If heated slightly above ambient temperature, such a structure can rise into the air, and attain enough lift to hold up a small city. We see a similar idea in the *ST:TOS* episode "The Cloud Minders," in which the sophisticated educated class of the planet Ardana lives in Stratos (the appropriately named cloud city) and essentially enslaves the Troglytes, who live below on the planet's surface.

We can learn quite a lot from other planets on this issue, even though we are fairly sure that industry has nothing to do with temperature increases or decreases on these planets. We have the most to learn from Venus. Based on recent observations, the atmosphere of Venus is much thicker than that of Earth, and comprised mainly of carbon dioxide. The temperature at the surface is extremely high, even higher than that of Mercury, which is much closer to the Sun. The higher temperatures are consistent with the high concentration of carbon dioxide. The carbon dioxide molecule is known to be an efficient absorber of infrared radiation. As ultraviolet radiation from the Sun makes it to the surface of Venus (or made it in the past), the ground heats up to the point at which it can re-radiate infrared radiation. This radiation then gets trapped by carbon dioxide in the atmosphere, warming it further. Any water that may have existed in the distant past would have evaporated, contributing to further warming by putting both water molecules into the clouds and releasing even more carbon dioxide into the atmosphere that may have been dissolved in the water. Any phase of Venus' past with significant water likely lasted up to hundreds of millions years, but the oceans would have dried up billions of years ago (Bullock and Grinspoon 2012). So, the Venus of the Ray Bradbury short stories such as "All Summer in A Day" and "The Long Rain," both of which feature a very rainy Venus populated by modern-day Earth settlers, have long been known (starting in the 1920s) to be unrealistic, at least if the stories are confined (more or less) to the present and beyond (Sagan, "Life in the Universe" 1969). In the 1950s we started to understand that Venus was actually extremely hot. Venus was much too hot for liquid water, and probably too hot for any kind of life-form we could dream up (Sagan, "Life in the Universe" 1969). Thus a somewhat more realistic view of what life could be like on Venus was given in "The Living Lights" episode of *Science Fiction Theater* from 1956. Here an astrophysicist (Dr. Lurie) attempts to recreate the conditions of Venus in a bell jar. In an attempt to show that Earth-bound life could adapt to these conditions, he accidentally creates a new, powerful and destructive life-form. Here Venus is described as being very hot, and then Dr. Lurie quotes a temperature of about 240 degrees, which is definitely hot to any human, but a bit lower than the 300 degrees (Celsius) that was actually observed for Venus in that same year. So, if the scientist in the episode actually meant 240 degrees Celsius, then this quoted temperature is only a little bit off. If he meant 240 degrees Fahrenheit, as would likely have been assumed by the viewers, then the quoted temperature was much too low (though at least he got it right that Venus was much hotter than Earth).

This general process of planetary warming due to excess carbon dioxide (and some other gases) is known as a runaway greenhouse effect. It may be that the atmospheric effects we see now on Earth are analogous to this runaway greenhouse, though hopefully not at a point beyond ability to return! A group of astrophysicists in Israel suggest maximum naturally caused runaway temperatures for exoplanets of 1200–1300 K, which, though hotter than Venus with a temperature of only about 740 K (Lewis and Prinn 1984), is a significantly lower temperature than what has been calculated prior. This also suggests that such planets, if bright enough as compared to host star, might be detectable in the near infrared range of the spectrum as discussed earlier (Shaviv, Shaviv and Wehrse 2011). Closer study of many such planets, if detected, could lead to a better understanding of natural effects that lead to extreme planetary warming.

We can learn the reverse lesson from Mars. In this case, the planet is cold enough, and with a thin enough atmosphere such that carbon dioxide just isn't concentrated enough to trap enough infrared radiation to heat the planet. Therefore, most water after a point stays frozen underneath the surface. Without extra gases in the atmosphere, the planet gets colder rather than hotter, leading to a reverse greenhouse effect.

Weird Planets

What about some of the more oddball planets that we see in science fiction? For instance, there is a planet of gold, Voga, seen in *Doctor Who* in "Revenge of the Cybermen" (Parsons 2010) and a planet with chlorine atmosphere in *Space: 1999* (in "A B Chrysalis" and in that same episode a reference was made to another chlorine planet, so we know there are a least two in that fictional version of the Galaxy). Chlorine planets were earlier seen in the Isaac Asimov short story "C-Chute," that featured the Kloros, a chlorine-breathing race. The two things these two very different kinds of planets have in common is that they would have to be rare. The reason is that gold and chlorine are rare elements in the Universe, and it's hard to imagine a particular star system that would have greatly enhanced amounts of these elements in a proto-planetary nebula that can form into planets or their atmospheres. To give you sense of how rare gold is in the Universe, all of the gold on Earth (including in the unmined crust) is about 10^{14} kg, which is approximately one tenth the mass of Mars's moon Deimos. That may seem like a lot, but it only amounts to less than one 10 billionth of the mass of the Earth. With only three other terrestrial planets in the Solar System (and some much smaller moons and asteroids), it would seem unlikely that very much more gold exists in the Solar System. Perhaps a larger "super-Earth" in another star system would have more gold, but it's hard to imagine that other much more common elements wouldn't also be enhanced. Chlorine is significantly more abundant, with about 10^{21} kg on the entire Earth (a bit more than one ten-thousandth of the entire mass of the Earth), however, much of it is in the form of salts, especially in the oceans (Sharp and Draper 2012). Free elemental chlorine is reactive, easily combining with many other elements, so would not exist in the atmosphere for long, before being "frozen" out in the form of salts and other compounds. In fact, if the early Earth had had more chlorine in its atmosphere, it would have likely led to saltier oceans, and thus overall making Earth less conducive to the development of life. Nonetheless, there are no physical laws that would keep these sorts of planets from existing if those elements were present as the planets in that system were forming. We do know that interstellar chlorine exists, but, again in low proportionate abundances (Harris and Bromage 1984). But are we likely to see anything like golden planets in the panoply of recent planetary discoveries? The necessity of these kinds of planets being rare would likely indicate that they won't be among the first thousand or more planets discovered. However, we've been surprised by planetary discoveries before, so we will have to wait to see what the actual observations bring.

Other types of "weird planets" are a bit closer to what we may see in reality. For instance, the *Doctor Who* serial "The Keys of Marinus" features a planet with acid oceans. The planet Venus in our own Solar System no longer is capable of having oceans due to the extreme heat at the surface, but the clouds have large amounts of sulfuric acid and smaller amounts of hydrochloric and hydrofluoric acid (Parsons 2010). In the *Lost in Space* episode "Space Creature," the Robinsons come across a planet that has atmosphere with 50% methane. Incidentally, the story line introduces a creature (or maybe creatures, though we see only one) that is a living blue mist on the planet. Planets in our own Solar System with a lot of methane look blue because methane absorbs red light very efficiently, letting mostly blue light pass through to the observer. Though the claim in this story is that the creature itself is part of the blue mist, perhaps these ideas came from the scientific discoveries (known at that time) that methane planets would be blue. Significant amounts of methane also exist on Titan; however, its mixture with nitrogen in the atmosphere leads to an orange haze, rather than blue (and it also exists in liquid form on the surface). On Pluto, solid methane has been detected, indicating a temperature less than -296 degrees F, about 90 K (Seeds 2005) and we know other dwarf planets of the Solar System, such as Eris, likely also have solid methane (Kay et al. 2013).

At other times in fiction, planets are pictured orbiting two suns. The most famous example is Tatooine of *Star Wars* (Luke Skywalker's home planet). In addition, the Doctor's home planet of Gallifrey is occasionally depicted as being in a binary system (the planet of the Gonds in the serial "The Krotons" is also in a binary system). In the original *Twilight Zone*, the fourth season episode "On Thursday We Leave for Home" depicts Earth colonists struggling for existence on an unnamed planet circling two bright suns that keep the planet eternally bathed in light and heat (and an earlier episode, "The Little People," also features a planet with two suns). In the *Space: 1999* episode "War Games," the unnamed world that has attacked Moonbase Alpha is shown to have two suns (though this is only revealed in two brief frames of the episode). In *The Outer Limits* episode "The Mutant," the planet Annex 1 is also depicted as being continuously bathed in light and heat, but it is unclear whether the planet is supposed to be in a system with widely separated suns (only one sun is ever shown), or whether the planet may be tidally locked (as described below). It may be the case that Annex 1 as depicted is in a densely packed cluster (such as a globular cluster) or near the center of the Galaxy. In such situations, the amount of starlight may be so extreme (as in the globular cluster M15) that there would essentially be no night as we know it (Ward and Brownlee 2000). However, the increased amount of radiation under such conditions would render the planet uninhabitable (Annex 1 does have a radiation problem). In a number of television episodes the dual suns are depicted as being very close together in the sky. If that is so, then the two stars should set together, and not always keep the planet hot (as in "On Thursday We Leave for Home"). The exception to this would be a tidally locked system in which the rotation rate of the planet is more or less equal to the time it takes to go around in its orbit, effectively keeping one face toward the two suns. However, if this were the case, one would wonder why they wouldn't seek a colder spot on the other side of the planet, or in a transition zone between the two sides.

For a time, it was theorized that the Sun might have a distant brown dwarf (very low luminosity) companion that could occasionally force asteroids or comets to collide with Earth and cause extinctions, as it went through part of its orbit closest to the Sun (Davis, Hut and Muller 1984). This theory inspired some fiction, such as Isaac Asimov's novel *Nemesis* (though in his novel, the star called Nemesis is not in a permanent orbit, but passing through the Solar System). Though this theory has been abandoned for lack of confirming observations (Luhman 2014), some planets in binary systems have been discovered.

Another strange planet would be that of Metebellus 3, referred to in many *Doctor Who* episodes, and first visited by the Doctor in "The Green Death." The planet is said to orbit a blue star and is bathed in blue light. It would appear to first have indigenous serpent-like creatures, and then far in the future from that point, was at least capable of supporting generations of humans and intelligent spiders. This planet and its star are perhaps similar to the Vega system. Vega is a blue star relatively near to the Sun (about 27 light years away), and has, over the years, shown some indirect evidence of planets, asteroid and comets, but to date there has been no direct confirming evidence of a major planet. Earlier we mentioned the "debris disk" around Vega, which has since been partially resolved into sections that may correspond to an outer region of comets and an inner asteroid belt, similar to our own Solar System. It should be noted that the total lifetime of such a star is likely to be significantly less than that of the Sun, so less total time for life to evolve. It's also generally accepted that Vega formed well after the Sun, and so would not likely have had time for even primitive life to have evolved on a planet.

Asteroids, Comets and Impacts

In one of Isaac Asimov's early novels, *Lucky Starr and the Pirates of the Asteroids*, as the title suggests, the asteroid belt of our Solar System is home to marauding pirates. Throughout the novel, Lucky travels from asteroid to asteroid, finding pirate hideouts, vacation spots, and then eventually ending up on the largest asteroid Ceres (which we'll discuss below). In the first episode of *Lost in Space* ("The Reluctant Stowaway"), the out of control spaceship *Jupiter 2* is said to be headed for a "meteor swarm" and then is seen to be colliding with what look to be boulders, roughly the same size as the ship itself. At the start of the "Golden Man" episode of *Buck Rogers in the 25th Century*, Buck's spacecraft, *The Searcher*, is caught in a very dense asteroid field in the Alpha Centauri star system. When we see the view screen looking outside the craft, the sky is filled with asteroids. They eventually find themselves partially lodged inside an asteroid. A spacecraft in the recent *Doctor Who* episode "Into the Dalek" meets a similar fate in a densely packed asteroid belt. Though smaller meteors are certainly a threat in space, the threat from larger asteroids, at least as presented in this way, is usually dramatically overstated. The first asteroid, Ceres, was discovered in 1801 in an orbit between Mars and Jupiter. In the years following, many other smaller asteroids were observed, the vast majority of which were also detected in orbits between Mars and Jupiter. Most are just a few meters in diameter, not miles. These discoveries later led to the term "asteroid belt" that refers to the asteroids detected in this region. It is perhaps this terminology more than anything else that has led to misunderstandings regarding how many asteroids there actually are in this region or perhaps in a similar region in another star system, and how densely packed they are in space. As Philip Plait states in *Bad Astronomy*, this is better called the "asteroid vacuum," since most space in those orbits is empty (Plait 2002). You would have to travel a distance roughly equivalent to the distance between the Earth and the Moon to go from one asteroid to another. Additionally, there have been some misconceptions regarding how Earth-like a typical asteroid can be. In two different *Twilight Zone* episodes ("The Lonely" and "I Shot an Arrow into the Air") the protagonists are said to be stranded on an asteroid, but these are clearly habitable with both breathable air and Earth-like gravity. Both of these properties strongly suggest an object that is both too warm and too big to be an asteroid. In fact, in "I Shot an Arrow into the Air," it turns out in the end that they really are on Earth. As Mark Scott Zicree comments in the *Twilight Zone Companion*, "Any astronaut who crash lands on a body within our solar system that has the same gravity and atmosphere of Earth and doesn't immediately realize he's on Earth, had better go back to astronaut school" (Zicree 1989). A similar sort of mistake occurs in *Lost in Space* when, after crash landing on a habitable planet in another star system, Will Robinson suggests that they have perhaps landed on the asteroid Cerberus (which, aside from being uninhabitable, is confined to our Solar System, and it seems that the premise of the show is that they have become lost in space in an unknown star system, nowhere near Cerberus).

A similar threat is often seen from comets, which, as with asteroids, is often overstated. Comets have been observed since ancient times, but for thousands of years, thought likely to be an atmospheric effect. Though some ideas regarding motion of comets on the scale of the Solar System were accepted as early as Tycho Brahe (Bailey, Clube and Napier 1990), it's only since Edmund Halley discovered a comet in 1705 (later to be named for him) to be periodic, and thus an object in the Solar System orbiting the Sun. In fact, this discovery was a triumph for both Kepler's and Newton's Laws of Motion. As many other comets were discovered into the 20th century, it was discovered by Jan Oort, after examining the orbits of many comets, that they originate in a reservoir that is almost one light year in radius (Bailey, Clube and Napier 1990), thus extending nearly a quarter of the distance to the nearest star system (which might have its own version of an Oort Cloud extending out towards us). There are thought to be nearly one trillion comets surrounding the Sun in this reservoir. If one were to travel into this region you would have to travel a distance equivalent to the Earth-Saturn distance between any two comets. In addition to the Oort Cloud there is an inner belt of comets (the Kuiper Belt). There are many fewer comets here; however, they do have much shorter orbital periods, bringing them closer to the Sun and Earth on a more regular basis. Although a comet collision could be very damaging, they are not a source of immense heat (and in fact, are quite cold), as would be suggested in several *Lost in Space* episodes, such as "The Derelict" and "The Condemned of Space." Interestingly, in *The Starlost* episode "Farthing's Comet," the astronomer aboard the *Ark*, Linus Farthing, states that their encounter with a comet is the first close-up sighting of a comet nucleus (this is supposed to be happening around the year 2800). In actuality, there have been robotic probes (Giotto and Vega) that investigated Comet Halley's nucleus in 1986 and the Rosetta probe also did so for 67P/Churyumov-Gerasimenko in 2014. However, it may certainly be true that no human will directly encounter a comet nucleus until 2800 or even beyond.

The 1990s brought us a revival of "doomsday" by impact films such as *Armageddon* and *Deep Impact*. In *Armageddon*, a rogue asteroid, tens of kilometers in diameter, approaches the Earth and threatens to lead to another mass extinction event. NASA's primary plan to stop the asteroid is to split it with a nuclear device planted by astronauts who are actually oil riggers (and would have the requisite experience in drilling needed to plant the device). The way this is presented is problematic, as the riggers only blow up the asteroid once it is fairly close to Earth. In this case, you'd likely just get two very big destructive collisions instead of one giant one. The amount you save the world is minimal. Interestingly, an episode of the British series, *Space Patrol* ("The Wandering Asteroid") got this right in 1963 when they said that an asteroid that was about to destroy a colony on Mars had to be completely obliterated and not just broken up into relatively large chunks that could still do damage. A similar plot was featured in *Deep Impact* in which astronauts are sent to detonate a nuclear device on a comet that threatens Earth. Though the comet is partly broken up, some fragments still hit Earth and cause a disaster.

Though many are killed in tsunami, many others also survive. A decade later, the television miniseries *Meteor* presented us with the scenario of a comet colliding with the asteroid Kassandra, splitting it in two, and sending the pieces on to Earth to cause calamity (which was averted at the last minute). This is largely a reworking of the 1979 feature film of the same name which also featured a comet hitting an asteroid and sending it on a collision course with Earth. NASA has warned for some time now that a destructive impact is possible, and this was brought further to our attention during the meteorite impact in Chelyabinsk, Russia, in 2013. There was an extremely bright fireball and smoke trail (probably from an asteroid 20 meters in diameter) and some destruction of property when sonic booms broke windows, but no deaths (Kring and Boslough 2014). In addition, in 2014, there was an apparent meteor strike in Managua, Nicaragua, producing a small crater. This particular strike is interesting as it seemed to be coincident with the passing of the small (20 meter diameter) asteroid, within 25,000 miles of Earth. Some have hypothesized that it was a chunk of this particular asteroid that fell on Central America, though there is no evidence of that yet and NASA has reported that the asteroid's direction and distance at that time would be inconsistent with the time and location of the meteor's fall (at the time of this writing no meteor has been found at that site). In recent history, we know of several such meteorites, such as the one that hit a car in upstate New York in 1992. Further back in time, there is evidence of even more destructive impacts from only somewhat larger (30 meters in diameter) and denser (iron instead of stony) small asteroids, such as the Barringer Crater in Arizona (though, at the time of the impact, about 40,000 years ago, there were likely very few inhabitants of that region). It's now believed that any animals within several miles would have been killed, and devastating effects would have been felt past 10 miles (Kring and Boslough 2014). Even more dramatic was the discovery of the submerged impact crater off the coast of Chicxalub, Mexico, which is now thought to have been created by an asteroid impacting about 65 million years ago and have been a major contributing factor to the demise of the dinosaurs. The crater is thought to have formed from by an asteroid that was about six miles in diameter and, upon striking, gave off nearly 10^{24} joules (equivalent of about 10^{14} tons TNT) in energy.

Telescopes

Since the time of Galileo, over 400 years ago, the telescope has developed to be the primary instrument of scientific discovery in astronomy. The basic concept behind a telescope has stayed the same over this period, though, of course, there have been many technological developments that have led to

2. Introduction to Astronomy 61

changes. First, a lens was used to collect and focus light in order to form images. For well over two hundred years, these images would be focused onto another lens, an eyepiece, and as the name suggests, the purpose would be for someone to look through this eyepiece in order to gain whatever information they needed on a particular astronomical object. The situation improved with the development of mirrors (beginning with Isaac Newton) as the primary light-collecting device in telescopes. Though it took another 200 years, this ended up being critical to the development of observational astronomy, as large lenses ultimately get too heavy to be used in telescopes, and much lighter mirrors are more effective. In fact no major research facility was equipped with a refracting (lens-based) telescope after the Yerkes Observatory was built in 1897 in Williams Bay, Wisconsin (operated by the University of Chicago).

Though the eye is fairly good at detecting dim objects quickly, especially with the aid of a telescope, it's not very good at collecting light over a long period of time (that is, we won't do better by looking at an object for a longer period of time). Also, save for memories, the eye can't create a good permanent record of what it views. This situation greatly improved with photography in the second half of the 19th century, and then about 100 years later, the CCD (charge coupled device) camera. Each of these allowed us to compensate for the weaknesses of unaided eye observations. They allow for us to collect light for longer periods of time in order to see dimmer objects, and also to keep a record of these observations in a photograph or digital image.

Additionally, telescope technology has developed at other wavelengths outside of the visible range over the last few decades. The first strides were in radio astronomy. Karl Jansky was able to develop a crude radio detector (able to detect the Sun, Moon, and the center of the Galaxy). Later, Grote Reber developed the first focusing radio telescope. Later, radio interferometers were developed, interconnecting many separate antennas and effectively increasing the resolution. In the more recent decades, the ability to get into orbit with rockets was critical for making X-ray, Gamma ray and infrared astronomy practical, since most light at these wavelengths are absorbed efficiently by the atmosphere. Gamma rays are too energetic to be focused by any practical mirror or lens we could build with current technology. Therefore, other techniques must be used for collecting gamma rays. One of these, historically, has been the spark chamber detector. A photon hitting the top of the chamber will create an electron-positron pair that tracks through the chamber. The path of these particles can then be used to find the location of the source to within several degrees (in this way it acts like a crude imaging telescope).

Telescopic discoveries are critical to the plots of several films, usually the ones that center on an astronomical object that will collide with Earth or has otherwise been discovered to be near to us. For instance, the discovery of the planets that will collide with Earth in *When Worlds Collide, Gorath, Melancholia,* and the mirror Earth of *Journey to the Far Side of the Sun* (and also *Another Earth*). It's also a telescopic discovery of a planet around Alpha Centauri that inspired the mission of the *Jupiter 2* in *Lost in Space* to colonize those planets.

To astronomers one of the fundamental reasons for using a telescope is to achieve the best resolution (ability to see fine detail) possible for the wavelength of light we are viewing. It turns out the resolution improves with bigger and bigger telescopes, which is a primary reason for building larger telescopes. However, we can see that in science fiction, the concept of resolution and what it really depends on is strained or ignored. For instance, in the *ST:TOS* episode "Assignment: Earth," from up in orbit the *Enterprise* was able to clearly see Gary Seven as he was tinkering with a rocket from the gantry before launch. Since we can clearly see his eyes, and even some details of his skin, the resolution is good enough that we can see down to about one millimeter or even better. The exact angular resolution will depend on how high up the *Enterprise* was, but if it were about 400 km above the surface of the Earth (similar to the current orbit of the International Space Station), this would correspond to a resolution of about 0.5 milli-arcseconds. This would be one hundred times finer that the resolution equivalent to being able to see the smallest writing on a penny that you have placed in California and viewed from New York (nearly 5,000 km). Theoretically, that level of resolution could only be achieved if the telescope onboard the *Enterprise* had a diameter of a little over 200 meters. The entire enterprise is said to only be a little larger than this size, so it seems unlikely that the resolution could possibly be that good. The situation would be even worse if the *Enterprise* were in an even higher orbit. In general, resolution can be improved by building an array of telescopes which work by combining the signals from multiple independent telescopes so that they will act as one. Though the *Enterprise* couldn't house such an array, it's possible they could access data from one. By the time we get to *ST:TNG*, we know that the Federation gets help from the Argus array; however, it's not clear whether or not this array existed in the time of the original *Enterprise*, and almost certainly not in 1968 (the date the *Enterprise* returns to when they encounter Gary Seven). Though in reality we know of no way they would have been able to communicate with this array anyway since it would be many light years distant (at least not in a way that would communicate high resolution images in real time); however, in the Star Trek universe, there was the ability to communicate through "subspace" which allowed for faster than light communication.

Chapter 3

The Physics of Space Travel

There is perhaps no topic that has inspired science fiction quite as much as space exploration. As the television series *Star Trek* (all versions) famously stated during its opening credits, space is indeed the final frontier. It is not only a vast physical frontier, but also an expansive frontier of the imagination. Many of the pioneers of space travel were themselves inspired by science fiction. The masters of science fiction have often dreamed up methods of travel that were deemed impossible at the time, but then were later to be shown to be full of possibilities. Here we start with a brief history of space travel as it stands today, followed by a summary of the basic background physics involved in rocketry, and then we review some possible methods for future space travel and how they have been handled in science fiction films, television and print.

History of Rockets and Space Travel

To better understand space travel in fiction, we need to first understand the history of space travel, which starts with the development of rockets over many centuries. Though rockets in rudimentary form may be over 1,000 years old, written records of their use go back to the Chinese of the 13th century, who used small rockets in warfare as fire bombs. Some of these records suggest that these crude rockets could have been used as early as the 12th century (Riper 2004). Though there is some further mention of rockets over the ages (particularly, the spread of these same sorts of rockets through to Poland and Spain by the 13th century), the next major development did not occur until the Napoleonic Wars of the early 19th century (which included the War of 1812 that was fought against the new United States), during which British inventor William Congreve developed small rockets that were comprised of iron-cased gunpowder (Rogers 2008). This was a significant improvement over centuries of previous rockets that were made out of tubes of paper pasted together. In addition, the powder for these rockets was prepared and packed consistently for each rocket (Van Riper 2004). These rockets had a range a bit over one mile (about 1.6 km), but with very limited accuracy, they caused some significant damage and fear, but had mixed results in the course of these wars. In fact, perhaps the most famously recorded use of these rockets was at Fort McHenry near Baltimore, Maryland, since this rocket attack was immortalized in the U.S. national anthem ("And the rockets' red glare / The bombs bursting in air"). However, as it turned out, the rockets were actually fairly ineffective in that particular attack. Though there were some further successes in the ensuing decades in stabilizing rockets during flight (an important step in achieving accuracy), the next major developments were some decades later in the late 19th century, and were primarily theoretical. Due to increased capabilities of artillery, rockets were not seen as being as effective in the warfare of the late 19th century and so practical developments were not seen much during this period (Van Riper 2004). In fact, it was at this time that Jules Verne's novel *From Earth to the Moon* suggested that the first flight to the Moon would use a giant artillery gun to send the astronauts there (it was Tsiolkovskii, who we introduce below, who showed that this would be impractical, since the gun would need too long of a muzzle in order to be sure that accelerations wouldn't be so high that they'd kill the astronauts). The Russian physicist Konstantin Tsiolkovsky wrote extensively on the design of rockets, and was the first to write about the use of liquid fuels to create hot gases for exhaust, as well as step rockets (staged rockets), which would be critical to the advancement of the American space program in the 1960s. Unfortunately, his work had only been published in relatively obscure Russian journals that were not translated until well after his death and thus had little impact on the developing field. The next major advancements were more practical. In 1926, Robert Goddard launched the first liquid propellant rocket. The general idea was to mix a liquid fuel such as gasoline from one tank with an oxidizer from another that would control the burning of the fuel and result in a high velocity exhaust gas. If the fuel is allowed to burn uncontrollably, then the spacecraft could explode, as is was the case with the space shuttle *Challenger* disaster in 1986. Goddard knew that solid fuels would not be as useful for his experiments since he would not be able to control their burning very well. The first flight was very brief (2.5 seconds) and did not go very high (41 feet), but the proof of concept was important in the serious development of rocketry, and Goddard himself was able to improve on his designs and flight over the next few years prior to the outbreak of World War II (by 1935 his rockets reached 7,500 feet and were the first to include gyroscopes for stabilization). In parallel to these developments, Hermann Oberth of Germany published the first treatise on rocketry that was to be taken seriously, since Tsiolkoviskii's publications were largely ignored on an international scale during his time. One of the most important developments as a result of Oberth's work was the establishment of independent rocket research in Germany (Moore 1969). Independent rocket research (which was regarded as military research) was not highly tolerated by Hitler's new government, so these independent research organizations (and their personnel) were effectively absorbed into formal military programs, where they could be monitored more closely. Not knowing of Goddard's earlier work, rocket developer Werner von Braun and his colleagues in Germany then perfected liquid rockets while building rocket weapons for Germany during World War II. The V2 rocket they built was impressive for the time, since it was able to reach just under 100 km altitude, the boundary of what we now think of as "space." Though the accuracy as a weapon was relatively crude, and did not change the outcome of the war as Hitler had wanted (thankfully!), it still killed thousands of Allied troops and civilians as well as indirectly leading to the deaths of forced laborers who worked on the construction of the V-2. As the war was ending, and it was becoming clear that Germany would be defeated, Von Braun gave himself over to the United States where the Americans were quite happy in using his knowledge in the establishment of their own rocket program in competition with the Soviet Union (Moore 1969). Thus, the American space program, especially the push toward the Moon, was largely dependent on Von Braun and the German war machine that had supported him. Moon voyages were a particularly popular subject of early science fiction (though that term didn't exist yet) in the 19th century and early 20th century, with Jules Verne's 1865 *From Earth to the Moon* and H. G. Wells' 1901 novel *The First Men in the Moon* being prime examples. Interestingly, the latter novel brings up the concept of a propulsion system that can counteract gravity, using some of the same principles used in blocking out radiation. Though this form of "anti-gravity" is not possible, it does pre-sage some notions about gravity (and similarity to other field theories) that we wouldn't see until Einstein came up with his theory of relativity a few years later.

Ethical Dilemmas

Von Braun's contributions remain controversial. He admittedly had been a member of the Nazi party (and, in particular, was an S.S. captain), and was later accused of personally abusing prisoners in the camp (Mittlebau/Dora) at which prison labor was used for the construction of the V2 rockets. As stated before, the rockets were effective in killing thousands of civilians in London, and many Allied troops (Neufeld 2007). We can ask ourselves whether it is ever ethical to use technology that was developed in this manner, and turn it around for good use. It is interesting to note that such ethical dilemmas often play out in science fiction as well. The most directly parallel situation comes about in the *Space: 1999* episode "Voyager's Return" in which the denizens of Moonbase Alpha come across a probe that had been launched by Earth many years prior. In order to obtain much needed information from the probe, this required interfering with the computer and drive systems of the probe. It had been revealed that this particular spacecraft had been created by scientist Ernst Queller, who created a similar probe that was responsible for killing hundreds as a result of an accident with the experimental drive system during testing. In addition, it was later revealed that the probe they were trying to recover was responsible for killing the Sidons, an alien race that lived in the path of this probe, Voyager One. The dilemma becomes two-fold: Is it worth putting Moonbase Alpha at risk by fiddling with the drive system of the recovered probe, in the hopes that they will better be able to retrieve its data? Also, can Ernst Queller (who had been secretly present on the base under an assumed name, Ernst Linden) be trusted to help with the probe? In the end, Queller redeems himself by using the probe's deadly drive system to fend off an attack by avenging Sidons. Queller is killed in the process (Muir, *Exploring Space: 1999* 1997).

Physics and Rockets

Up to the present day, and likely well into the future, the physics of space travel really just depends on one fundamental concept, and that is Newton's Third Law, the principle of action and reaction as discussed in Chapter 1. From the point of view of conceptual physics, it doesn't matter whether you are throwing hot gas, baseballs or rocks outside the bottom of your spacecraft to get it going upward. But, as a practical concern, the only things we can throw back at high enough velocity are hot gases, so that's what we use for now. Keep in mind that all of the gas is not exhausted at once. There is a continuous release of the gas as it is converted from fuel. Thus, it is actually more analogous to slowly pouring sandbags out off the back of a boat to get it to move forward than throwing one big heavy item overboard (Moore 1969). An equivalent method for thinking about rockets is in terms of conservation of momentum, which we discussed in detail in Chapter 1. That is, for every step along the way, as the rocket is losing mass in terms of fuel converted to exhaust gas thrown out the back of the rocket, the rest of the mass lurches forward with a new velocity that is related to the velocity of the exhaust gas. However, it's cumbersome to solve for the velocity at every step along the way. In this case, it's actually easier to use calculus to determine the final velocity. This has been the method used in modern rocketry since Robert Goddard had his first successful flight in 1926. However, there is a limit to

3. The Physics of Space Travel 67

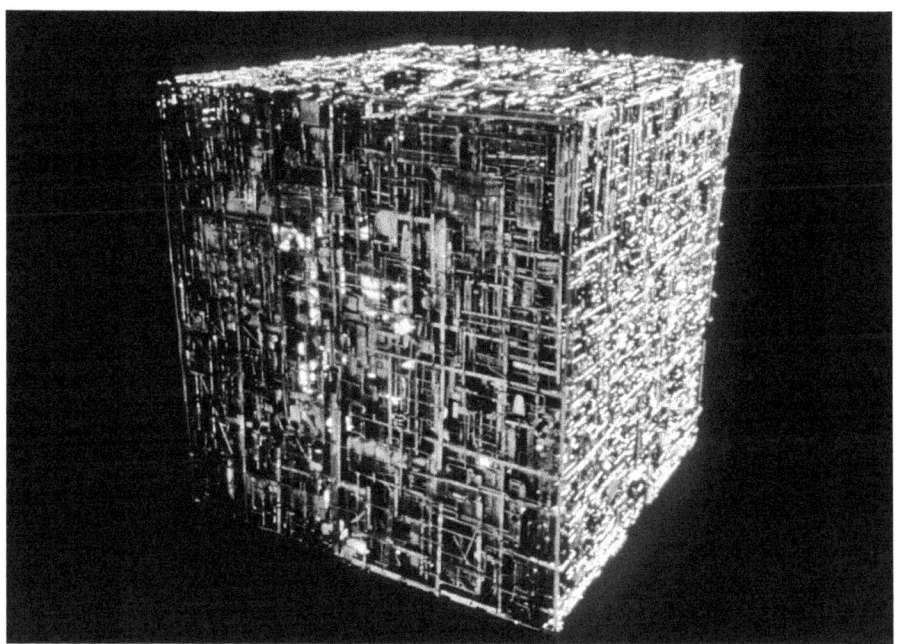

The Borg spacecraft, here as depicted in *Star Trek: Voyager*. Photofest.

how fast these gases can move, and the maximum velocity is about 6,600 miles/hr (about 3 km/sec). We refer the interested reader to calculations in the endnotes,[1] but the final speed of the spacecraft depends on how much fuel is being expelled out the back as hot gases, and how much mass is left over (as rocket, passengers and payload) to be sent through space. Practically speaking, we can reach rocket velocities about two times greater than the gas exhaust velocity. We have probably reached the limit of how fast we can expel gases, so if we ever want to go significantly faster through space, we will have to think of what we can expel at higher velocity with significant mass. We can gain a little bit of extra final velocity for the amount of fuel we put in by ejecting some of the rocket's own mass as the rocket becomes emptied of fuel. This process, known as staged rocketry, has been used in the worlds' rocket programs for decades. Much of science fiction, especially that which deals with the near future, depends on this same concept for chemical rockets.

Also, since, for now, we are sending rockets from the Earth's surface, both gravity and air resistance act against the upward motion of the rocket. The second effect is very important for designing rockets. Air resistance is stronger if the object has more contact with the air (bigger surface area) and if the object is moving fast, since air resistance is proportional to the velocity

68 The Physics and Astronomy of Science Fiction

The Jupiter 2 spacecraft from *Lost in Space*. Photofest.

squared for large fast-moving objects. The former is the essential reason for giving rockets a tapered look and pointed "top" so that there is reduced contact surface of the rocket with air, especially in the direction of motion. For similar reasons, a rocket solely traveling through the vacuum of space need not have this sort of look at all. Thus, oddball designs, such as the starships and the cubical Borg craft from *ST:TNG* are perfectly reasonable, although would make it more difficult to take off or land on a planet with an atmosphere if that is ever required. In fact, the creators of *Space: 1999* purposely used "boxy" looking Eagle spacecraft, knowing that the intention would be to only use these spacecraft on the Moon (though during the series they often have to land on planets with atmospheres, which can be very inefficient for this sort of spacecraft).

Exploring the Solar System

We will soon discuss the technologies that could get us to other star systems, but a considerable amount of science fiction has been dedicated to travel within our Solar System so we will start closer to home. For decades,

3. *The Physics of Space Travel* 69

The starship Enterprise from *Star Trek: The Original Series.* **Various incarnations made it into various films and television shows of the** *Star Trek* **franchise. NBC/Photofest.**

the focus was on Mars and Martians, in such classics as H.G. Wells' (1898!) *War of the Worlds*, Arthur C. Clarke's *The Sands of Mars*, Ray Bradbury's *Martian Chronicles*, Philip K. Dick's *Martian Timeslip* and Robert Heinlein's *Stranger in a Strange Land* (just to name a few). Even some updated texts focus on Mars, such as Kim Stanley Robinson's *Mars Trilogy* concerning terraforming Mars, and the 2001 film *Mission to Mars*. An early film, *Rocketship X-M* (1950), shows the difficulty of space travel and speculates about what we might encounter on a first accidental mission to Mars (incidentally, this was the first film to show a female astronaut, and also showed a red-tinted Martian surface in an otherwise black and white film that is close to the real thing). In addition, 1960's *Angry Red Planet* features another ill-fated adventure on a (less realistic) orange-tinted Mars with tentacled plants and "rat bat spider crabs." The film *Robinson Crusoe on Mars* shows how a lone astronaut must survive on the inhospitable surface of the planet after his escape capsule crashes. Sending humans to Mars need not be confined to fiction. As Robert Zubrin and others have noted, we could potentially get to Mars with current technology; however, it requires commitment to certain types of flight paths

(Zubrin 1996). The primary reason why only certain specific paths can be taken is that fuel usage will be considerably higher in certain cases. As Earth and Mars travel in their orbits around the Sun, we might think it would be best to travel between the two planets when they are closest together (*conjunction*). However, this would have serious negative consequences. The problem is that the Earth would be traveling quickly in its own orbit around the Sun. To overcome this velocity and "jump" toward Mars would take a considerable amount of fuel. Since most fuel is used at launch and in immediate post-launch maneuvers, this sort of very expensive maneuver would be insurmountable, and is rarely ever seriously considered. The most economical choice is actually the opposite case, when each planet is in a position directly on the opposite side of the Sun from the other. In this case, a rocket can easily get into an orbit that is in the same direction as the Earth's orbit around the Sun. With small corrections, the rocket can then curve in a more highly elliptical orbit that meets up with Mars. The recent television series *Defying Gravity* keeps to Mars and Venus. Before astronomers realized that Venus would be far too hot to support life, Venus was also a fixation of science fiction. Venus was the focus of such B movies as *The Doomsday Machine,* in which a team of male and female astronauts are sent to Venus in order to restart the human race, which is about to be killed off by a "doomsday" weapon set off by the Chinese. There was also the adaptation of the Russian film *Planeta Burg* (released in the U.S. as *Voyage to the Prehistoric Planet*) in which a team of astronauts and their robot meets up with difficulties from dinosaur-like creatures on the Venusian surface and eventually discover the remnants of an ancient Venusian civilization. The possibility of life on Venus stuck around long enough to make it into the *Outer Limits* episode "Cold Hands, Warm Heart." Here Colonel Jeff Barton (William Shatner) returns from an exploratory mission to Venus. He almost immediately exhibits the symptom of perpetually feeling extremely cold. Eventually he shows more obvious signs of genetic mutation, such as hands that now look to be that of some unidentifiable creature and there are also changes to his blood. In the end it's realized that he started mutating after an encounter with a Venusian that he had since forgotten (presumably any Venusian would find our temperatures to be unbearably cold therefore the mutations also explain the earlier symptoms). An episode of the British action/mystery/science fiction television series *The Avengers,* "From Venus with Love," starts with amateur astronomers mysteriously dying off. All had been interested in observing Venus, and look to have been murdered. At first some investigators conjecture that there is something, maybe even intelligent life, on Venus that is somehow causing the deaths. To the credit of the writers, the characters do mention that life as we know it would be impossible on Venus because it is so hot. This theory is eventually abandoned when a more conventional murder plot is revealed. In the "Journey with Fear" episode of *Voyage to the Bottom of the Sea*, executive officer of the submarine *Seaview*, Chip Morton, is teleported to Venus by aliens who call themselves Centaurs, and by their own admission, are not originally from Venus, but another star system. Unfortunately, the common factor in most of these treatments is inaccuracy (often severe).

However, film and television haven't just confined themselves to the inner Solar System. *Journey to the 7th Planet*, though interesting in places as a film, unrealistically depicts encounters with a powerful alien on Uranus (although one thing they get right is that Uranus should be extremely cold. When they start encountering much warmer areas with breathable air, they suspect something some entity is projecting illusions, which turns out to be so). Improbably, in the *Doctor Who* episode "The Sunmakers," the TARDIS lands on Pluto, finding a highly technological society there. As the Doctor learns, Pluto is made habitable by artificial suns created by an alien society, supplying these suns at great cost to the humans eking out an existence there.

The Future of Human Spaceflight in the Solar System

Trips to Mars and the rest of the outer Solar System may no longer seem much like science fiction (our interplanetary probes have landed on a moon of Saturn, and the most distant ones are now almost 10 billion miles from Earth). However, we have not yet achieved human spaceflight past the Moon. Accomplishing this now seems decades off even if there were to be a present-day commitment to using current technology, so it is definitely not a certainty. It's certainly a matter of debate whether we should spend the effort and dollars on human spaceflight. Robotic probes tend to be many times cheaper than similarly destined ships with personnel. Robotic probes would also be safer, since they don't require anyone to go into space. In the *ST:TOS* episode "The Ultimate Computer," the inventor of the M5 computer (Dr. Richard Daystrom), the greatest computer of his generation (in the 23rd century), states that he created this computer that will be able to eventually fully automate starships in order to keep people from needing to meet harm in exploring the Galaxy. However, we must at least consider the option of manned space flight for understanding science fiction that will devote itself to travel to the outer Solar System and beyond. In addition, we may also have to consider whether we are missing our only opportunity to build up space travel while we can. Ultimately, living separately from Earth may be the only way that the human race can survive. For instance, we may fall victim to global climate

72 The Physics and Astronomy of Science Fiction

The crew from the 2000 film *Mission to Mars* (Touchstone Pictures), a film about a modern journey to the red planet: Phil Ohlmeyer (Jerry O'Connell), Luke Graham (Don Cheadle), Jim McConnell (Gary Sinise), Woody Blake (Tim Robbins), and Maggie McConnell (Kim Delaney). Buena Vista/Photofest.

change or nuclear conflict. Even if we avoid all possible calamities, we must eventually face the fact that the Sun will become a red giant that will engulf the Earth within five billion years. J. Richard Gott makes a strong case for there being likely only one "space age," and that we are in it now, and that if we don't make the most of it now, we will have to remain on Earth and be forced to accept our fate (Gott 2002). In that instance, living on Mars would also be seriously be compromised, but perhaps by that time we would have been able to move out of the Solar System completely. One way of potentially overcoming this danger is to build colonies in space or to colonize a reasonably suitable planet, such as Mars. Most official long-term plans for going to Mars over the years have had the same problematic similarities in that they depend on extremely large infrastructures that take decades to create. At the time of this writing there is some uncertainty over both the immediate and long-term goals of the human spaceflight program of NASA. The U.S. Space Shuttle program that started in 1981 has now been ended, with incomplete plans for a follow-on vehicles and potential follow-on programs. The future may lie with a number of other nations, especially Russia and China, who have potential for going back to the Moon and then perhaps on to Mars. There are also a number of other countries with unmanned space programs (India, Japan, Israel, Iran) as well as private U.S. companies that have invested in rocketry (such as Elon Musk's Space Exploration Technologies Corporation, better known as Space X, and Orbital Sciences). Another effort is being led by Dutch entrepreneur Bas Lansdorp. His intention is to raise funds for a one-way mission to Mars (dubbed Mars One) with volunteers who will build a colony and stay there. Though some have dismissed this effort as underfunded and foolhardy (or even suicidal), strategies involving non-traditional funding sources and approaches may indeed end up being the best way to get to Mars (or anywhere else) without constantly kicking the can down the road until two decades in the future (Engber 2014).

Some other destinations have also been emphasized, such as the enigmatic moon of Jupiter, Europa, long thought to have conditions suitable for life underneath a thick surface layer of ice. An ill-fated mission to this moon is subject of a recent film, *Europa Report* (2013). The realistic, yet fictional, footage of Europa gives some credibility to the film, as well as the fact that they never really understand exactly what has confronted them. A similar mission with a similar fate was the subject of the recent film *Astronaut: The Last Push*.

Traveling to the Stars

So, what would prevent us from using today's rockets to go to the stars? We might expect that one solution would be to use brute force. That is, we can supply a rocket with a large enough amount of fuel to accelerate it to near light speeds, regardless of how low the exhaust velocity is. The rocket equation, at least at first glance, would seem to allow this. However, using the rocket equation and the typical exhaust velocities for rockets today, we

Rocketship X-M, the first Hollywood film about a trip to Mars. Depicted here are Dr. Lisa Van Horn (Osa Massen), Col. Floyd Graham (Lloyd Bridges), Harry Chamberlain (Hugh O'Brian), Dr. Karl Eckstrom (John Emery), and Maj. William Corrigan (Noah Beery, Jr.). Lippert Pictures Inc./Photofest.

see that this mass ratio (the mass of the full rocket divided by the mass of the empty rocket) would be approximately 10 raised to the 40,000th power! Aside from being an untenable number on most calculators and computers, we know that in the lifetime of the Universe we would not be able to come up with this amount of fuel, let alone actually carry it with us in an interstellar rocket. As we will see later, the problem is even worse as we get to near light speeds. Clearly, this would be an unacceptable solution. In principle, we could go a long way toward making this possible if we were able to send material out the back of the rocket at much higher velocities than we can with hot gases. Today's rocket exhaust velocities are only two thousandths of one percent of the speed of light, and thus it would take over 200,000 years to get to the nearest star system. Alpha Centauri is the closest star (actually, a double star system) with planets but Proxima Centauri is about one trillion miles closer. Proxima may actually be a third star in the Alpha Centauri system, widely separated from the other two stars, but we have not yet found conclusive

3. The Physics of Space Travel

The Angry Red Planet (American International Pictures, 1959), another early film attempt at depicting Mars, which in this version is full of carnivorous plants and rat-bat-spider-crab monsters. Depicted are the crew: Colonel Tom O'Bannion (Gerald Mohr), Dr. Iris Ryan (Naura Hayden), Professor Theodore Gettell (Les Tremayne), and Sam Jacobs (Jack Kruschen). American International Pictures/Photofest.

evidence to support this hypothesis (Beech 2015). Each of these stars would leave us with similar approximate numbers, assuming relatively low (and probably realistic) mass ratios (Goswami 1983). We could get there faster if the spacecraft could get some gravity assists from passing by massive planets in our own Solar System, such as Jupiter. During such a pass, momentum is transferred between the planet and the spacecraft. The spacecraft gains momentum by speeding up, and the planet must then lose momentum, though the amount of momentum loss by the planet is insignificant and will not change the path of the planet in a measurable way. Alpha Centauri (for now, including Proxima) is not only the nearest star system besides the Sun but also the nearest with a planetary discovery and is a bit more than four light years (24 trillion miles) from Earth, and the next closest, Epsilon Eridani, is more than two times farther than that. Lawrence Crowell discusses other stars within about 20 light years of the Sun. Most such stars either do not have any detected planets (and thus would make less interesting targets) or are potentially unlikely to have habitable planets due to being M dwarfs, though as we see in Chapter 9, life in such star systems may be possible after all, perhaps even abundant (Crowell 2007). For more possibilities, we could always go further into the Galaxy and within 20–30 light years there are several more Sun-like stars with planets, but these aren't very likely to be the first targets for space travel unless further observations show that they are the only stars to have Earth-like or otherwise habitable planets. Clearly, for practical interstellar travel, we'll need much higher exhaust velocities. In 2013, Kite and Howard called for more research into the technologies (mostly funded through the Department of Energy) that would allow for a robotic probe to the Alpha Centauri planetary system (Kite and Howard 2013). They argue, for instance, that funding this probe could lead to a new, and presumably successful, focus on fusion research. Ben Zukerman of UCLA replied to this article with his own letter to *Physics Today*, suggesting that there would likely be very limited public buy-in to interstellar travel of any kind unless the star system in question was known to be habitable (if not actually habited). A similar point was made a few years earlier by Lawrence Crowell in *Can Star Systems Be Explored?* (Crowell 2007). As Zuckerman points out, this would likely require a next generation telescope dedicated to planet finding, such as TPF discussed in Chapter 2 (which could be more than a decade off). In any case, we discuss progress on various technologies that can be used for interstellar travel below (B. Zuckerman 2014).

We should note though, that even if we can achieve high exhaust velocities, we want to be careful not to accelerate too fast, especially if we are interested in human space travel. Typically, we will want to keep acceleration to about the same as Earth's gravity so that the humans aboard won't feel any extra strain on their bodies. This acceleration will then put an additional limitation on how quickly we could get to the nearest stars. For instance, even if a rocket had an exhaust velocity close to the speed of light, and taking into account a typical mass in fuel, it could take about two years to accelerate to greater than 99 percent of the speed of light (Crowell 2007). Adjusting the mass in fuel we wish to use, and allowing for either slightly lower or higher final speeds can allow us to accelerate toward the speed of light a bit faster or slower, but practically speaking, we can't do this in less than a year because we wish to avoid harmful accelerations, and would not want to extend it past tens of years in order to avoid taking up too much time in one astronaut's life and avoiding the necessity of a generational ship. Considering time dilation effects that we discussed in Chapter 1, it will probably be impractical to go much faster than about 85% of the speed of light. Once we get to higher speeds, the differences between how time passes for someone on board the fast spacecraft will be dramatically different than on Earth. Even for an unmanned probe, it seems unlikely that the public will get behind funding a probe that may not return any results for 100 years, even if from the perspective of the probe, it reaches the target star in just a few years. This problem is exacerbated with people. It seems unlikely that most human astronauts will be able to tolerate returning to an Earth on which almost everyone they knew, including their youngest relatives, would have likely died long before their return.

Ion Drives, Plasma Drives and Atomic Rockets

One option that is already in development for small spacecraft is the ion drive, for which a beam of ionized atoms is created by a hot filament to be used as exhaust (Kaku, *The Physics of the Impossible* 2008). Though at present the exhaust velocities of ion drives are very low, the ion beam can operate for years (as opposed to the seconds or minutes of a chemical rocket), leading to large change in momentum over the duration of the flight. Thus, though the original exhaust velocities are low, these drives are much more efficient at achieving a desired final velocity. This makes such drives poor for initial launch from a planet's surface, but ideal for continuing on in space. We can then imagine a probe intended for the outer Solar System that is initially lifted into space by a chemical rocket, but then continues on with the ion drive (Crowell 2007). An alternate method for this type of drive is to ionize hydrogen and have the plasma guided out of the rocket as thrust using magnetic fields (Crowell 2007). Though *ST:TOS* (e.g., "Spock's Brain") occasionally discussed various spacecraft that ran on ion power, it seems unlikely that they were thinking of this type of ion power, since it can't push a very high mass object very far. However, it is possible that they were thinking of a considerably more scaled up version that could have been used for certain maneuvers. Another possibility for fuel is the use of either fission or fusion reactions (as we discussed in Chapter 1, and which also applies to the Sun, as discussed in Chapter 2 and weapons as discussed in Chapter 8). As we saw in Chapter 1, controlled nuclear fusion is very difficult to achieve, so first there was much consideration given to nuclear fission rockets, since fission reactors had already been developed. The idea was to use fission reactions to heat up hydrogen gas that could then be used as an exhaust gas to propel the spacecraft. As we have seen, in nuclear fission, an atomic nucleus is split to result in a new atom and a tremendous amount of energy as well as other resultant particles such as neutrons. However, many safety issues plagued these early projects. Chief among them was the possibility of the reactants going into an uncontrolled chain reaction (a bomb, essentially). Nuclear fission propulsion was revived again during early discussions of a manned mission to Mars; however, was eventually cut from the plans. During the late 1950s, serious consideration was given to another type of nuclear rocket, and one such project was Project Orion (G. Dyson 2002). Though the original scope of the project was to stick to interplanetary travel, one of the top scientists working on the endeavor, Freeman Dyson, now of the Institute for Advanced Study, has published work on a potential scaled up version that could go to the nearest stars (F. Dyson 1968). In principle, it is possible to accelerate a rocket to about one-tenth of the speed of light using nuclear fission and fusion explosions (from bombs already in stock, or similar ones produced for this purpose). In a fusion reaction, two atomic nuclei combine to create a new heavier element and energy. Some reactions are much more efficient at producing energy than others, and furthermore, some only occur under very extreme conditions (ultra-high temperatures and densities). Dyson's idea was to use the shock waves produced by nuclear bombs to drive the starship. A great advantage of this design is that it makes use of an energy source that we already possess. However, as Dyson explains, nuclear bombs are great at releasing fantastic amounts of energy, but not comparatively fantastic amounts of momentum. In the end, a "pusher plate" was designed that could absorb much momentum from the explosion by purposely directing a jet of gas from the explosion toward the pusher plate.

However, a major concern in planning such a spacecraft was figuring out how it could survive numerous nuclear explosions. Certainly, if two cities (Hiroshima and Nagasaki) had been devastated by 15-kiloton nuclear weapons, how could a spaceship survive a one-megaton explosion, let alone a series of them? The answer is in the design of the outer hull of the ship. One idea would be to cover the hull of this ship with a material that can absorb the energy well. If the outer hull can absorb heat well (without melting) it can survive such explosions. However, it would probably take billions of kilograms (millions of tons) of copper to do so (and that is just the outer part of the ship). For comparison, a full Space Shuttle had a mass of about one million kilograms. Perhaps a better solution would be to cover the hull with a thinner substance that can slowly ablate after each explosion. This would protect the ship without adding so much mass. In fact, this was the basic idea behind heat shields in spacecraft such as the ones used in the Apollo program. Still, this spacecraft is ultimately limited by the fact that it is a traditional reaction rocket that must carry along the fuel, and would become far too unwieldy for going to any but the nearest stars. However, the greatest disadvantage of this design is that the Nuclear Test Ban Treaty would not allow us to test these weapons for use in a spacecraft, and thus the idea has long been abandoned. Additionally, this program and other alternative ideas for space travel became victims of the success of the chemical rocket program that was already making significant progress in getting us toward the Moon. Even the effort towards the Moon was known to be complex and expensive, and not much credence was given to alternative ideas that would add their own complexity, and of course, expense. Nonetheless, in the 1970s the core idea behind the Orion Project was revived by the British Interplanetary Society in the form of the Daedalus Project. Though only ever studied conceptually, the Daedalus concept replaced bombs with fusion pellets. Unfortunately, the type of fusion reaction proposed, that between deuterium and Helium-3, though possible theoretically, has never been achieved. Furthermore, the sheer amount of Helium-3 needed could only be found by "mining" the atmosphere of Jupiter first (Matloff 2012). These difficulties prevented the project from really getting off the ground. However, this study did show how much more efficient a spacecraft such as Orion could be if it were to be updated with cutting edge (or beyond cutting edge) energy sources (Kondo 2003). In 2009 the BIS started an updated version of Daedalus called Icarus (Icarus being the mythological son of Daedalus) that would include, among other things, updated fusion technology (though no one process has been selected, it is unlikely to involve Helium-3, since the collection of rare Helium-3 from the gas giants was one of the main aspects that led to the Daedalus project's demise) and better scientific return for the proposed mission (Obousy 2012). The 2014 Syfy mini-series, *Ascension*, starts with the supposition that an atomic rocket of this variety (named *Ascension*) actually secretly was sent out to the nearby star, Proxima Centauri, in the 1960s on a 100-year mission as a generational spaceship (the concept of which is discussed further below). A twist is eventually introduced that reveals that *Ascension* never left Earth, and the pretense of a generational spaceship was being kept up (at least to the inhabitants) as a social experiment. This sort of plot twist (of "the space flight was all really just an experiment" variety) has a long history in science fiction, such as in *The Outer Limits* episode "Nightmare" (one of the few episodes that were redone as part of the 90s reboot of this series).

Another related idea is to create a nuclear fusion reactor that scoops up hydrogen from space as its fuel, thus obviating the need to bring fuel along for the ride. This concept was first proposed by Robert Bussard in 1960. This drive system is featured in Poul Anderson's 1970 novel, *Tau Zero*, in which a ship of this type loses its ability to decelerate on its way to the relatively nearby Beta Virginis star system. A similar idea is alluded to in several *Star Trek* episodes. For instance, in *ST:TNG* episode "Night Terrors." At the end of this episode, they must release hydrogen into space to start a reaction that will free an alien species into space. Initiating this release, Data states "activating Bussard collectors." At first glance, the implication is that the

Enterprise would use normal hydrogen collected from space in its fusion reactors. However, we know from *Star Trek: Voyager* (*ST:V*) episode "Unforgettable" that the collectors are also used for deuterium (however, we'll soon see that in reality, this would be far-fetched). Though the Bussard "scoop" solves one problem, it creates others. Firstly, an extremely large scoop would be needed. Using Bussard's original assumptions about the density of hydrogen in interstellar space and speed of the spacecraft, he determined that a scoop 100,000 km² in area would be needed. However, since that time, it's been discovered that the density of hydrogen within a few light years of the Sun is much lower (perhaps more than 100 times) than the average for the Galaxy (Cox and Reynolds 1987), which is the number that Bussard used and is widely quoted in texts (Spitzer 1978). It's likely that this local cavity was created by a supernova explosion in the vicinity of the Sun about one to ten million years ago. This would clearly require an even more immense scoop. An even larger scoop would be needed for the rarer isotopes of hydrogen, such as deuterium, or for other gases, such as helium. Perhaps one way around this is to purposely ionize the hydrogen atoms in the path of the ship, and then use a magnetic field as a scoop. However, this process may end up taking in more energy than it delivers. In addition, the direct fusion reaction of a proton with another proton is not very efficient, so we would have to make up for this deficiency by being able to collect more and more hydrogen from space. Furthermore, though fusion research has continued for decades (primarily through research in thermonuclear Tokamak reactors, inertial confinement, and beam confinement) we have not yet achieved any kind of controlled fusion reaction on Earth for more than a fraction of a second, and none yet can produce more energy than they take in, so it will have to be some time before we make use of controlled fusion reactions in space. Despite this fact, several science fiction television series have focused on nuclear fusion reaction to power starships. In *Lost in Space*, the interstellar spacecraft *Jupiter 2* is described as running on "atomic motors" and possessing "reactor chambers," and perhaps a fusion concept is what they were embracing, though few coherent details are given throughout the series, and conflicting details have been presented in fan publications in more recent years (though some do indeed at least mention "fusion reactors"). Similar concepts are introduced for the "impulse" engines of *Star Trek* (the engines used on maneuvers that don't require exceeding the speed of light). The Ark of *The Starlost* was supposed to have been driven by a controlled fusion reactor as well.

Naively applying the rocket equation, if we wanted to get to a final velocity that is 99% of the speed of light, and we could attain an exhaust velocity of about one tenth of the speed of light using a nuclear pulsed rocket like that discussed above, we would need a fuel supply that is about 20,000 times the mass of the rocket and payload. This would be prohibitive, especially if we wanted a massive payload, such as a band of intrepid space explorers and all of their equipment. However, even so, it's only about 20 times the mass ratios used for the Moon landings (though these started with huge rockets full of fuel, eventually shed in stages, and the ended with the comparatively tiny capsule of the Apollo spacecraft landing in the Pacific Ocean). In reality though, the mass ratio problem is even worse than that stated above. Including the effects of special relativity, which we must do once something moves at speeds within a few percent of the speed of light, the amount of fuel needed would really need to be about 320 billion times the mass of the rocket and payload.[1] As a rocket (or anything else) accelerates closer and closer to the speed of light, the amount of energy needed for even small increases in speed becomes exorbitant. The problem is exacerbated even more for interstellar flight, since we would likely need to decelerate the rocket at its destination, then speed back up (and once again slow down) to get back home. Without showing further calculations here, it is important to note that even modest increases of the exhaust velocity will lead to huge savings in fuel, as would lowering the final velocity a bit. The largest sacrifice in lowering the final velocity would be in adding total time to the voyage.

The ultimate solution may be to use anti-matter, since the reaction of matter with anti-matter is the most efficient known reaction, and is thus able to produce generous amount of energy for low amounts of fuel. Thus, for similar mass ratios as with chemical rockets, we would be able to start with much higher exhaust velocities and end with velocities approaching the speed of light. The reaction between protons and anti-protons is known to create energetic particles called pions, and these could be potentially used as the exhaust for a matter/anti-matter rocket (Forward 1986). Alternatively, the high energy light itself created in such reactions can be used as exhaust, or perhaps used to heat a gas that can be used as exhaust. A major disadvantage of this method, even though it is extremely efficient, is that anti-matter is extremely rare and only now created as a by-product of high energy particle experiments. Furthermore, anti-matter is generally very rare in the Universe. Though there are some locations in our Galaxy where anti-matter might be more abundant, none are close to the Earth, so would not be feasible sources of anti-matter. Another disadvantage of this method is similar to the problem we would have had in using nuclear weapons to fuel the ship. That is, if we use this drive when on or close to a planet, we could do tremendous damage to life there (or even to the crew, if we aren't careful). It has been suggested by Charles Adler, among others, that this can be used to be an advantage, if the drive of the ship were used as a weapon against threatening foes (Adler 2014). We discuss similar subjects further in Chapter 8. Michael O'Brien's recent novel *Voyage to Alpha Centauri* focuses on the first manned mission to Alpha Centauri made possible by the discoveries of (fictional) Nobel prizewinner Neil de Hoyos, making the use of anti-matter in the spacecraft engines more practical. Anti-matter has made a journey to Alpha Centauri of nine years possible. As pictured here, the spacecraft is immense, with nearly 1,000 crew/passengers, including de Hoyos.

Solar, Laser Sails and Rail Guns

Instead of using a reaction rocket, we could think of other means of propulsion. One possibility is the use of a solar sail made of a very thin aluminum sheet (Rogers 2008). That is, pressure from light of the Sun can act against a large deployed sail to push the craft into deep space. In some sense, this is still dependent on the conservation of momentum, since the momentum of the light is being transferred to the sail. However, it is fundamentally different from a traditional reaction rocket because fuel is not being carried along for the ride. This is the same process that leads to dust tails of comets being pushed away from the direction of the Sun as the comet orbits. In addition, there are several possible sail shapes that would have advantages, such as being more easily deployable. Since sunlight would greatly weaken as the spacecraft goes to the outer Solar System and beyond, solar light would not be a reliable means of propelling the spacecraft to another star system. However, in the future, such technology could be extended to the point at which powerful lasers could be set up on the Moon to help accelerate the sail to a large fraction of the speed of light. Such a sail is featured in Stephen Baxter's novel *Proxima*. However, the sail itself needs to be extremely large (hundreds of miles across), the lasers need to be thousands of times more powerful than the current power usage of the entire Earth, and with no current means of getting to the Moon (though we had the capability 45 years ago), this project will certainly have to be put off for decades. An additional problem is that the spacecraft would need to decelerate and then re-accelerate as it approaches another star system. This would require having a similar sort of laser set up in the other star system, which of course is not possible if no other craft have been there before! One possible solution is to focus light from a laser on our Moon onto the spacecraft even up to a few light years away. This is considerably easier said than done, since this would require building a lens larger in diameter than the Sun, with the mass of a large asteroid. On the bright side, efforts such as this can be scaled down if we make the spacecraft as small as possible (such as for a stellar probe, instead of a manned spacecraft). Also, in more modest form, the craft could be a method for reaching trans-Neptunian objects (TNOs) at hundreds of astronomical units from the Sun without taking decades (the New Horizons probe got to

Pluto, itself classified as a TNO, in nine years). Though there have been some successful tests of deployment of solar sails, none have resulted in a craft that was actually propelled by a sail. Yet, because development of the craft itself is a matter of improving upon current technology, and because the energy requirements, though extremely large, are not as large as those required by other means of interstellar travel, this might be one of the more hopeful ideas for getting to another star system. Another possibility for "rocketless rocketry" (a term coined by Robert Forward) would be a magnetic rail gun. A rail gun can be created by sending a large current through conducting rails. The rails then set up a very strong magnetic field that can then apply a force to a metallic object, acting like a gun. Velocities with known rail guns are great enough to potentially send an object into orbit around the Earth. Though the idea is very enticing since the object of interest can be accelerated at Earth, this leads to some difficulties as well. The biggest problem is that a rail gun does most of its accelerating over a relatively short distance (and short period of time), and thus the experienced "g" forces will be too great for a human to withstand. However, a completely inanimate probe might be able to survive this more readily. A related problem is that when objects coming out of a rail gun hit the air, they become deformed. If used as a means for accelerating a spacecraft, we could perhaps place the rail gun in space or on the Moon to avoid this problem. To go to another star system, however, would take an enormous space-based rail gun that would accelerate to about 5,000-g. Since no human could survive this sort of acceleration, this mode of transportation, at least for now, would be reserved for the heartiest of probes (Kaku, *The Physics of the Impossible* 2008).

We might be able to approach this problem from another direction. That is, instead of being concerned completely with the nature of the fuel and the exhaust speed or even using a sail as described above, we can focus on making the vehicle and payload very small. Both Frank Tipler and Michio Kaku separately discuss the possibility of these nano-ships. Tipler shows that an anti-matter powered nano-ship could accelerate to one tenth the speed of light and coast to a nearby star with less than 2 kg of exhaust gas and less than 4 milligrams of anti-matter (Tipler 1994). The focus here has to be in getting a device that is very small to be very useful, because if it cannot relay information back to us, then it will be useless. We have to keep in mind here that even just to send signals back to Earth (or to receive such signals) would require a large radio dish, so communications would not be possible with a very small probe (at least not an independent one). To mitigate such problems as many molecules as possible have to be directly related to the functioning of the probe. Another focus of these nano-ships is to get them to be self-replicating. In this way, we could potentially indirectly create a much more effective probe, or set of probes, by making a small number of self-replicating nano-ships. The new nano-ships can then take on either very similar functions, or be programmed to take on new functions. However, there are additional problems with nano-ships. The primary problem is that they can be easily deflected off course.

Using Mach's Principle for Thrusters

Broadly stated, Mach's Principle essentially states that the mass distributed through the Universe influences the inertia of any other individual mass (say, for instance, a rocket launching here on Earth). In this sense, the principle has been absorbed into general relativity, and as stated in Chapter 1, we know that the geometry of space is dependent upon the distribution of mass in the Universe, and, this in turn will affect any other individual mass in the Universe. However, the details of Mach's Principle, as calculated in general relativity say a bit more than this general statement. Essentially they would lead us to conclude that the mass of the rest of the Universe would lead to any other individual mass feeling just a little bit of resistance to any other force applied to it. In engineering terms, the rest of the Universe out there can lead to extra thrust on an object here. But is this a "real world" effect? Calculating the precise effect on an individual extended object (that is, a real life object and not just a "point mass") is complicated. However, James Woodward has determined that there can be small, but measurable Mach effects on objects the size of typical desktop lab equipment. Confirming this effect, and then scaling up by factors of up to one million for practical use as a rocket thruster may take decades or more, but it's encouraging to know that reconsidering "old physics" for practical engineering usage in rockets could lead to alternatives to either chemical rockets or some of the other long considered alternatives mentioned above that have not come to fruition (Woodward 2013).

Microwave Thruster

Recently there have been tests at NASA's Johnson Space Center of a resonant cavity thruster. The device works by bouncing around microwaves in a cavity. In tests it has shown a very small thrust of about 40 microNewtons. Similar to the thruster described in the previous section, these forces are about one millionth of that experienced by a book feeling the Earth's gravity. The investigators admit to not having an understanding of the physical effects that might be causing the thrust though they do appeal to the possibility that this is related to a "quantum vacuum virtual plasma."

Navigation at Near-Light Speeds

Just as traveling near to the speed of light can change how we measure both time and spatial dimensions, there are other effects that will have direct consequences on how we perceive light coming from stars. Both the color of light and the direction from where the light is originating will be highly distorted if the observer (an astronaut aboard a spacecraft) is approaching the speed of light. For stars in front of the ship, light will be blue-shifted, meaning that the stars will appear to be bluer than they actually are. For the stars in back of the ship, light will be red-shifted, thus these stars will appear to be redder than they actually are. The effect on measured direction of the light is called aberration, and leads to the angle between the ship's direction and the direction of the starlight being compacted toward the direction of motion of the ship. This effect is described in detail in Poul Anderson's 1970 novel, *Tau Zero*, and more recently in Peter Cawdron's *Galactic Exploration* in which several ships traveling near to the speed of light explore separate parts of the Galaxy. An opposite effect will occur in the direction of the rear of the ship: stars' light will appear to be coming from well away from the rear direction of the ship. Though these effects may seem extreme and hard to overcome, any navigation system controlled by computer can carefully take these effects into account and properly navigate the ship. However, as the spacecraft accelerates, it would be extremely difficult for an astronaut to make any attempt to recognize individual stars or constellations with the unaided eye (Goswami 1983).

Faster than Light

Perhaps the most dramatic solution of all is that of faster-than-light travel. This sort of method is casually mentioned in such classics as *Star Wars* and *Battlestar Galactica* and in much more detail, in the various incarnations of *Star Trek*. Though often posited as impossible by physicists, this is only strictly true if an object itself is moving faster-than-light within local space. However, faster-than-light travel with respect to the global surroundings (the very distant Galaxy) might be possible if it is local space itself that is changing in order to get a starship from point A to point B. One benefit of this kind of faster-than-light travel is that it avoids time dilation. That is, time won't seem to be slowed down for the crew, as compared to the outside world, which is quite important for a show such as *Star Trek*, as the crew does not want to receive an emergency order to go to a very distant planet, potentially to save lives, only to find out that everyone involved in the crisis had died decades or even centuries ago. A potential real life version of the warp-drive of *Star Trek* was first theorized by Miguel Alcubierre in 1994. Before we understand the details of Alcubierre's theory, we must first understand some concepts behind Einstein's General Theory of Relativity. One primary idea is that a particular distribution of mass and energy will dictate the geometry of space around it. Perhaps the most famous case of this a black hole, which will create a deep "well" of space around a very dense concentration of matter. However, any mass at all will distort space and time to some degree. In the Alcubierre theory, space is warped in a fashion that allows a traveler to move faster than light if they remain in this "warp bubble." This bubble can contract ahead of the ship, and expand behind it. However, there are a number of important drawbacks. Firstly, the warp bubble can only be created by negative matter or energy. Negative matter would be unusual indeed, and it is not known if any exists anywhere in the Universe. Negative energy only exists in very small quantities as a result of the Casimir Effect. The quantity of energy needed to create these bubbles is enormous and you have to have these bubbles created in advance of traveling. Therefore, it seems that "on demand" warp drive would be difficult to manage (Krauss 1995). However, this remains a very interesting case of how science fiction helped to inspire a theoretical physicist to come up with valid equations that could explain Warp Drive and faster-than-light travel, even if it is not practical due to vast energy requirements.

Another related concept that could also help with space travel in the far future is that of wormholes. The original theorizing of wormholes goes back to Einstein himself, and his student Nathan Rosen. In studying general relativity of black holes, they realized that a natural result would be a "bridge" to another part of the Universe (or possibly another Universe entirely) where a "white hole" could open up. It was soon realized that nothing manmade could make this journey, since the tidal forces at the black hole would become infinite and rip apart any person or spacecraft as the black hole is approached. Over time however, some interest in wormholes increased as gravity theorists were wondering whether it was possible to create a wormhole that would not necessarily destroy a space traveler. As the story goes, Carl Sagan was looking for a way to get a character in a novel he was writing (*Contact*) to take shortcuts through space. His original idea was to somehow make use of black holes and Einstein-Rosen type wormholes. However, talking to a theoretical physicist friend, Kip Thorne of Caltech, it became clear that tidal forces near the black hole would probably kill Sagan's protagonist before she got anywhere else, and a more hopeful avenue would be a different type of wormhole (Thorne 1994). Wormholes are essentially shortcuts through space that could take matter from one point in the Universe to some other point, possible many light years away from the first wormhole mouth. Like the warp bubbles discussed earlier, stable wormholes can only exist as a result of configurations of negative matter or energy. Therefore, they will meet with the same difficulties: finding negative energy or matter in the first place, and finding vast amounts of it. We will revisit wormholes in more detail when we discuss time travel in a future chapter. However, this is yet another interesting case of how research in theoretical physics was directly inspired by science fiction.

Suspended Animation and Generation Ships

The world of science fiction has offered some potential solutions to work around these problems of space travel in the future, and some seem promising, in the sense that they are allowed by physical laws, but are likely still far too costly in terms of energy. A workaround that was introduced early in science fiction is that of cryogenic suspended animation (sometimes also called cryonics), that is, the slowing down of metabolism by dramatically cooling the human body. Probably the earliest example in film is from the 1954 film *Gog*, which has numerous items we'll be discussing in future chapters. The film is set in a testing facility for a future space station. Among the experiments is one testing the "freezing" of astronauts, to be used in space. In fact, one of the first unexplained deaths that occur in this film is one of the scientists running this experiment. Mark Glassy discusses two early films that dealt solely with the topic of cryogenic suspended animation, *The Man with Nine Lives* and *Frozen Alive*, both addressing the topic of re-animating people after they have been frozen (Glassy 2001). Another early example from television is *Science Fiction Theater*'s "The Long Sleep" episode (Ivan Tors was the producer of both *Gog* and *Science Fiction Theater*), in which a doctor experiments on inducing hibernation in non-hibernating animals. This doctor is forced to apply his technique to a dying child in order to save him. One early example is in the British sci-fi marionette series from 1963, *Space Patrol* (this was called *Planet Patrol* in the U.S. to avoid confusion with a series that had the name *Space Patrol* already). They used what they called "freezing" (suspended animation) as a way to avoid excess accelerations during interplanetary travel (this has some similarities to the laser stasis field used for similar purposes in the 1956 film, *Forbidden Planet*). In the 1964 *Twilight Zone* episode "The Long Morrow," an astronaut is sent on a 40-year mission to another star system (and back). He is placed in suspended animation to help prevent aging during the trip. In the end, he purposely comes out of suspended animation early so that he will be the same age as the woman he fell in love with just before the mission. However she, also thinking of the age difference upon his return, purposely went into hibernation on Earth to reduce her aging (in this sense, it's a science fiction re-working of the "Gift of the Magi"). "Freezing" is also a key element in the 1965 pilot episode of *Lost in Space* and was returned to from time to time during the series. The intention was to put the entire family in suspended animation during what was to be a five-year voyage to a planet orbiting Alpha Centauri, one of the closest stars to Earth. The Robinson family in *Lost in Space* only stayed in suspended animation for a short time before their mission was derailed by a saboteur, Dr. Zachary Smith, but the "freezing tubes" were used briefly in other instances, such as to reduce the effects on the human body during hard landings. A similar "freezing" device was used by the astronauts in the original *Planet of the Apes* (and led to one crew member dying when her freezing compartment was breached). Another type of suspended animation using drugs during a six-week space mission was implemented in the film *Journey to the Far Side of the Sun*. Similarly, an "eternity drug" was used for this purpose in the aforementioned short story, "Far Centaurus." In one way or another, this made it into many different science fiction series, including *ST:TOS* in the episode "Space Seed" that introduces Khan, Kirk's nemesis who reappears in the second *Star Trek* film as well. In *The Starlost* episode "Lazarus from the Mist," an engineer is revived from suspended animation to potentially help in getting the Ark back on course. However, it turns out that this engineer had a fatal disease, and would be terminal upon revival. In addition, he has no knowledge of nuclear reactors that would be needed to fix the Ark. In another space-ark themed episode, the *Doctor Who* episode "The Ark in Space," a space station orbiting the Earth has kept a large number of personnel frozen over time. In the *Space: 1999* episode "Earthbound," we see that an advanced species, the Kaldorians, have developed a very advanced form of suspended animation that can preserve the full essence of a person's soul and body. In a later episode of this series, "The Exiles," one of many capsules suddenly orbiting the Moon is taken in for inspection. Upon opening it, they realize that the capsule contains a humanoid (named Cantar), apparently frozen. They are successful in reviving him and find out he is from the nearby planet Golos, having been exiled for political reasons 300 years prior. They then go out to retrieve his wife, Zova. It is soon realized that they were actually exiled violent criminals from Golos. In *Space: 1999* there were also similar plots involving reviving aliens who were long ago placed in a form of suspended animation (always turning out to be more than they bargained for), such as in "The Mark of Archanon" and "The End of Eternity." As part of the premise of *Buck Rogers in the 25th Century*, the titular character becomes accidentally thrown into suspended animation when his spacecraft gets thrown into a distant orbit of the Sun and he becomes frozen, only to be thawed out hundreds of years later.

For decades in biological research and medical research glycerol (glycerin) has been used to protect tissue in cryogenic preservation. Ethylene glycol, commonly used as an automotive antifreeze, is a very similar compound. Both act to inhibit crystal growth of water as it cools to form ice. Some research with mammals has been conducted, and there is some evidence that people may be able to survive if their body temperature is brought below freezing. Such research has called for dramatic procedures, such as replacing blood with a special fluid that acts like a natural anti-freeze. Some of these animals were revived successfully (Kaku, *The Physics of the Impossible* 2008). A major problem is in seeing that everything from internal organs to skin is kept from forming ice crystals, as this will destroy the tissue (Glassy 2001). In the future, this may be a way to prolong the life of those who have inoperable or otherwise incurable conditions (though probably not for years, as portrayed in fiction). The 1973 comedy *Sleeper* featured an ordinary man, Miles Monroe (Woody Allen), frozen for 200 years after an unsuccessful operation, who was then later revived. Though treated in comic fashion, the film does show the difficulty such a person would have in adapting to society upon coming out of this kind of hibernation. Not surprisingly, such techniques also have the possibility of being abused. For instance, in the *Twilight Zone* episode "The Rip van Winkle Caper," three criminals steal gold, and then wait out 100 years in suspended animation, hoping that there will be no one left interested in capturing them once they awake (they forget to take into account the possibility that gold will completely devalue in that amount of time, which is precisely what happens).

A second popular workaround discussed at length by Simon Caroti is the intergenerational starship or "space ark" (Caroti 2011). On television, this concept was most famously presented in *The Starlost*. With Ben Bova as science adviser, there were some initial attempts to bring serious science into the story. For instance, it was understood that a nuclear fusion reactor would be necessary to power the ship and that the reactor would get its nuclear fuel from hydrogen in space. Unfortunately, extreme budget cuts led to a much more stripped down version of what was originally intended and attention to these sorts of scientific details was severely compromised. A considerably more effective presentation of a similar story was given in *Space: 1999*'s episode "Mission of the Darians." In this episode the crew of the ship had suffered a nuclear accident and was faced with a dilemma of how to survive without sufficient food supply. The survivors resorted to a form of high-tech cannibalism, by converting their mutant compatriots to energy and basic proteins (Muir, *Exploring Space: 1999* 1997). A more updated version is presented in the web based series, "The Ark." Though this is perhaps the easiest way to circumvent low ship speeds, it introduces a host of other problems. The primary concern, as with most other forms of interstellar travel, is that this would require large amounts of energy. In fact Simon Caroti, quoting the result of Frank Drake's calculations, shows that a 100-year journey to a star within about 10 light years, and with 100 crewmen, would use as much energy as a major country would in 100 years (Caroti 2011). This is thousands of times more energy than a typical nuclear power plant could possibly create, so clearly we would need a very efficient energy source. Another issue is that it may not be worth it to send out such a slow ship when over such a long period, human progress is likely to lead to a much more efficient technique. This exact problem is the premise of the classic 1944 A E. van Vogt short story "Far Centaurus," in which the crew of a 500-year mission gets to Alpha Centauri, only to find out that many generations of people from Earth have set up colonies on all the planets of the Centaurus system of stars (there is a similar turn of events in the *Twilight Zone* episode "The Long Morrow"). Though the crewmen in some sense are treated like mythological figures, they are not able to function in the much more advanced society. Some of these themes and plot lines are further explored in Van Vogt's novel, *Rogue Ship*. Something of a concern that is often introduced as a plot device in science fiction is that folks over many generations in such an intergenerational spacecraft may lose knowledge of how to navigate and repair the ship. In fact in many plot-lines, such as in Heinlein's *Orphans in the Sky*, Brian Aldiss' *Non-Stop*, and Ellison's *Phoenix without Ashes* (the story behind television's *The Starlost*) and *Star Trek: TOS* episode "For the World Is Hollow and I Have Touched the Sky," inhabitants forget they are on a ship at all! In the latter case, the ship was disguised as a habitable asteroid. In the aforementioned mini-series, *Ascension*, the twist is near to the opposite of this: the crew thinks they are on an intergenerational space ark, but are actually all participants in an Earth-based experiment, and the spaceship is a fiction that has been perpetrated for decades.

Peter Cawdron had a different purpose for generational ships in his *Galactic Exploration* novellas. Here, because extraterrestrial civilizations are discovered to be quite rare, one must go on extragalactic voyages to find intelligent life. The long voyages require a number of generations to act as crew even traveling near to the speed of light to the Andromeda Galaxy (there was a similar concept in the *ST:TOS* episode "By Any Other Name," in which the Kelvans, from Andromeda, appropriate the *Enterprise* to take it back there to help in their colonization efforts).

Issues in Space: Bringing Air with You

Since humans have to breathe oxygen and said oxygen has to be at an acceptable pressure, temperature and density, if we don't have those conditions where we intend to go, then we have to create them artificially. In early space travel, as is true today, the main concerns were with the compartments of small spacecraft, as well as with space suits. The primary concept of a space suit is to inflate an airtight suit to atmospheric pressure (or some reasonable fraction at which humans can survive) so that the astronaut won't be exposed to the vacuum. In addition, the suit must protect from extremely high and low temperatures, micrometeorites, and blinding light. The space suit matured from earlier developments in pressure suits for high altitude airplane travel with the first inventions coming out of necessity between World War I and World War II as planes needed to go to increasingly higher altitudes (Thomas and McMann 2006).

The space suit as depicted in science fiction has been discussed at length by others, including Westfahl (2012) and Gooden (2012). An early Ray Bradbury short story, "Kaleidoscope," depicts astronauts thrown into space with only their space suits after their ship is torn open in an accident. The astronauts slowly die off as they run out of oxygen and then burn up in the atmosphere. This story seems to have influenced a scene from the *Space: 1999* episode "War Games," in which Commander John Koenig is ejected from his Eagle spacecraft, alone and dying in just his space suit, left to think for an hour and half about his existence. However, most depictions of space suits were fairly crude for several decades of film. Even the television era only saw minor improvements in realistic depictions. For instance the many space walks of *Lost in Space* never saw the crew wearing a true pressure suit. Particularly as Westfahl points out, the critical point in realism for depiction of space suits was soon after television coverage of the U.S. space shots. For instance, the space suits of *2001: A Space Odyssey* (released in April 1968) were more realistic than those that came before.

In early space missions, for use within the capsules, oxygen under pressure was brought up in canisters. For later missions, such as the ISS, oxygen is created via electrolysis of water, which is made of both hydrogen and oxygen. However, these methods both depend on supplies brought from Earth (Rogers 2008). Clearly, this could be a problem for future space travel that may extend into the farther reaches of the Solar System, or even deep space. The early science fiction television series, *Fireball XL5*, though intended mainly for children, tried to solve this problem by having the astronauts take "oxygen pills" with no attention to how the astronauts would deal with pressure and temperature differences in space without pressure suits (though the thought of oxygenating astronauts' blood has been given serious study).

Issues in Space: Simulated Gravity

Other than the means for traveling in space, in science fiction (and also, to an extent, in reality) we encounter various other issues. For instance, for any voyage of substantial length, simulated gravity would be highly preferred to living in a low gravity environment. We know that long periods of time living in microgravity can lead to severe muscle atrophy and bone loss in astronauts, as well as many other issues related to health and comfort, such as sleeping, eating, and using the toilet (Rogers 2008). Though "simulated gravity" is often mentioned in science fiction, it is less often understood how it is accomplished. Simulated gravity can be accomplished by spinning the spacecraft (or part of the spacecraft). To a person who is within the rotating environment, there will be a centrifugal force felt that would act to push the astronaut toward the wall (if the surface of the walls are parallel to the spin axis). If we set up the craft so that the astronaut can begin to walk on what might originally be perceived to be a wall, he can walk all around the spacecraft on this outside wall, so long as there is sufficient spinning. Near the axis of spinning, the forces felt would be zero, and the astronauts would still be weightless, but there would be increased weight felt as the astronauts approach the outermost walls of the craft, where weight would reach its maximum. This centrifugal force felt by the astronaut is often referred to as a "fictitious" force, since it does not have its origin due to the interaction of objects. However, this term is somewhat deceiving, as it implies that what is felt is somehow unreal (Goswami 1983). We see a repeated example of this in the British series *Space Patrol*. Their regularly used spacecraft is a rotating torus, and the astronauts are definitely shown moving around in the ship under Earth-like gravity. However, it would have been more realistic had they actually shown crew members walking on the curved inner surface of the spacecraft.

In addition to being concerned about the effects of low gravity, we also have to be concerned with accelerations that are much stronger than normal surface gravity on Earth. This will particularly be a concern at launch, when accelerations can be at their greatest. But for any of the methods of travel discussed, a major concern will be that you must not accelerate the spacecraft so greatly that you will kill the occupants! As an example, we might be tempted to "put our foot on the gas" to get to the nearest star with known planets. However, if the ship is manned, it is very important not to accelerate too much at any point in the voyage. Usually, these forces felt are quantified in terms of multiples of the acceleration due to gravity here on Earth ("g"). We know that at several g, people will start to feel significantly heavier and begin to have difficulty moving around. Finally, at about 25 g, no movement even at the extremities will be possible. No human has ever been tested under conditions greater than 45 g, but it is suspected that before 100 g, a human would not be able to survive (Rogers 2008). In fact, by the time *ST:TNG* was on the air, the creators realized that quick acceleration as pictured in the *ST:TOS* would lead to g-forces that would certainly kill our favorite characters (as well as the usual group of red-shirts). Therefore, writers cleverly invented "inertial dampers" that would somehow cancel out the g-forces. Though this is really just an ad-hoc solution with no satisfactory explanation, at least they were aware that they had to address a serious issue of physics that came to the attention of many fans (Krauss, *The Physics of Star Trek* 1995).

Issues in Space: Space Colonies

Perhaps one of the more famous intended applications of simulated gravity discussed above were the space colonies (also sometimes referred to as space habitats) first proposed (at least from a serious technical perspective) by Konstantin Tsiolkovsky (as we can see from him also having proposed staged rockets that he was quite a visionary) and then popularized by Werner Von Braun, Arthur C. Clarke (especially in his novel *Islands in the Sky*). These colonies went beyond the notion of space stations that were largely intended for relatively small numbers of astronauts and space scientists to either use as a transport way station or scientific research. The colonies would essentially run as small self-sustaining cities in space. However, much of the applied physics is similar for either a smaller space station or a full-fledged colony. The colony concept was most famously backed by Gerard K. O'Neil of Princeton in the mid–1970s. He suggested that immense cylindrical colonies (about 17 miles long and four miles in diameter) could be sent into orbit in the Earth-Moon system (which we will discuss more in a moment). Based on the materials needed, it is estimated that the mass would be at least 5×10^8 kg, about 1,000 times more massive than the considerably more modest International Space Station now in orbit around the Earth. Some other alternatives have been discussed, such as toroidal (doughnut-shaped) colonies, but physics and economics will limit the shapes we can have for our colony. For instance, simulated gravity via rotation will make it most practical to have people walking on the inside surface that is perpendicular to the axis of rotation. In addition due to the need for a pressurized atmosphere, there will be a stress on whatever material is used for the hull. This stress will be greatly reduced for curved surfaces, hence the double need for curved shapes (Johnson and Hebrow 1977). It turns out that a toroid will have less useful "floor" space as compared to a cylinder of the same total inner surface area. A spherical shape could work, but would not have uniform gravity throughout the inner surface as it rotates. The simulated gravity would especially be much lower as you would go toward either of the poles.

It has been argued that such a colony would best be placed at the L4 or L5 point of the Earth-Moon system. These are Lagrange points and are thought of in the following way. The Earth and Moon orbit around a common center of mass which happens to be closer to the Earth because the Earth is more massive than the Moon. Normally, studying such systems further by understanding what would happen if additional bodies were to enter the system (such as an asteroid) could be very complicated, however, Lagrange studied an interesting limiting case. In this case, if you assumed that a third body was much less massive than either of the other two bodies in the system (which is absolutely the case for even a very large colony) then there are fixed points where a third body will remain in the same position relative to the other two bodies. For instance, at the L4 and L5 points, the space colony would be either 60 degrees behind the Moon or 60 degrees ahead of it, in the orbit about the common center of mass. There are a number of advantages of placing a colony at one of these points. One of them is that if we expected to have to make use of the Moon's resources, then the colony would never be too far from either the Earth (the source of colonists) or from the Moon (the primary source for materials). Also, in such a position, the colony would not have the Sun blocked out as much by Earth, which can lead to more efficient use of solar energy. Another logical placement would be low Earth orbit, for reasons of keeping the colony close to the ground for a number of reasons. The primary reason is that fuel costs to low Earth orbit are relatively cheap, which would be especially important if Earth remained the primary source for materials as well as colonists. In addition, evacuation or response to other emergencies would be easier.

O'Neil argued that these colonies could be made economical by mining the Moon for necessary minerals. The Moon has much lower gravity than the Earth, so as long as the requisite materials can be found there, sending these materials into space requires much less fuel and is therefore cheaper. The main hindrance is that we still do not have a cost effective method for getting to the Moon with the proper mining equipment, and then sending it into space. Rather than using rocketry, O'Neil proposes a device which is similar to a conveyor belt, but working magnetically, to send small buckets of material into space. An alternative might be a rotating launcher that shoots small pellets into space (to be collected at the target). Once constructed, these colonies could be self-sustaining through solar power and agriculture. He even suggested that societies in space could essentially hit a cultural reset button and avoid wars, poverty and pollution (O'Neil, "The Colonization of Space" 1974). Furthermore, such a colony would not face all of the problems a similarly sized "space ark" would since it will remain in orbit, and have easier access to resources of a planet or moon, if needed. One additional option would be to equip enough of the space habitats with propulsion adequate for bringing them over one trillion miles from Earth in the outer reaches of the Solar System. The reason for this isn't so much for exploring the outer Solar System, but as an outer bound for where these habitats can be placed. Though NASA took research into this matter seriously for a few years, it was eventually dropped for being far too expensive, especially after some intense skepticism from Congress. Soon after O'Neil published his popular book on the subject (*The High Frontier*), the topic made its way into science fiction in Ben Bova's *Colony*, about such a space habitat built 100 or so years in the future to escape overpopulation and pollution on the Earth. It should also be noted that Arthur C. Clarke's 1972 novel, *Rendevous with Rama*, featured an alien spacecraft that resembled one of O'Neil's colonies in that it was an immense rotating cylinder with contained environments. More recently, similar colonies have been featured in Kim Stanley Robinson's novel *2312*, though here they are in the form of hollowed out asteroids, rather than bringing the materials closer to Earth and having the colony constructed. The 2013 film *Elysium* focuses on a future society on Earth that has been ravaged by overpopulation and poverty, and only a small group of elites have settled in an orbital space colony. Though Elysium resembles the sorts of toroids that have often been discussed in serious discussions of space stations as well as being depicted frequently in science fiction, we don't ever see Elysium spinning in the film even when we clearly see motion shots of other spacecraft approaching the outside of the colony, though we do see the effects of artificial gravity within the station. In addition, we clearly see that some of the atmosphere is directly exposed to space. On a planet such as the Earth the atmosphere is "held down" with the pressure we are familiar with at sea level because there is an entire massive atmosphere extending above for tens of miles. In a volume as small as Elysium, there wouldn't be enough mass to contain a gas. There would have to be an artificially pressurized atmosphere.

An even more ambitious example of a space colony is the Dyson sphere. In 1960, the Institute for Advanced Study physicist Freeman Dyson suggested that it would be possible to collect a large percentage of the energy of the Sun by surrounding it with satellites that would collect the energy. Among the variants of the idea are to place all of these collectors at a distance that is equivalent to the Earth-Sun distance. In this way, all of these collectors could also potentially be extended into full-fledged colonies taking the energy for their own use. The most extreme interpretation of the so-called Dyson sphere is a literal hard sphere of material completely surrounding the star. If such a structure were at the Earth-Sun distance, people could build their colony onto every square meter of the surface! This idea made it into the *ST:TNG* episode "Relics" (though, disappointingly, it didn't figure into the storyline very much). The primary problem with such a shell is that a shell of matter doesn't interact gravitationally with anything inside of it (this is a standard problem to be solved in junior level undergraduate physics courses). Therefore, the shell can drift and potentially crash into the star.

Another twist on space habitats are alien space stations and colonies.

One such example is in an early episode of *Lost in Space*, "The Derelict." The Robinsons encounter a space station that is inhabited by bubble creatures. In fact, this was one of the very few times that *Lost in Space* dealt with a non-humanoid intelligent species.

Generally speaking, we should not be confined to so-called "freely floating" colonies in space, but could also colonize planets, the Moon, and asteroids. In fact, this would be the primary intention for terraforming Mars or other planets as discussed in Chapter 2. One advantage of colonizing a planet is that the colonists would be closer to resources that they might need. A clear disadvantage is that they would be in a fixed orbit (either too far or too close relative to the Sun), farther from Earth (so more of a commitment to leaving the home planet). Though we have discussed terraforming, it should be clear that this is an extreme process, both time and energy consuming. Manipulating a planetary atmosphere and surface, if it is even ethical, is not easy or cheap. An orbiting colony could be manipulated more easily to have acceptable atmosphere, gravity and relative location to Earth.

Issues in Space: Getting Around on a Planet

In the 1965 James Bond film *Thunderball*, and in several early episodes of *Lost in Space* from the same time period, we see the use of personal jet packs (more precisely here, rocket packs) to both get around on Earth and other planets (Montandon 2008). In both of these cases, these jet packs are the "rocket belts" developed by Bell Aerosystems in the early 1960s (with the team led by Wendell Moore). In fact, the company's test pilot, Bill Suitor, was used in the two instances mentioned above for the stunts. The development of the rocket belts was primarily funded by government agencies, though only at a relatively low level, due to their apparent potential to become useful to the military in transporting troops over small distances, especially in rough terrain or in a battlefield (although that was determined to be impractical decades ago). The concept here is very similar to that of the rockets we discussed earlier, except applied on a smaller scale to a single individual wearing a pack. Here, hydrogen peroxide was used as fuel, and could be relatively easily (through chemical reaction) heated into rapidly expanding steam that could be vented out of the bottom of the pack worn by the pilot very effectively for thrust (Lehto 2013). Also, in *Lost in Space* we see the use of a set of "parajets" (small thrusters attached to the arms) that allow an astronaut to maneuver independent of a spacecraft and even to enter a planet's atmosphere independently (though as portrayed in this series, this is farfetched, since an astronaut without any kind of shielding will burn up on re-entry). Some may object to this last claim, remembering Felix Baumgartner and others, who have jumped from a 27-mile high capsule attached to a balloon without burning up. However, these cases are significantly different than astronauts, primarily because astronauts will be coming in with a much higher velocity, from having been in orbit. The progressive drag from the atmosphere as the astronaut comes in from 60 miles up at high velocity would heat him up until he gets burnt to a crisp.

Issues in Space: Radiation and Meteorites

Another potential issue is that of radiation levels, which can be both problematic due to solar flares (or flares of another star in other star systems), or in some of these cases, radiation due to the drive system itself. In particular, when using the term "radiation" here we are referring to high-energy light (such as X-rays and gamma rays) as well as energetic subatomic particles. Solar flares in particular could be deadly to unshielded astronauts on a space walk or on the surface of a planet without significant atmosphere and magnetosphere. A spaceship without sufficient shielding could also lead to short- or long-term radiation exposure. Another serious issue can be meteor strikes, especially micro-meteor strikes, which can slowly destroy the outer shielding of the spacecraft and create holes that can de-pressurize the spacecraft. Though the chances of a relatively major strike are small, small strikes are common enough and can do enough damage and are worth worrying about (Rogers 2008). In the context of space colonies mentioned above, O'Neil downplays the threat of meteorites. In particular he states that "it would be several thousand years between strikes by a meteoroid big enough to break a window panel" (O'Neil, *The High Frontier* 1989).

Issues in Space: Psychological Effects

In addition to the purely physical problems, we would surely also have to be concerned with the psychological effects that long missions could have on astronauts. There has been extensive research into this. In particular, astronauts aboard the ISS and Mir for long periods (about six months or more) experienced more than normal amount of irritability and nervousness (Rogers 2008). Nick Kanas of the University of California at San Francisco reports that astronauts on long missions begin to feel isolated and develop adversarial attitudes toward some workers at Mission Control. These attitudes can be exacerbated by cultural differences between crew members (such as would be the case on the International Space Station) and between crew and members of mission control. Astronauts on much longer future missions to Mars, the outer Solar System, or even other star systems will be less able to communicate with home due to long time delays in communication (limited by the speed of light), plus will have to live with the idea of only returning home after many years, or perhaps never returning at all. Some of these psychological issues, especially in dealing with others' frailties over time, were explored in the *Outer Limits* episode "Counterweight." Here a group consisting of several scientists, a journalist and a real estate developer (who has his eye on developing a new colony on another planet) are selected for a simulated interstellar flight (a bit less than a year) as part of a practice run for future real flights to other stellar systems (the fictitious Antheon is mentioned in the episode). Unknown by them, aliens from Antheon have taken over the simulation, influencing the passengers to become anxious over their own fears and paranoia. The overall intent of the Antheonians would be to keep mankind from being overly eager to explore space. The premiere *Twilight Zone* episode "Where Is Everybody?" starts with a man who finds himself alone in what appears to be a completely abandoned town. He runs around frantically, looking for signs of anybody at all. Eventually it is revealed that he is actually in an isolation chamber as a test for astronaut training for missions to the Moon. He has been in there for almost two weeks and has now suffered a complete breakdown, shrieking for help. Poignantly, this episode showed that perhaps some of the greatest demons in conquering space are in those that are created by the human mind. Though psychological factors turned out not to be significant in relatively short missions, the above evidence does indeed show it as a possible concern.

Additionally, if we go the way of sending out generational starships, we must think about how the first generation will handle their permanent separation from Earth, and how future generations will regard Earth and fellow Terrans having not ever lived there themselves (Kanas 2011). There may also have to be consideration given to astronauts who wake up from a long hibernation in suspended animation, or who experience time dilation effects. How will they feel if they are decades younger than compatriots left behind on Earth? Or perhaps family members have died in the meantime? Perhaps then it is a little bit shortsighted to ignore or give little attention to possible psychological difficulties during long missions.

Chapter 4

Universes, Dimensions and Space

Alternate Universes in Science Fiction

Parallel Universes have been a mainstay of science fiction for some time, particularly in television. As science fiction critic John Kenneth Muir states in his work *A Critical History of Doctor Who*, "If one were to judge a genre show solely by how well it tackles the standards (androids experiencing emotions, the generational space ark, the sentient machine, time travel, etc.) then the alternate universe category would certainly be one of the most important benchmarks. The alternate universe category has become one of the most enduring and popular clichés within the realm of science fiction television" (Muir 1999). In fact, in 1967 alone, *ST:TOS* aired two separate episodes on the subject. The most famous of these episodes was "Mirror, Mirror" in which several crewmembers of the starship *Enterprise* swap places with their evil doppelgangers from an alternate Universe (fortunately, evil duplicates usually possess facial hair and hideous scars so that we are able to tell who is who). This plot line continued in a number of future installments of the *Star Trek* franchise, including the *Star Trek: Deep Space Nine* (*ST:DSN*) episode "Shattered Mirror," *Star Trek: Enterprise* episode "In a Mirror, Darkly," as well as a number of fan produced episodes, including one that is a direct sequel of "Mirror, Mirror" (called "The Fairest of Them All") and another in which it is implied that this alternate Universe was created accidentally during a time travel experiment ("In Want of a Nail"). Additionally, *Doctor Who* also had its requisite "evil duplicates in an alternate Universe" in its "Inferno" episode. Shortly afterward, *Space: 1999* aired one such episode, "Another Time, Another Place," although here the duplicates have simply followed another timeline and aren't necessarily "good" or "evil." A similar alternate Universe with an alternate Earth is a fundamental part of the novel *Twistor* by John Cramer in which a "shadow Universe" is discovered serendipitously during a study of the physics of superconductors.

More recently, in the *Farscape* episode "Through the Looking Glass," the living spaceship *Moya* starts to experience problems in going into "starburst," its natural ability to go faster than light. This malfunction leads to the creation of portals to alternate Universes. Trips to and from a parallel Universe have been part of an ongoing story arc for most of four seasons of the recent television series *Fringe*. Many of the aforementioned episodes of all of these series have allowed for excellent special effects (considering the time at which they were created), showing misty corridors between Universes and some interesting choices for representing what a parallel Universe would look like. Some particularly interesting choices were made with *Fringe*, in which we see duplicates of entire cities, such as New York, yet with a World Trade Center which has survived the September 11 terrorist attacks, and zeppelins used as a popular mode of transportation (we also see "old-time" bicycles with large front wheels and tiny back wheels being commonly used). With these choices, there is just enough "sameness" to make the alternate world seem recognizable and believable, yet also enough "strangeness" for viewers to appreciate the differences and easily be able to distinguish the two Universes. As part of an inside joke for science fiction fans noted by Mike Brotherton (2011), the character Olivia Dunham's first contact in the alternate Universe (usually referred to as "The Other Side" within the series) is with rogue scientist William Bell, played by Leonard Nimoy (the image of him as Spock's doppelganger in "Mirror, Mirror" with beard and all, has practically come to represent alternate Universes). Alternate Universe episodes are often particular favorites among fans, due to their showing different sides to favorite characters (usually the same actors are also playing their own alternate Universe doppelgangers) and showing different sides to a familiar world. In science fiction literature, alternate worlds are featured in Clifford Simak's *Ring Around the Sun*. Isaac Asimov's *The Gods Themselves* features the discovery of a parallel Universe. After discovering an isotope of plutonium that couldn't have possibly formed in our Universe under our physical laws, a physicist concludes that the atom must have been formed in a parallel Universe. The consequences of these different physical laws at first seem to be a boon to mankind, as the physicist can use his new invention to extract energy from the parallel Universe. Unfortunately, a major consequence is that the Sun will become unstable and explode as a supernova! In the John Cramer novel, "Einstein's Bridge" particle experiments at the Superconducting Supercollider (SSC), an American version of the LHC that never got built, leads to a bridge being created between Universes. In addition, Stephen King offers the alternate Universes of "The Territories" in *The Talisman* and "Boo Ya Moon" in *Lisey's Story*. Though these novels are primarily fantasies, these worlds are in many ways indistinguishable from such alternate worlds offered in "hard" science fiction. Certainly, we could even potentially go a step further and

4. Universes, Dimensions and Space

consider Oz and the worlds of many animated films or comic books to be alternate Universes of sorts or certainly worlds separate from our normal plane of existence. However, herein we'll stick to texts that at least claim to be rooted in the science of alternate Universes and dimensions.

One particularly popular take on the alternate Universe is the anti-matter Universe. In another *ST:TOS* episode, "The Alternative Factor," a man chases his anti-matter self through two Universes, our own and an anti-matter version of our Universe. Tremendous amounts of energy are released when one or both of the counterparts travel between the Universes. There are other mysterious effects, such as the planet around which the *Enterprise* is orbiting apparently losing its mass as the Universe around them apparently "winks out" (in science officer Spock's own words). In addition, in December of 1967, perhaps inspired by the previous two *Star Trek* episodes that had aired earlier in that year, *Lost in Space* aired its own "The Anti-Matter Man," which also featured evil duplicates (once again using this particularly popular plot device which was to become especially common for *Lost in Space*, even very separate from alternate Universes). In this particular episode, the duplicates of the anti-matter Universe attempt to switch places with their counterparts so that they may live a free existence. In their Universe they have been imprisoned for "thousands and thousands of years" (though by whom, and for what reason, and how they could live such a long life span, was never revealed). *Space: 1999* had two such episodes that focused on anti-matter worlds, "A Matter of Balance" (though anti-matter is described as being in "anti-space" and this description is incorrect) and "A Matter of Life and Death" about an anti-matter planet. *Doctor Who* got in on this in 1973 with *The Three Doctors*, within which Omega, a rogue Time Lord, is trapped in an anti-matter Universe within the event horizon of a black hole and uses this as a vantage point for attempting to target the Doctor, and conquer our Universe. In the 1975 *Doctor Who* episode "The Planet of Evil," a monster has made its way from an anti-matter Universe to our Universe. Many of these renderings, in particular those focusing on anti-matter, have their roots in the 1937 John Clark short story "Minus Planet." In this short story, the Earth is threatened by a small anti-matter planet, presumably from an anti-matter Universe (this origin is suggested in the story itself. Interestingly, some have proposed that the 1908 Tunguska event in Siberia, which knocked down trees for miles and followed a very bright fireball in the sky, was due to a small amount of anti-matter colliding with the Earth). In the end of the story, the solution is to purposely drive the Moon into the planet with special engines attached to the Moon. This last plot device was to appear nearly four decades later as the premise for *Space: 1999* (albeit in the form of a nuclear accident) and also was an important component to the Japanese film *Gorath,* in which immense rocket engines are activated at the South Pole to direct the Earth away from

Gorath, a dense planet that was set to collide with Earth. Considering that the anti-proton, discussed in this story as the "anitron," was not even theorized by Dirac until 1933, and not to be discovered for many years, it was certainly at the forefront of science fiction of the day to be integrating anti-matter into a short story. Possibly the subject of anti-matter was so often re-addressed in science fiction in the 1960s and 1970s because the discovery of the anti-proton (a negatively charged version of the proton) in 1955 was still relatively fresh. This discovery made the news again in 1959 with the awarding of the Nobel Prize in Physics. The position, or anti-electron, was discovered over two decades earlier. However, the primary constituent of matter is the proton, so we could not envision any kind of anti-matter world that looked like ours until an anti-proton was discovered. Anti-matter in science fiction is often portrayed as having extreme properties that normal matter does not possess. However, in reality, the only difference is that anti-matter has opposite charge. But, it is important to note that when a proton and anti-proton come into direct contact (or any particle and its anti-particle), they completely annihilate and create energy. The amount of energy is stupendous. In fact, this is the most efficient way of creating energy and one kilogram of matter/anti-matter annihilating can create enough energy to power a modest city for about one year (about 1,000 times the energy released by the Nagasaki atomic bomb).[1] At the time of that discovery, it had been suggested by prominent physicist Maurice Goldhaber, in a 1959 *Time* magazine article, that there could perhaps exist a parallel Universe made completely of anti-matter. In 1966, Hans Alfven and Oskar Klein (who had earlier proposed theories of multiple dimensions that we will be discussing soon), as discussed in Alfven's popular book, *Worlds-AntiWorlds* (Alfven 1966), proposed a theory for our Universe suggesting that the Universe started off with equal amounts of matter and anti-matter. The matter and anti-matter would be drawn to each other, annihilating, and then driving the observed expansion. However, the theory is problematic for a number of reasons, primarily because we do not see anywhere near equal amounts of matter and anti-matter. A slightly later theory of Roland Omnes proposed to resolve these differences between this theory and observation by evoking islands of anti-matter in the overall Universe. However, this type of theory as a whole has now been abandoned (Peebles 1993).

The Truth About Anti-Matter

Anti-matter does exist in our Universe, but apparently in extremely small amounts as compared to the regular matter we are more familiar with since only small amounts of isolated anti-matter have ever been detected in space, and all current evidence suggest that even this anti-matter was all created as transient by-products of high energy reactions. That is, there is absolutely no evidence of anti-gas clouds, anti-stars, anti-planets, and so forth. This is counter-intuitive, since we might expect that the Universe started with equal amounts of each. However, it is possible that asymmetries in matter and anti-matter at the time of the Big Bang led to the asymmetries we see today. In fact, some asymmetries must have existed in the early Universe, because equal amounts of matter and anti-matter would have completely annihilated each other, leading only to high energy light, but no particles, in the end (Close 2009). Recent experiments with high-energy particle accelerators suggest that nature slightly favors some reactions that lead to matter as opposed to the anti-matter counterparts.

We do know that in the center of our Galaxy, a "fountain" of positrons was detected in 1997, but there is no evidence of anti-protons there. In addition, the only anti-matter we know of on Earth has been created in very small amounts in particle accelerators. This discovery had led to continuing searches for anti-matter, particularly with the research satellite PAMELA. One discovery has shown an "excess" of positrons over what would normally be predicted. Some astrophysicists think these positrons can be from pulsars; however there are some who think these can be as a result of dark matter annihilation. However, as this field stands now, it's not particularly certain how much anti-matter there is (although we know it's low) or how it got here (Close 2009).

Why Anti-Matter in Science Fiction?

However, these plots involving anti-matter readily lent themselves to science fiction television writers in particular thinking in terms of "opposites." In particular, we see this enhanced in "The Anti-matter Man" episode of *Lost in Space* when we see the evil duplicates dressed in black and white outfits that are very similar to the Chinese Yin and Yang symbol (representing the comingling of contrary forces) and this is further discussed by Sarah Stuart in the context of the parallel Universes (though not necessarily anti-matter Universes) of *Fringe* (Stuart 2011). Members of one Universe could be "good," while their opposites would be "evil." In fact, these character traits can be explored in dealing with two sides of one person. In the earlier series, this tended to be dealt with at the most simple level with duplicates being very clearly delineated as good or evil, but by the time *Fringe* came along, these themes became significantly more complex, due in part to the devotion of multiple seasons to the "alternate Universe" format. Unfortunately, the one thing most of these episodes had in common was they were not particularly accurate, or even consistent in how they dealt with the facts of anti-matter. One particular problem was that we can often see no immediate ramifications of a normal matter human stepping foot on an anti-matter world. In reality, the energy created in the annihilation of this person with an equal amount of anti-matter would be enormous, as suggested by our earlier calculation. More egregiously, the effects of anti-matter would just be invented, such as suggesting that one could pass through an object made of anti-matter, or that some sort of electrical discharge similar to lightning would take place near anti-matter. Although these effects made for exciting episodic fiction, they didn't help in properly educating us on anti-matter.

Mirror Universes and Reversed Time Universes

We have already seen that science fiction writers are keen on "opposite" Universes, particularly ones in which charge is reversed (an anti-matter Universe). Another type of Universe that has been shown is the mirror image "reversed" Universe (physicists call this a parity reversed Universe), for which left and right are transposed. A very early example of this is in Lewis Carroll's 1871 novel *Through the Looking Glass*. However, though we see some evidence of reversals (such as Alice needing to hold "reversed" writing up to a mirror to read it correctly when in the Looking Glass World), these notions are not consistently applied throughout the novel. In modern science fiction, we see something similar to this in the 1969 Gerry and Sylvia Anderson film, *Journey to the Far Side of the Sun*, though strictly speaking, this involves visiting a parity reversed planet within our own Solar System. In this film, astronauts crash on a planet on the opposite side of the Sun from Earth and begin to realize it is an exact replica of Earth, save for reversal of left and right. A similar idea made it into the *Space: 1999* episode "The Last Enemy" in which Moonbase Alpha faces conflict with two planets that are in the same orbit, but on opposite sides of their Sun. The planets are locked in a bitter war. There isn't a literal mirroring of the inhabitants of the planets, yet those on planet Betha appear to be all female and the residents of planet Delta appear to be all male. In addition, one planet is pictured as blue and the other is red (opposite ends of the spectrum). Historically speaking, the idea of a planet opposite from Earth's position has its roots in the concept of Counter Earth (Antichthon), attributed to Philolaus of Croton, who is thought to have lived about 2,400 years ago. Though his model is not heliocentric, it is thought to be the first non-geocentric model. It does involve Earth, Counter-Earth, the Sun, and other planets, revolving around a central fire (Huffman 1993). Though this model does not have some of the mathematical power to explain phenomena as other models later did, it's widely thought to have still been a serious attempt at describing the world, and not just a mythology. More recently in science fiction, similar plot devices are seen in a 1951 episode of *Tales of Tomorrow* called "The Duplicates," and an early *Doctor Who* episode, "The Tenth Planet," explaining the origin of the Cybermen on the planet Mondas, a mirror planet of the Earth (Parsons 2010). In "Invaders from the 5th Dimension" (*Lost in Space*), the strange invaders are explained as being from "anti–Earth." Though the script of this episode offers no further explanation, Mitchell and Anchors explain in *The Lost in Space Encyclopedia*, the concept of anti–Earth probably refers to the theory of a hypothetical planet such as Anticthon (sometimes called Clarion in more recent incarnations of UFO enthusiasts). However, as they point out, such a planet would reveal itself soon by changing its own orbit relatively quickly, and also perturbing the orbits of other planets, particularly Venus (Mitchell and Anchors 2010). No such planet has ever been detected. It turns out that the proposed position of a "counter-Earth" corresponds to the L3 Lagrange point of the Sun-Earth system (see Chapter 3 for a discussion of Lagrange points). In the Sun-Earth system, L3 will always be directly opposite from the Earth, on the other side of the Sun, and at the same distance from the Sun. In the Sun-Earth system this point will be unstable because of the differing interaction of each body with the rest in the Solar System, acting to pull the body at L3 away from the fixed point opposite the Earth (Adler 2014).

The general idea of an "opposite" planet also likely has its recent roots in the treatment of Bizzaro World in the Superman comics (introduced in the early 1960s). For example, Bizzaro World is treated as being in all ways opposite to Earth (and is even referred to as Htrae, Earth spelled backwards). Here, for instance, people invest to lose money, and take insults as compliments. In addition, the 2011 film *Another Earth*, though more about second chances at life than planets with doppelgangers, has some of these elements. For instance, after the duplicate Earth is discovered, we see a scientist trying to contact the other planet. It is soon revealed that she is engaging in a circular conversation with her counterpart. However, on a grander scale, can such a Universe, with charge reversed or parity reversed even exist? How would we be able to tell the difference?

Such questions have been asked by Michio Kaku (in *The Physics of the Impossible*) and others. In 1957 it was discovered by T.D. Lee and C.N. Yang (and confirmed by Wu) that parity can be violated, meaning that our Universe and a mirror image Universe can be distinguished from each other (in terms of the laws of physics) if the proper experiments are conducted. Furthermore, it was discovered that CP (charge and parity) together can be violated, and thus such a Universe with parity and charge reversed would also reveal itself as fundamentally different from our own. However, a CP reversed Universe with time also reversed can't be distinguished from our Universe. Such a Universe was actually suggested in *Star Trek: The Animated Series* (*ST:TAS*) in the episode "The Counterclock Incident." In this episode, the *Enterprise* goes into a supernova explosion, only to realize it is the portal to the CPT reversed Universe. In this Universe, people talk backwards and are born as old men and women, and then end their lives as children. Stars are dark and space is bright (I can't help but think of a "negative" of a picture made from film when I see this, and that's perhaps what inspired these images). Though this made for an interesting show, it can't be what a "real" CPT reversed Universe looks like, since it is distinguishable from our Universe. An element of this theory also made it into the aforementioned *Space: 1999* episode "A Matter of Balance," in which the main character states that his race of anti-matter people on the planet Sunim (which happens to be "minus" spelled backwards) started off evolved and is now "descending into the slime" in a manner opposite to the course of human evolution on Earth. Similarly, in "A Matter of Life and Death," Lee Russell, a man the Alphans encounter, who ends up being an anti-matter man, ultimately has the ability to reverse time. The implications seem implausible, as they run so strongly against our common experience. In addition, as presented in the typical science fiction episode, there are only kernels of truth presented. For instance, though some of the laws of physics do allow for time to be reversed, on the realistic macroscopic level, large-scale processes tend to lead to a disorder that cannot be reversed, as dictated by the second law of thermodynamics as seen in Chapter 1. So, though Newton's Laws for a projectile allow time to run backwards or forwards, we cannot take this to the level of "unbreaking" a glass or resurrecting the dead.

Perhaps we should not be surprised by the lack of CPT violation (that is, that a CPT reversed Universe is not distinguishable from our own). In 1948 it was realized by Richard Feynman that an anti-matter particle could be treated as its matter counterpart, but traveling backward in time. Motion in space for anti-particles could then be completely reconciled with matter particles if left was transposed with right. That is, as this theory implies, if you make a video recording of a charged particle, such as an electron, and play it backwards, it would, according to the laws of physics, appear the same as the particle's anti-matter counterpart, the positron, moving forward. One ramification of this symmetry (the precise physics is beyond the scope of this work) is that if charge, left/right and time symmetries are together preserved after a reversal, then any of these symmetries individually is not enough to preserve the laws of physics after reversal.

The Multiverse

To consider whether or not parallel Universes are even possible, we have to consider what a Universe really is in the first place. The term certainly

4. Universes, Dimensions and Space   107

suggests something all-encompassing and possibly infinite. Within physics, the term has often been used similarly; however, there can be multiple Universes if each represents a separate physical realm that may only be weakly connected or not connected at all to another realm of existence, including our own Universe. Therefore, the physical conditions (if not physical laws) can be different from one Universe to another. In *Our Mathematical Universe*, Max Tegmark of the Massachusetts Institute of Technology (MIT) uses the term "our Universe" to describe that physical reality that we can observe (Tegmark, *Our Mathematical Universe* 2014). In that sense, the simplest way to describe any other Universe is that it is any extension of physical space that is not (even in principle) observable by us. Somehow though that's not totally satisfying, and we need to look for more physical explanations beyond this one. The term multiverse is now used to include all possible Universes. There are a number of theories for multiverses, and not all are mutually exclusive. We will discuss these possibilities roughly in the order of what naturally (from simplest and most accepted to most complex and most speculative) may arise from currently accepted theory and outlined in a taxonomy by Tegmark ("Parallel Universes" 2011). Since a separate Universe is defined as being causally disconnected from another Universe, we can essentially have a "Universe within a Universe" if expansion within one Universe is so rapid that parts of the Universe become causally disconnected over time. These separate Universes cannot then be seen from any of the others and are thus often labeled as "beyond the horizon Universes" (Tegmark refers to this as a Level I multiverse in his taxonomy). Interestingly, because there can be an infinite number of these Universes, one might eventually stumble upon one that is an exact copy of our own. The distances would be immense (much greater than even the distance to the horizon of our own Universe), but it is possible. Furthermore, if one was only interested in finding a near copy of our own Universe, say one that had an Earth that was similar in some ways, but different in others, the chances are we'd bump into such a Universe at a slightly closer (but still quite immense) distance. In fact, in the *ST:TOS* episode "Miri," the *Enterprise* stumbles upon just such a copy. At beginning of the episode, its clear that they have encountered what looks at first to be a replica of the Earth. However, upon beaming down, the city they land in appears to be similar to Earth of the mid–20th century, but in detail, life has progressed in dramatically different ways. Though this find of theirs captures the spirit of being able to find a distant Earth replica, within the concept of "beyond the horizon Universes," such a copy would have to be considerably more distant from us than Miri's planet (save for a couple of notable exceptions, we are to assume that the *Enterprise* stayed within our Galaxy). Also related to the expansion of the Universe from the Big Bang, it is possible to get another type of multiverse that is related to the beyond the horizon multiverse.

During the early expansion of the Universe, it is theorized that there would have been an extremely brief period of rapid inflation, during which the overall expansion of the Universe was much more rapid than what we see today. In fact, this is not a onetime occurrence even in one location, but there can be different times of inflation in different parts of the Universe (called "chaotic inflation" and developed by Andre Linde). Thus, there can be Universes such as our own that have survived an initial inflation, and gone on to support life, or there can be Universes still undergoing inflation, or where inflation stopped at a point that rendered the Universe with physical laws that are inconsistent with habitability. The effect would be then to create separated off "bubble Universes" that can then have very different physical conditions (Tegmark refers to these as Level II multiverses). Each of these "bubble Universes," which have also sometimes been referred to as "pocket Universes," can then also have an assortment of "beyond the horizon Universes." *ST:TAS*, in the episode "Time Trap," specifically uses the term pocket Universe (one of the earliest uses of the term) for an alternate Universe in which several members of various alien societies have been trapped by a Utopian society, Elysia. In physicist John Cramer's 1997 novel, *Einstein's Bridge*, an intelligent civilization in another bubble Universe creates a bridge to our Universe via a recently activated particle accelerator on Earth. One interesting aspect of bubble Universes is that their presence may be observable through gravitational effects on our Universe. In particular, many have looked for distortions in the cosmic microwave background that cannot be explained by gravity within our Universe. In particular, there has been some controversial evidence suggesting what is called a "dark flow," or an unexplained "flow" of clusters of galaxies (detected by their distortions to the CMB) toward a particular region of sky. The ultimate origin might be the pull of another bubble Universe.

Another interesting option has been theorized by Lee Smolin. It is possible for new Universes to be created during the evolution of black holes due to quantum gravity effects that allow for expansion of space-time within the black hole. Thus, it could be possible that we live in a Universe created by a black hole (and inside the event horizon of the black hole), a proposition that made it to the previously mentioned *Doctor Who* episode "The Three Doctors." Since black holes can only be created in a Universe that favors star formation, and also such a Universe would favor planet formation, and thus potentially formation of life, it could be that many Universes that favor life are being created by the development of black holes (Manly 2011). A fascinating ramification is that this can lead to a natural selection of Universes that favor black holes, star formation, and life. Universes created in this manner that favor production of black holes less than others will not create as many black holes, and so on. The path that leads to the most black hole Universes (and thus life, etc.) is the one that will keep on creating more and more favorable Universes over time. However, there are some problems with this idea, as pointed out by John Barrow. One problem is that this theory assumes that the black hole production would have maximal values as you change these constants, and thus, such Universes could only have these specific values of nature's constants if black holes are to be maximally created. However, the gravitational constant does not behave in this manner. In one case, that of the gravitational constant, changing the gravitational constant could either lead to an increase in black hole production, or just a Universe with stronger gravity (Barrow 2011).

For a significantly more comedic introduction to the multiverse, there is *Family Guy's* eighth-season episode "Road to the Multiverse," in which Stewie (the baby and child prodigy of the Griffin family) and his dog Brian (who can talk, write books, and have a troubled love life with human women) visit numerous Universes by switching back and forth with a special remote control device. This is one of many sci-fi oriented *Family Guy* episodes (and Seth McFarlane himself has had sci-fi cameo appearances). Though some of the multiverses are obviously played for satire or even typical *Family Guy* crude humor, it does give a sense of the multiplicity of possible Universes. For instance, in one Universe the usual characters are all animated in the style of classic Disney films. In another Universe, Japan did not lose World War II and is the dominant culture in the U.S.

What Is Space?

There will be other potential types of multiverses that naturally derive from considering space with dimensions beyond the familiar three. However, before we consider dimensions of space, it will be worthwhile to consider what space actually is and to consider the early philosophical discussions before we get into the physics. We tend to take the definition of "space" for granted, just essentially assuming "everyone knows what it is." For instance, just going by intuition, we could think of space as just being a completely featureless void and not go much further (Dainton 2010). Or we think of space as being three-dimensional and linear in its geometry. However, now we know that neither is true in general, even if it seems that way to us under most circumstances. The nature of space was the subject of much debate between the mathematician Leibniz and physicist Newton in the 17th century. Leibniz took the view that space only has a meaning in terms of the relationships between objects, such as "what is the distance between Object 1 and Object 2?" That is, space is not an independent container for objects, only a set of relations between objects. This view also holds for relationships between potential objects. That is, for instance, a point anywhere between two objects can just be seen as the potential place for a new object that is part way between the others. There is no "empty space," just potential places for objects that are at distinct positions relative to other known objects (Sklar 1992).

Newton took the alternative view that space can and does exist by itself as a container of sorts. Certainly a number of science fiction texts consider space to be substantive in and of itself, or phrases such as "a rip in the fabric of the space-time continuum" that we see so often in episodes of *Doctor Who* or *Star Trek: TNG* would have no meaning (whether they make sense in terms of the actual physics is something we'll address later). But are they just speaking metaphorically or taking some artistic license? Operationally speaking, we may consider space in both ways at different times. For instance, we often speak solely of the distances between objects or the volume or area. However, at other times, we are clearly speaking of space as some sort of container, especially when speaking of outer space beyond the Earth. In some ways, Einstein's relativity (which we will discuss in more detail in moment) makes the matter more difficult. The theory of general theory of relativity clearly equates distributions of mass with curvature of space. In this formulation, space is something that can be curved, and the effect is that how things move in space depends how much "stuff" there is in that space. It is important to realize here that matter and space are always interrelated in this formulation. The distribution of matter anywhere will uniquely define the geometry of space. Though the distribution of matter may not uniquely define the nature of space, since it may also depend on some other assumptions, the geometry of space does nonetheless depend on the distribution of matter. However, it still may not be meaningful to say that relativity theory is clearly either relationalist (Leibniz) or substantivalist (Newton) (Huggett 1999). In that sense, the original debate between Leibniz and Newton is perhaps moot, but philosophers and scientists alike are constantly considering the nature of space.

Invaders from the 5th Dimension

"Invaders from the 5th Dimension" is actually the title of a 1965 episode of *Lost in Space*. Though this episode actually does give a little bit of insight into extra dimensions, it doesn't really discuss the sort of invaders (in this case, hideous disembodied aliens) we are interested in. As it will turn out, most of the sort of extra dimensions we'd be interested in won't be very good at hiding a monster (or in the case of Ken Shufeldt's *Tribulations*, a faster-than-light space ark) of any appreciable size. We will eventually be interested in looking for particles (the "invaders") that could show evidence of an extra dimension, or more than one extra dimension. These extra dimensions could show evidence of other Universes. But before we proceed too far with extra dimensions, let's think more deeply about the dimensions that we already know and love. We are most familiar with three spatial dimensions which we can think of as being height, width, and length, but might be defined a little bit differently depending on geometry. In any case, for a three-dimensional object, you can define and measure three coordinates that tell you where you are at within that object. The fourth dimension refers to time. At first this seems odd, because time certainly seems a lot different from space. There are two ways of thinking about this. On one hand, time gives you the one extra piece of information that defines a location. For example, an airplane might only be in a very precise spot in 3-D space above your head for a fraction of a second. Certainly, one hour later, the plane may be very far away, or even have landed elsewhere. Another perspective comes from the special relativity theory of Einstein. If we only take into account spatial dimensions, then as an object approaches the speed of light, then any length recorded by someone moving with the object will be different than that measured by someone on the ground. However, an effective length that also takes time into account is the same for all observers. When going beyond these well-known dimensions, we will soon see how the existence of extra spatial dimensions might lead to other types of Universes.

A Stringy Universe

A third type of Universe within the multiverse derives from consideration of developments out of string theory, which we discussed in general at the end of Chapter 1. An important ramification of the theory is that it calls for 10 spatial dimensions (of course, there has never been any evidence for the additional seven beyond our regular experience). This result shouldn't be taken for granted, and requires some additional reflection. We can easily grasp the notion of three spatial dimensions, since we, and apparently everything else, exist in three spatial dimensions. But can there be additional spatial dimensions? As Michio Kaku relates in his 1994 work, *Hyperspace*, mystics and scientists alike considered and popularized a fourth spatial dimension in the 19th century and early 20th century (chief among them was mathematician Charles Hinton). The spectacular trial of Henry Slade in London brought the fourth spatial dimension to the attention of the public as Johann Zollner in particular, and other physicists he brought on to defend Slade explained how certain feats could be possible if enacted in a fourth spatial dimension (Kaku, *Hyperspace* 1994). Though the concept is correct, we now know it is not possible for a single person to accomplish this due the enormous energies that would be involved in accessing these additional dimensions. One of the first fictional accounts to address these ideas was Edwin Abbott's *Flatland*. In Flatland, two-dimensional creatures are taken aback when their world is visited by a three-dimensional creature. This manifests itself in a bizarre manner, as the two-dimensional creatures see a three-dimensional spherical creature change his apparent form in their world as he crosses from the third dimension. Though this work was originally written as satire, it does give us some insight into how we in a three-dimensional world might experience someone crossing into our world from a fourth spatial dimension. *The Outer Limits* featured a two-dimensional being that is trapped in our three-dimensional Universe in its second season episode "Behold, Eck!" We see a more recent example in the *ST:TNG* episode "The Loss." The two-dimensional beings in this episode are naturally attracted to a cosmic string, a mass that is highly concentrated into one dimension (they have been hypothesized but none have been discovered). The two-dimensional beings first draw the *Enterprise* toward the string. In devising a way to escape, the crew finds a way to cast a reflection of the string in back of them, drawing the creatures in the opposite direction. Fortunately, the creatures are sufficiently confused that the *Enterprise* was able to escape. These ideas are further treated in Robert Heinlein's short story "He Built a Crooked House." In this story an architect builds a house that is in the shape of a tessaract, a cross figure that is comprised of six cubes. Just as a 3-D cube can be unfolded into a two-dimensional set of squares that make up a cross, the tesseract could potentially be folded up into a hypercube, though the trick is that in order to do this, there needs to be a fourth dimension. In the story, an earthquake causes the tesseract to fold in on itself into one cube. As the story later reveals, this is really a four-dimensional hypercube. The *Voyage to the Bottom of the Sea* episode "The Death Clock" seems to have been partly inspired by this story. The premise is that a villain has trapped some crewmembers of the submarine *Seaview* in a fourth spatial dimension. As Captain Crane and Chief Sharky are looking to escape their trap in the fourth dimension, they first see through the viewport that they don't see water as they should, but just darkness. As they try to go through one door that they expect to lead to a hallway, they encounter the ocean, and through another, a glacier. Through still another door, they encounter a fire. A more modern example of a similar effect is played out in the *ST:V* episode "Twisted." The effects described in these stories are very bizarre, and perhaps exaggerated; however, the main idea is correct in that you could take apparent shortcuts through our three dimensions if you had access to a fourth dimension (though it would certainly take much more energy than even a very strong earthquake would provide). A similar effect leads to an ongoing gag in *Doctor Who*: the TARDIS (his time machine) is much bigger on the inside (looks to be a substantially sized room with control panel in the center) than it is on the outside (looks like an old style London police booth, which is about the same size as an old style American phone booth). In the episode "The Three Doctors," Patrick Troughton as the Doctor explains the phenomenom: "You know, relative dimensions and all that." A similar explanation is given in the aforementioned "Invaders from the 5th Dimension" for the difference between the outside and inside appearances of the alien spacecraft.

A "Brane"-y Universe

A significant breakthrough came with the theory of general relativity. Though this theory as Einstein conceived it only deals with three spatial dimensions and the one dimension of time, Theodor Kaluza realized that if he considered this theory in one extra spatial dimension, he could actually unify gravity and electromagnetic forces. The most immediate problem with this formulation is that no fifth dimension has ever been observed, so to many physicists, this seemed to be a useful mathematical abstraction with no further use. Some physicists hypothesized that this fourth spatial dimension could indeed exist, but be "compactified." In such a dimension, you could only travel an extremely small fraction of a millimeter before you start to go around in a circle and come back to your starting point. A few years after Kaluza's work, Oskar Klein concluded that such compactified dimensions could only be about 10^{-35} meters in radius, the Planck length we introduced in Chapter 1, and dictated by the unification of quantum mechanics and gravity. Thus such dimensions are unfathomably small and undetectable. Clearly, this is not the sort of dimension that could hide some of science fiction's best monsters very effectively! To probe small length scales it is necessary to use particles of extremely high energy. To understand why this is so, we need to understand another principle of quantum mechanics, the Heisenberg Uncertainty Principle. In one form, the principle states that you cannot simultaneously know both momentum and position to high precision. That is, if you want to examine very small distances, you need to use a broad range of momenta, particularly including very high momenta. Since energy of a particle is directly related to its momentum, this also implies that we need high energies to examine small distances. In particular, for the Planck scale, this corresponds to an energy that is orders of magnitude greater than what will be achieved by the Large Hadron Collider (LHC). It has recently been suggested that some compactified dimensions could be very small, yet still orders of magnitude greater than the Planck length. One way to potentially detect the existence of such a dimension is to see how the force of gravity behaves over small distances. That gravity drops off with the square of the distance between gravitating bodies is a direct consequence of the force acting over three dimensions. If it acted over only two dimensions in a Flatland type of Universe, then gravity would only drop off linearly with distance. Likewise, if there were extra dimensions, then the force of gravity should drop off more quickly. So far, no such effect has been observed. Given these results, some expected there to be multi-dimensional versions of strings; however, for many years this did not seem to be an acceptable ramification of the theory. However, some mathematical results of more recent String Theory revealed that there could be multi-dimensional membranes, now called *branes*, lying within a multi-dimensional substrate. These branes aren't individual objects, but a (potentially infinite) space in which an entire existence (a Universe) can be contained. Furthermore, there can be a large number of branes, some of differing numbers of dimensions, each with different Universes, and each with potentially different properties. The consequence of these branes is that there can be many total dimensions in a Universe, but all can be divided up among three-dimensional branes, all separate "brane worlds" that look like separate three-dimensional Universes. It has been suggested that all particles of the standard model could be confined to a brane and that the only force allowed to work over the bulk would be gravity (gravity in general is the one force that can't be confined to a brane). In such a model, gravity could act over extra dimensions. One ramification of this theory is that if gravity acts over one extra dimension, then the effects of gravity dilution would have to be compactified over very large distances (millions of miles). This seems prohibitively large since we would surely see the effects of a dimension that encompasses a good chunk of the Solar System. However, if gravity were to only act over two extra dimensions, then the extra dimensions could be compactified to about one millimeter, and much smaller still if there are three or more extra dimensions. In a recent sensitive gravity experiment, two disks were stacked on top of each other, and would only tend to twist if gravity was acting over more than three (and probably more than four) spatial dimensions. The disks were never seen to twist, and thus extra dimensional gravity can be ruled out down to about one tenth of a millimeter (Randall, *Warped Passages* 2005).

Kaluza-Klein (KK) particles are proposed extra-dimensional particles that can manifest themselves in three dimensions by looking much like a new particle in three-dimensional space. One suggested KK particle is a multi-dimensional partner to the graviton, but can only exist if there is extra dimensional space. Though the probability of detecting any one of these particles is very small, the expected particle flux might be large enough for us to expect to detect these using the LHC. One such model suggests that KK particles are created in a relatively large extra dimension and then detected in our three-dimensional space. Though this is possible, it could end up being

4. Universes, Dimensions and Space

problematic if no large extra dimensions (for these purposes, "large" would be any dimension larger than the atomic scale, but less than about 0.1 mm) are ever found by the means discussed above. Another type of extra-dimensional particle model has been developed to potentially solve the hierarchy problem in particle physics discussed earlier. From these earlier considerations, it is expected that any solution to the mass hierarchy problem would also answer why gravity is so much weaker than any other forces and vice-versa. In one model, a brane may exist on which gravity is very strong, and as a result, the Planck mass is much lower, and closer to the masses of other particles. If we exist on a separate, but very nearby brane (the distance might be much smaller than a centimeter), we can experience gravity from the other brane, but in much diluted form. This model can be confirmed by detecting certain types of KK particles (Randall, *Knocking at Heaven's Door* 2011).

At this time we should mention that string theory is not the only potential theory of quantum gravity, so lack of evidence of dimensions may or may not be a blow to string theory, but even so, would still leave other theories of quantum gravity as possibilities.

It has been suggested that the Big Bang itself was a collision of pre-existing brane worlds (never mind for now how they got there in the first place!). This theory has received the unfortunately difficult to pronounce title of *ekpyrotic* multiverse. As a result of the collision described above, conditions similar to what we expect from the observed Big Bang would be set up in each separated brane world. It is also possible that this type of multiverse is also a cyclic multiverse. That is, after the branes collide, they would separate, and then, come together again in a collision. This process would repeat itself indefinitely. It's also possible that this theory can be tested. Such a brane collision would not be expected to release strong gravitational waves as the inflationary model would predict for the Big Bang. Even with great improvements to our ability to detect gravitational waves over the next few years, if none are detected from the Big Bang, it would be a blow to the widely accepted inflationary model. Though it wouldn't in and of itself confirm the ekpyrotic model, it would certainly then be allowed, if not confirmed, by the data. At first look, the ekpyrotic model seems to be a revival of the old idea of cyclic Universes, theorized by, but dropped once it was realized that such a model would violate the Second Law of Thermodynamics.

An additional ramification of string theory is that there can be up to 10^{500} possible ways in which extra dimensions can be arranged involving complicated geometries called Calabi-Yau shapes that define possible branes (this number made its way into popular culture when *The Big Bang Theory*'s Dr. Sheldon Cooper's string theory research was criticized for resulting in such an intractable number). Calabi-Yau shapes can have "open regions" that limit how extra dimensions can be arranged. However, branes can also have an associated flux, just as other fields do in physics. These fluxes can be threaded through the open regions of Calabi-Yau shapes, increasing the way that extra dimensions can be arranged. Also, based on string theory, we know that these fluxes can be threaded through the open regions in roughly ten different ways. If we have 500 open regions, with 10 possible threadings for each open region, then we have 10^{500} extra dimensional arrangements. This suggests that there can be unfathomably many Universes in the multiverse. However, though there are this many possibilities, it does not necessarily mean that all are physically instantiated. Though at first this may be discouraging and lead us to abandoning string theory, there is one clear advantage. There has always been some difficulty in explaining the "fine tuning" of the constants of the Universe. Some say that if it weren't for fine tuning we wouldn't be here to ask such questions. In other words, it's just a selection bias that makes us think there is something special to these values. Still others hold this up as evidence for intelligent design, that is, design by an intelligent creator (God). Though I suppose it's possible, it's certainly not a testable scientific hypothesis. But why should the constants of the Universe have the precise values that they do? This is much less of a problem if a tremendous number of possibilities exist, and our Universe is just one example of the possible Universes. The problem has been discussed for decades, and the solution involving a multiverse pre-dates string theory, or at least pre-dates the advent of string theory's relationship to multiverse theory. Nobel laureate Steven Weinberg discusses this vexing problem as early as 1987 as part of his own grappling with the anthropic principle, which states, in summation, that we, as humans are here because of a number of confluent special circumstances, physical constants, and physical laws; otherwise, we wouldn't be here to talk about it. Weinberg determined that there can only be a small range of possible values of the cosmological constant. If the cosmological constant were much greater than the present matter density of the Universe, then the Universe would collapse in on itself without giving a chance for galaxies (and stars, planets, life) to evolve. If the cosmological constant were much smaller, then galaxies wouldn't be able to coalesce. He determines that's if there are about 10^{124} Universes in the multiverse, then the chances of having at least one of many being able to produce galaxies (and then, possibly, life) would be reasonable, and we don't have to rely on there being anything particularly special about the values of fundamental constants. Still, there are detractors who say that if we start our search by looking for a single theory for everything (string theory), but instead find that there might be separate theories for everything that exists, we have a legitimate reason to be highly discouraged (Smolin, *The Trouble with Physics* 2006). In addition, Smolin is critical of some of Weinberg's assumptions and analysis that lead to his results.

On the Fringe of Many Worlds

Another type of Universe derives from consideration of quantum mechanics and the Many Worlds Hypothesis of Hugh Everett (Tegmark refers to these as Level III multiverses). In 1959 Hugh Everett proposed an alternative to the Copenhagen interpretation by stating that the probability of each possible state (or "reality") evolves separately, and for each of these states there is a separate world (i.e., a Universe, in modern parlance). The separateness of these Universes leaves them unobservable from each other. As stated by Steve Manly in *Visions of the Multiverse*, "There is no way for an observer in one stream to perceive what is happening in another" (Manly 2011). At times this seems to be the theory for the parallel Universes encountered in *Fringe*. In the episode "The Road Not Taken," Walter's explanation of potential alternate realities does have commonalities with the Many Worlds Hypothesis (he repeats part of this explanation in later episodes). Later, it's not completely clear whether "Many Worlds" applies to *Fringe* because the plots only deal with one other alternate Universe. We don't know whether that's because it's the only Universe that exists, the only that's accessible, or the only that the characters are interested in. We also see a similar theory of "Many Worlds" espoused in the *ST:TNG* episode "Parallels," in which the *Enterprise* security chief, Worf, experiences an energy surge that shifts him between these "many worlds." In one "world" he is at a birthday party with chocolate cake, and in another world he shifts into, with what appears to be angel food cake (a similar plot develops in the 1934 short story "Sideways in Time," though without reference to anything quantum mechanical and is close to the premise of the entire run of the television show *Sliders*). In the climactic scene of this episode, the states start to combine, and we see hundreds of *Enterprises* appearing from these worlds, including one that had just experienced a fierce battle and was virtually destroyed. This also appears to be the premise for the similarly named film, *Parallels*. Here, a brother and sister team, in search of their missing father, encounter evidence for many alternate Earths, and are eventually transported to one themselves. Unfortunately, one primary ramification of the theory is that there can be no interaction at all between the possible worlds. Therefore, this unfortunately would be one of the least tenable theories for alternate Universes as are typically encountered in science fiction, at least if one has any hope of traveling between them.

Tegmark noticed that both the "infinite space" multiverse mentioned earlier and the "quantum multiverse" seem to be accounting for the same thing, many slightly differing copies of us, albeit with very different origins. However, after some calculation, he realized that a multiverse of many differing copies, all with different "collapsed wave functions" is the same thing (as far as the math is concerned) as a multiverse spawned by not collapsing the wave function. So, it would seem that if the Many Worlds Hypothesis is correct, there is no need to appeal to new Universes being created. These Universes already exist. Also, if you prefer to be loyal to the Copenhagen interpretation (collapsing wave function), you could keep all of the calculations, and so long as you accept the infinite space multiverse, you'd come to the same conclusions as someone who decided to accept the Many Worlds interpretation of quantum mechanics.

The Universe Is Math

In the entirety of physics we assume that the equations are the best approximation available for describing the world around us. But what if mathematics can exactly describe the structure of our Universe (or any other Universe)? There is some precedent for this elsewhere in physics. For instance, considering general relativity, space is completely defined by geometry and this geometry is in turn determined by the configuration of mass. Now, this idea has been expanded by Max Tegmark to be one of the many theories for the multiverse. The philosophical underpinning behind the physics is that behind all physical descriptions there is some external reality that is in most cases not fully understood and described because of the way humans need to interpret the world around them. Incidentally, the interpretative element would be there even without humans. That is, there would likely be some element of interpretation even if there were only computers, or even some alien intelligence, doing the observing, experimenting, and theorizing. The concept of an external reality isn't universally ascribed to, but most scientists accept some version of this. That is, that they accept that there is some absolute reality out there, and it is the scientists' job to get to the heart of it. However, Tegmark further hypothesizes that a mathematical structure is the only kind of structure that is a pure external reality. That is, mathematical structures have no properties that can be ambiguously interpreted and there is thus no barrier between the actual physical reality and the math. The math is the reality. He further hypothesizes then that our Universe and thus other Universes are mathematical structures. Our Universe can potentially be described by an exact mathematical structure, and so can many others. Furthermore, these mathematical structures would be the key to a Theory of Everything (ToE) as they would be unfettered by the interpretive descriptions that are likely getting in our way to this theory now. There may be infinitely many mathematical structures that can define separate Universes. Tegmark goes so far to suggest that if the mathematical structure for a Universe exists, than this is tantamount to saying that this Universe actually has a physical presence (*Our Mathematical Universe* 2014). Steven Manly categorizes this type of multiverse theory as a "faith based multiverse" due to the need to accept certain pre-conditions on faith, and then accept the results of accepting these conditions (Manly 2011). Perhaps, to a scientist, the term "faith based" is a bit too pejorative; however, some elements of the theory and its assumptions stated above are problematic, and reminiscent of St. Anselm's ontological argument for the existence of God, for instance. As that (nearly one thousand year old) argument goes, "if we have the concept of God's existence in our mind, and there can be no higher than God, then he must exist in reality as well." I personally find such "proofs" unsatisfying, whether applied to God, Universes, or anything else. String theorist Brian Greene also cast some doubts on this particular theory, having preference to theories that involve physical processes (Greene 2011). However, though Tegmark's concepts are more in the category of philosophical underpinning than physical process, there is nothing about this theory that divorces itself completely from physical processes. In fact, they could and should reveal an ultimate theory of everything.

Am I a Real Author or Just a Simulated Author?

We can even go further and imagine a multiverse that is created by computer simulation as we see in films such as *The Matrix*. In the *ST:TNG* episode "Ship in a Bottle," a captured holodeck character, Moriarty, is left to live out the rest of his existence in a holodeck program, unbeknownst to him (he's been tricked to believe that he can live out his life in "the real world"). In the recent novel *Dark Matter*, by S.W. Ahmed, the Galaxy is divided into several empires, and one of the ruling species is the Volona. The Volona are unique, in that the vast majority live out their lives in virtual realities. Even some of those going about and conquering the Galaxy are actually, from their perspectives, living out their lives in a virtual world. The general idea of a simulated multiverse goes something like this: Once a civilization becomes advanced enough to have created complicated simulations, they can eventually get to the point at which they can simulate a Universe. In fact, they can simulate a multiverse. Furthermore, we can even conclude that the number of possible simulated Universes that can support life will be much greater than any number of real Universes that support life, and we can thus conclude we are more likely to be in a simulation. However there are some problems with this idea. One is that it seems impossible to create a simulation as complex as our entire Universe without some glitches. That no such glitches seem to be observed would either indicate an incredible simulation, or, of course, just indicate that we are real after all (Barrow 2011). Additionally, the entire discussion completely undermines all scientific discovery, for if we are within a simulation, then understanding the nature of the Universe, really just corresponds to figuring out the nature of the simulation, which may or may not resemble anything real. Though this may seem far-fetched, let alone not being testable scientifically, we include this as one of the more outlandish possibilities that has been discussed, and clearly it has made its way into various science fiction venues.

Chapter 5

Time Travel

What Is Time?

Before we go too deeply into the specifics of time travel, we need to consider the nature of time in general. Philosophers and physicists alike have wondered about the nature of time. The ultimate question, "What is time?" is very difficult to answer in terms of tangibles that we are all used to. We certainly think we have a grasp of time, but when it comes down to putting it in words and definite terminology, trouble arises. There has been a tendency to explain time by use of metaphors and analogies, such as "time marches on" or "time is like a flowing river"; however, since "marching" and "flowing" are types of motion, which inherently refer to a distance traveled in a certain time, they're unacceptable as parts of a true definition, both essentially being self-referential and thus lacking in explanatory power. Furthermore, there can be the difficulty of how time is perceived by the human mind, and how that compares to a more objectively determined time. Some philosophers, such as John McTaggart, have gone so far as to say that time is completely illusory (Dainton 2010). Others, including philosophers and physicists alike, insist on reality of time, including the reality of the passage of time (Smolin, *Time Reborn* 2014). Lee Smolin further insists that the reality of time has many practical consequences in politics as well as physics. On the social and political stage Smolin makes the case that the reality of time discourages us from putting off pressing societal problems such as global warming to the undefined future. In the case of physics he argues (not completely convincingly) that the reality of time demands that physical laws evolve in time, and furthermore we cannot accept physical laws as timeless, in the sense of existing unchanged, outside of time. He does show that such a general interpretation will have observable consequences, so we should eventually be able to determine its merit. Many other physicists simply accept that time is a dimension used to measure changes in a system. Since changes cannot be simultaneous, it necessitates different moments for separate events, and thus a differentiation in time (Dainton 2010). Beyond that, most physicists would accept that the passage of time (dynamic time) is at best unexplained, and at worst, an illusion. These challenges make understanding time one of the most vexing issues of philosophy and physics.

In addition, there have been many discussions on the perceived (or actual) direction to time. It turns out, that at first glance, physics seems not able to provide a natural direction to time. That is, some of the basic equations of motion show no bias towards time moving forward or backward. Based on these equations, we'd have no preferred direction for time. But then on further consideration of some important concepts in physics, such as the laws of entropy, a direction is provided (Carroll, *From Eternity to Here* 2013). Furthermore, it would then seem natural to call a previous state "the past," and an approaching state "the future." However, some philosophers object, and say that it is not that entropy leaves time with a direction, but that entropy happens to have the property of increasing with time (Maudlin 2012). I will leave the resolution of that last particular debate to the philosophers, but note that since all matter has the property of entropy and that entropy of a closed system must increase, then entropy will dictate the progress of everyone's life, and the evolution of the Universe. In our Universe, the nature of existence depends on time being pinned to entropy or vice versa (Carroll, *From Eternity to Here* 2013). The essential reason for this is the very low entropy of the initial Universe. Thus, the highest probability (by far) is for the Universe to have progressed from lower to higher entropy. So then, the philosophers have a point after all: It is not so much time itself, but the initial conditions of the Universe, that have driven time in a particular direction. If there are other Universes with different conditions, the nature of time may also be different.

One of the most dramatic aspects of Einstein's Theory of Relativity is that time has to be treated as a coordinate and dimension on par with spatial positions and dimensions. At first glance, this may seem like an arbitrary designation that only matters to physicists, but the consequences are quite dramatic. The most dramatic ramifications are that both traveling close to the speed of light, and traveling near a very massive object can lead to significant differences in how time is perceived. In the most dramatic case, time can be distorted to a great enough extent that time travel into both the future and the past may be allowable. Time travel to the future is relatively easy, at least if you are a small particle or don't wish to go more than a tiny fraction of a second into the future. We know already that particles moving close to the speed of light see the passage of time differently than slower particles going at everyday speeds. This isn't a distortion or illusion. The timescales actually are different, and shorter amounts of time will have appeared to go by (from the point of view of the particle) than for observers. A couple of famous experimental results show the reality of this theoretical result. For instance, as discussed a bit in Chapter 1, fast muons (a type of elementary particle) are known to be able to reach the ground intact, even though they should have decayed by the time they reach the ground from 10 km or so up in the atmosphere. The explanation is that though the decay lifetime of the muon is what it should be from the point of view of the particle, for an outside observer the decay time is much larger (more than 10 times larger, at highly relativistic speeds). This gives the muons enough time to reach the ground from the perspective of an outside observer. You might then wonder why the muon doesn't think it's going to decay before it hits the ground. It turns out that from the muon's perspective, the ground appears to be at a shorter distance from it than what would be measured by an outside observer (another relativistic effect called length contraction). Thus, even from the point of view of the muon, it can reach the ground without decaying (Beiser 2003). But it's not totally satisfying to confine ourselves to particles and puny periods of time. What about spaceships or some other sort of time machine that can bring us to the future? We can now measure these effects very precisely, and know that clocks running on an airplane will show that less time has passed as compared to clocks on the ground. However, these effects can be measured in microseconds. For the astronauts who have logged a year or more in space, the discrepancy between time frames (for a speed of a little over one thousandth of the speed of light) is about 10 to 20 milliseconds (Gott 2002). We can see this clearly that if we think about an astronaut stepping into a spaceship and traveling to a nearby star at a speed close to the speed of light, this could lead to a much larger discrepancy of years. He then returns to Earth at a similar speed. From the perspective of the astronaut, he would be stepping years into the future upon returning to Earth. However, in order to get something very massive, such as a spaceship, up to near light speed, we need tremendous amounts of energy and in fact, this can be more energy than the entire Earth currently uses in one year (Everett and Roman 2012). In the *Space: 1999* episode "Journey to Where," it may be that this (a trip into the future) has happened with the entire Moon! Surprisingly, Moonbase Alpha receives signals from Earth, but those on Earth explain that it is the year 2120. Though no details for the time difference are given, we are to presume that either time dilation due to the high bulk speed of the Moon, or some other kind of unexplained "time warp" (such as going through a wormhole), is responsible. As we will soon see this theory (and even the energy constraints) are far more optimistic than what we will need for backward time travel; however, for now, even forward time travel for macroscopic matter (i.e., people and spaceships) will likely be prohibitive for centuries. I should add that all of these models for future time travel (as well as most of the science fiction) assume that the time traveler is simply skipping ahead in time, and there is no alternate version of you living out life at the normal pace with everyone else on Earth. That is, it is an Earth that has progressed without you on it.

It has long been a fallback topic of science fiction, perhaps even a cliché, to depict backward time travel. Perhaps this is because time travel provides the opportunity to correct the past. Who doesn't have something in their own past they'd like to reverse? Or perhaps a more magnanimous soul would like to prevent the rise of Hitler, or evacuate thousands before a devastating tsunami. This line of reasoning is exemplified in Irwin Allen's *Time Tunnel* for which it was a common plot device for the protagonists to attempt reversing a catastrophic fate. In the series pilot, a military experiment in time has gone awry and leads to a young scientist being hurled back in time to the ill-fated *Titanic*. His attempts to get the captain (played by Michael Rennie, of *The Day the Earth Stood Still* fame) to veer even slightly off course are in vain and the *Titanic* sinks (of course, our hero and his co-star are able to escape in the nick of time). In later episodes they try to warn people of the bombing of Pearl Harbor, the eruption of Krakatoa, the massacre of Custer's troops, and the fall of the Alamo. A joke mentioned by Princeton physicist J. Richard Gott in the Discovery Channel series *Through the Wormhole* is that perhaps the *Titanic* sunk because it was full of time travelers looking to either gawk at the incident or warn the captain!

Similar plots were normal for *Doctor Who* as well (such as in the episode "Genesis of the Daleks," in which the Doctor and his companions have the opportunity to go back into time and kill the engineer, Davros, who created the murderous Dalek cyborgs). And who can forget (among those who are old enough to have seen *Back to the Future* in first run) Marty McFly trying his hardest to be sure that his parents really do meet back in the 1950s? Furthermore, he saves the life of his mentor by warning him of what appears to be his eventual murder by terrorists. To a more nefarious end, in 2004's *Primer*, two young engineers experimenting in their garage serendipitously invent a very limited sort of time machine. However, the writers confuse a physical effect that can counteract the local force of gravity from the Earth with the manipulation of ultra-strong gravity that would be needed to affect time. In particular, they are said to be making use of the Meisner Effect, which can lead to a superconductor expelling its magnetic field, which can be exploited for levitation. However, even with these limitations, they are able to manipulate the stock market to their advantage. So, is it physically possible to travel in time?

Avoiding Paradoxes

First, we must consider the logical possibilities and restrictions, and then go on to discuss specific physical models. From our previous discussion of the nature of time, it is a clear stance amongst most physicists that even if time travel is possible, changing the past is likely not possible (Maudlin 2012). This stance is taken in order to deliberately avoid troubling paradoxes such as the grandfather paradox. This paradox is summed up as follows: a time traveler goes back in time to kill his grandfather (it really can be any ancestor, but grandfathers have been the traditional victims of time travelers). However, if he is successful, then clearly the time traveler can never be born, and thus not able to go back into time to kill his grandfather. In the *Outer Limits* episode "The Man Who was Never Born," an attempt is made to go back in time to assassinate the man who inadvertently created a plague that wiped out most of humanity (though here, the time traveler himself is not a descendant, though he has been mutated by the plague). He mistakenly is taken back to the time of the man's father and mother. He then gets the idea of preventing their wedding (this was aired in the early 1960s, so we can assume that was essentially tantamount to the couple not being able to have a child together). He does also seriously consider killing Bertram Cabot, Sr. (father), though, interestingly, he only seems to very briefly consider killing Noel (mother), even before he falls in love with her himself. He is successful. Though in attempting to return to the future, he fades into nonexistence (perhaps implying that he was indeed part of this family line, or at least that the chain of events that was to lead to his birth had now been prevented).

Another interesting related example of this is in the finale of *ST:TNG's* "All Good Things." In this episode, the *Enterprise* inadvertently creates a time disturbance, which among other things, emits dangerous radiation. It eventually is revealed that the time disturbance was actually larger and more disruptive in the distant past. Q (a powerful alien who spent the run of the series toying with the *Enterprise* crew) reveals to Captain Picard that this disturbance will be so large in the past that it will prevent the early evolution of life on Earth. In a similarly plotted early episode of *Doctor Who* ("City of Death"), an alien (Scaroth) crash-lands on Earth during the period of the beginning of life. An explosion sends the alien into multiple time periods (somehow, copies of himself were able to exist this way and were also able to communicate with each other through time). His (their?) primary goal is to re-unite all of his selves back in the time period just before the initial explosion, and then do what he can to avoid it. The Doctor, realizing that the burst of radiation from the explosion was the catalyst that started life on Earth, prevents Scaroth from re-integrating himself by sending him back to the future. In this case, Scaroth was about to be the assassin of all mankind (as in the grandfather paradox), yet was ultimately stopped by the Doctor (Muir, *A Critical History of Doctor Who* 1999). In the 1984 film *Terminator*, a computerized weapons network (Skynet) becomes self-aware and seeks to destroy mankind, and is partly successful in setting off a nuclear holocaust. Eventually,

The TARDIS of the *Doctor Who* television series, the time- and space-traveling craft of the Doctor (here portrayed by Peter Davison), was purposely built to look like a 1950s London police box so that it would blend in as "ordinary." BBC/Photofest.

a resistance movement against the controlling Skynet is started by John Connor. Seeking to end the resistance before it even starts, Skynet sends a terminator (an android assassin) to kill off Sarah Connor, John's mother, before he's conceived. However, perhaps Skynet need not have expended so much effort especially considering its lack of ultimate success in its goal. We find out in *Terminator 2* that from the Terminator's arm left behind when it was mostly destroyed, the engineer Myles Dyson uses the advanced microchip to later design Skynet. Though we'd think that it might end there and that the intervention didn't change the course of history, we do see that Dyson is sufficiently convinced of the negative ramifications of his work, that he completely destroys (along with himself) the lab work using the advanced devices copied from the original terminator.

Though killing your ancestor (or yourself) in a visit to the past is problematic for time travel, simply visiting yourself or ancestors is less problematic, and can lead to some interesting encounters. In the "Day the Sky Fell In" episode of the aforementioned *Time Tunnel*, scientist Tony Newman encounters his father as a young man in Hawaii and tries to warn him of the impending attack on Pearl Harbor (his father is killed in the end anyway).

Newman also is able to encounter his younger self (who of course is able to escape the attack). Spock visits his younger self and saves his younger self's life in *ST:TAS* episode "Yesteryear." A humorous example is from the film *Bill and Ted's Excellent Adventure*. The general premise is that society of 700 years in the future is based on the music of Bill and Ted, amateur teenage musicians from the 1980s. Knowing that the present-day Bill and Ted will jeopardize their music career (and thus future society) by failing a history course and thus failing out of school (with Ted being sent away to military school in Alaska), a representative of the future society (Rufus) aids Bill and Ted in passing history by helping them go through time to meet various historical figures. They encounter their future selves who encourage the present versions to continue on with their adventure so that they can save future society. Their past selves don't really believe that the look-alike visitors they encounter are really their future selves, so ask, "If you're us, what number are we thinking of?" They then guess correctly and are accepted as the future Bill and Ted. There have been similar encounters in *The Simpsons* and *Family Guy* (such as "Stu and Stewie's Excellent Adventure").

The only other choice in order to avoid these logical inconsistencies, rather than allowing for time travel, but barring changing of the past, would be to conclude that no time travel at all is allowed (and that may yet be shown to be true). At first this interpretation may seem contradictory. Surely, if you are traveling into the past, you are changing it by being there! But this view is overly simplistic. In actuality, if you go back to the past, then it is always the case that you were part of that past event. Nothing has been changed. As an illustrative example, say you go back in time to the assassination of Julius Caesar. Though history does not record that there were any mysterious time travelers on the scene, all that means is that you were good at hiding yourself! You were always a part of that past (even though you never knew you had been before you went back in time). Thus, you cannot go back in time particularly to stop the assassination of Julius Caesar (or at least, not actually be successful), as it has always been the case that he was killed. It is, however, possible, that you, the time traveler to the past, handed a certain knife over to Brutus, which he then used to stab Caesar. That is, you can be part of the known past, but as stated before, it would have always been the case that you were part of that past. *ST:TOS* seems to have an inconsistent view of interfering in the past. In "Tomorrow Is Yesterday," the *Enterprise* accidentally gets sent to the past Earth, and, after tampering with the past in what seemed to be a minor way, they decide to attempt to go back to the time before they interfered, and avoid the incident. Since ultimately no claim to have changed the past was made (though they did imply to have had that ability), this view is consistent with currently accepted physics. In "Assignment: Earth," the *Enterprise* purposely goes back to 1968 to better study the Cold War period and how nuclear war was avoided at that time. In the midst of their work, they encounter a human agent of an alien society, Gary Seven. At first Seven appears to be sinister, trying to start a nuclear war (though Kirk and Spock should have known better and realized that the past couldn't be changed). Seven eventually detonates the nuclear warhead before it could do any damage. Apparently, it was the last-minute detonation of the nuclear weapon that made the superpowers realize that they had been on the brink of destruction, thus encouraging them to put off World War III for some time (it did indeed eventually occur within the *Star Trek* history). At the end of the episode Spock reveals that the *Enterprise* was always to have been part of the incident (again, a truism in standard physics). Likewise, in the *Twilight Zone* episode "No Time Like The Past," a physicist, Paul Driscoll (played by Dana Andrews), disgusted with the events of the 20th century, tries to use a time machine to go back and correct some of the worst moments. For instance, he tries to evacuate Hiroshima on the day the first atomic bomb was dropped, attempts to assassinate Hitler, and also tries to get the *Lusitania* to avoid the torpedo that sunk it. In each case, he fails. Upon return to his present, his collaborator says, "You must know that the past is inviolate." A similar principle is expressed in the earlier *Twilight Zone* episode "Back There." After discussing the possibility of time travel with friends, Paul Corrigan ends up mysteriously transported back in time to the evening of Abraham Lincoln's assassination. Though he tries to warn people of the president's assassination, he is not taken seriously. He is even abducted by a man who turns out to be John Wilkes Booth, who wanted to be sure Corrigan didn't interfere with his plot. After Booth successfully kills Lincoln, Corrigan concludes that it is not possible to change history. Upon his return though, he notices some small changes. For instance, he sees that a man who he remembered as a servant at the men's club is now a member. He further concludes that small changes to time are possible, but that grand events are immutable. There are some additional examples of how it's clear that going back to the past affected events in some way, but did not change the events from what they always were. For instance, in the *Lost in Space* episode "Visit to a Hostile Planet," it is suggested at the end that the term "flying saucer" was originated by one of the 1950s town folk who observes the *Jupiter 2* as it goes back to the future. A similar idea was adopted by *Back to the Future*. When a member of the band playing at the school dance hears Marty McFly playing his guitar, he's inspired to call his cousin, who happens to be Chuck Berry, and has him listen to what he thinks is a new sound (the implication being that Marty inspired the beginnings of rock music by bringing it from the future). It's even less problematic if your only intentions are to visit the past, perhaps to learn a bit of history or just experience a time period without affecting it ("time travel tourism," more or less). Though it's likely more problematic if you pluck historical figures *from* their lives and into your own time period, as in "The Kidnappers" episode of *Time Tunnel* and the "Time Lock" episode of *Voyage to the Bottom of the Sea*. In such cases, it would seem difficult for the historical figure to then continue their lives as historically recorded. This particular problem was avoided in at least one case, in which the alien from the Canopus system in "The Kidnappers" says that he acquired Hitler just as he was about to commit suicide in his bunker in Berlin. Considering all of these issues, we now know that we need not have "time police" or anything or anyone else science fiction writers like to conjure up to protect us from folks who would like to change the past, since it is most likely not possible to do so (one episode of *Lost in Space* pre-supposes that time in the Universe is controlled by a flamboyant "time merchant"). These restrictions do not themselves prevent time travel to the past, but they do pose serious restrictions, many of which eliminate the possibility of some favorite science fiction plots mentioned above.

Causal Time Loops

One particularly popular manifestation of time travel is the closed (causal) time loop. That is, we are able to travel back in time, but eventually are able to get back to the point at which we are at our time machine, ready to go back into the past, and so on. The loop has to be self-consistent, always getting the time traveler back to the point of getting into the machine to the past. To do otherwise would be incoherent. Even so, some physicists and philosophers still debate the possibility of causal time loops. A fun example of this is the original five *Planet of the Apes* films from the 1960s and 1970s, which together all form a causal time loop. In this scenario, astronauts from Earth in the near future embark on a deep-space mission at near light speeds. However, something goes wrong, and they crash-land on what they think is a remote planet in another star system. Their chronometer tells them that they are over 2,000 years in the future. They have some bizarre encounters, but by far the most disturbing is that they are on a planet of intelligent apes that clearly have the power of speech and some crude technological abilities. Furthermore, the native future humans appear to be mute, docile, and not nearly as intelligent. Eventually it is climactically revealed that they are actually on the future (about 3700 AD) post-apocalyptic Earth. Unfortunately, as the plot collectively evolves through all of the films, the future Earth suffers an even more devastating, and apparently final, nuclear blast. The only survivors appear to be a band of ape scientists who have the forethought to launch into space using one of the spacecraft left by the human astronauts when they crash-landed. Eventually, they make it back to the past Earth (roughly speaking, present day) with the dominant humans. The offspring of these apes lead the rest of Earth's apes to a rebellion that eventually leads them to be the dominant species that leads to the future that our original astronauts encounter. This time loop is completely consistent, though somewhat perplexing. For example, what is the ultimate origin of the rebellious apes? Do they originate in the past? Or, do they originate in the future? Some feel that it is an affront to logic not to have a clear beginning, and for this reason, a number of philosophers and physicists alike do not think time travel to the past is possible. Another example occurs in *Terminator*, as we mentioned earlier. John Connor sends Reese into the past to stop the terminator from killing his mother, Sarah Connor. However, Reese then fathers John Connor with Sarah. So, how did John come into being? Was there ever a John Connor that existed without Reese being his father? In addition, was there ever a Skynet that hadn't been indirectly created from an artifact of the first destroyed terminator? The standard view of physicists as presented earlier would say "no" to each, though it does strain logic to have something or someone with no clear origin.

We also note that in science fiction, such time loops are not always treated consistently. For instance, in the *Voyage to the Bottom of the Sea* episode "A Time to Die," the submarine *Seaview* is mysteriously brought to the distant pre-historic past. Shortly thereafter the villain, the quirky inventor Mr. Pem, reveals that he is responsible. The rest of the episode is spent with Pem revealing his mastery over time by showing Admiral Nelson glimpses of the past, and then the future, where Nelson sees that he will be killed. Intent on having a different future, Nelson sets out to stop Pem, and he is ultimately killed. Though there are no time loops yet, there are some problems with how Pem presents Nelson with a future that never comes to be (suggesting, of course, that it can be changed). In addition, though the episode seems to end with everyone happy in the present, we never clearly saw the *Seaview* return to the present from pre-history (though perhaps this was implied). The real problems start when Pem returns in the final episode of the series, "No Way Back." Here, the *Seaview* explodes, killing all. It's revealed throughout the episode that this was the act of Mr. Pem. Evidently, he has planted the bomb in the past in order to convince the present-day Admiral Nelson to go back in time and try to save the vessel and crew (of course, without revealing that he was ultimately responsible). Pem then had plans to seize the submarine for his own purposes. This is in itself problematic, since it shows once again that they are convinced that the past can be changed. Also, there's no clear start to this part of the loop. On one hand, Pem has somehow gotten to the past to plant the bomb. However, we see soon after that the only way he was able to get to the past was to convince Nelson to help him only after Nelson has seen that *Seaview* was destroyed. Nelson had agreed to let Pem use the nuclear reactor at his headquarters as a power supply for his time travel. We're then distracted by a plot in which Pem, now in control of *Seaview*, has brought it deeper into the past to the time of the American Revolution. Though it's clearly Pem's intention to side with Benedict Arnold in allowing the British to take West Point, it's never made clear how this turn in the Revolution would benefit Pem (however, it is stated in the first episode that Pem is erratic and impetuous, and often acts without a real plan). Clearly again, Pem firmly thinks he can change the past. Eventually, this plot is exposed, and Pem is killed while the crew regains control over *Seaview*. Nelson finds the bomb that was planted and ejects it from the submarine. Thus, this is an incoherent time loop (or at least, opens the possibility of not being consistent). In the end of this episode though, it appears as if *Seaview* is brought back into the future, or at least significant time has passed with no explanation given. The inconsistencies are unfortunate, as it is an otherwise entertaining episode of this series. In still another *ST:TNG* episode, "Cause and Effect," the *Enterprise* goes through a repeating causal loop, always ending in the *Enterprise* being destroyed, but still sent into the past to begin the process over again. Eventually, the crew is able to figure out that they are trapped in this loop, and in order to get themselves out, they must send messages to themselves in the next loop (using fictional particles called "dekyons," probably chosen to sound like "tachyon") to avoid the events that led to the *Enterprise* exploding. The main problem here is in thinking that you can change the loop, since that amounts to a change in the past, which is widely believed to be impossible. Also, there may be no valid method for leaving messages for the next loop (though tachyons, to be discussed later, are the best bet).

In the recent film *Looper*, time travel becomes outlawed, and only mobsters have control over the time travel devices. They use time travel for purposes of assassination: They send the person they want killed into the past where a hit man is waiting to shoot them. The body is then disposed of in the past by the assassin. However, problems arise because of a proviso that the assassins agree to: if they are to live 30 years into the future, when time travel is invented, they are to be sent into the past to be assassinated (by their past self, apparently). Problems arise when the future "self" (assassins refer to their future selves as their "loop") escapes assassination. Though some inconsistencies arise with this concept as presented in the film, it's likely that the writer-director (Rian Johnson) fully intended to bend some of the commonly accepted notions of time travel. That is, these are unlikely to be careless errors. However, some of the inconsistencies are still worth discussing for the sake of understanding the underlying concepts. For instance, it would seem that the present "self" fears punishment, even up to being killed if he lets his "loop" go, either intentionally or unintentionally. This would seem to be incoherent. Clearly, if he sees his future self has lived up to 30 years, then he knows he will definitely be alive in the future, and has nothing to fear, at least not regarding being killed. Also, it would appear, that at times in the film, a present self is able to send his future self a message by, say, carving a note into the skin of his forearm, and then it appears on the forearm of the future self as a scar. This seems far-fetched, since if it's really his future self, he would have had this scar for decades. However, it would seem that Johnson takes the position that in time travel mechanics, anything goes, and all of our rules of causality go out the window. The characters themselves seem to be somewhat aware of these issues. When Young Joe confronts Old Joe (it is the convention of the many websites that discuss this film to refer to the present and future Joe in this manner) in their favorite diner, Old Joe responds with, "If we talk about time travel we'll be here all day making diagrams with straws," and further responding with a vehement, "It doesn't matter!" The end of the film takes this even father. The future Joe is obsessed with going back in time to kill the Rainmaker, a future mob boss responsible for killing Joe's wife. He firmly believes he will be able to change history, and more importantly, the happy course of his life by doing this. Young Joe becomes aware of Old Joe's plans and goes to the farm where a young child named Cid lives, one of several children who might be the future Rainmaker. He becomes close to both Cid and Cid's surrogate mother. Eventually, Old Joe catches up to them, and attempts to kill Cid. Realizing that Old Joe will likely succeed in killing Cid, Young Joe kills himself, terminating his timeline, "erasing" old Joe, and letting Cid's life continue. This in itself is acceptable to most time travel experts. However, this would also mean that any evidence that Old Joe ever existed would also have to be erased, such as the injury to Cid's jaw from Old Joe's gunshot. Such evidence does remain in the last moments of the film.

Physical Models for Time Travel to the Past

Soon after Einstein announced his results of his theory of general relativity, a number of theoretical physicists began to work on models of the Universe that would be consistent with the equations that govern the theory. One such scientist was Kurt Goedel, who devised a model (published in 1949) that would allow for time travel, particularly, time travel into the past. Although not initially intended as the dominant feature of his model, he received much criticism for this time travel feature. In fact, we will soon see that all "time machines" are actually the way physicists refer to solutions of Einstein's equations of general relativity that allow time travel. However, the one catch is that this particular model of Goedel's is that it would require that the Universe itself was rotating. To travel back in time in such a Universe, one would have to circumnavigate the Universe. In an immense Universe, this circumference could be at least 100 billion light years. Therefore, time travel, even with fast spacecraft discussed in earlier chapters, would be impractical. However, the possibility for backward time travel that was opened up was still intriguing and thereafter, it became a mission of Goedel's to see if astronomical data available at that time indicated a rotating Universe. Though an early study by Vera Rubin (who figured prominently in determining the amount of dark matter in galaxies) show that there might be a systematic velocity effect that could be due to rotation of the Universe (Panek 2011), no such effect has been observed in any modern data, so Goedel's model is mainly presented as an early possibility discussed for time travel, even though it does not seem viable today (Nahin 1999). But in this case, the legacy of the solution was more important than the solution itself. This type of solution (rotating mass) led to an entire class of solutions that allow for time travel. Building on this idea, Frank J. Tipler introduced the possibility of time travel into the past by traveling around an infinitely long, extremely dense cylinder at nearly light speed. This may have been one of the ideas to most quickly make it into science fiction. Larry Niven almost immediately published a short story that had the same title as Tipler's journal article. Though nothing can be infinitely long, and perhaps no matter can be quite as dense as Tipler required (up to 80 orders of magnitude greater than the density of a neutron star), it may be possible to be close enough (very, very long and very, very dense) to achieve the possibility of time travel. However, some criticisms of such "approximate Tipler cylinders" abound, and it just may not be possible due to the cylinder essentially crushing itself. Furthermore, the tremendous accelerations felt by anything at the surface due to the rapid spinning would likely lead to most matter disintegrating. Though we did already mention that such a cylinder would have to be made of superdense matter anyway, so perhaps that's a saving grace, at least for the machine itself, if not for the time traveler.

As explained in an earlier chapter, Kip Thorne revived his interest in wormholes while helping his friend Carl Sagan develop a plot device for his first (and only) science fiction novel, *Contact* (and the idea has been revived, with Kip Thorne as adviser, in the 2014 film *Interstellar*). While working out the details, Thorne not only realized he could create a safe tunnel through the Universe with a wormhole, but that with two connected wormhole mouths, he could potentially create a time machine. If somehow, one wormhole mouth can be relativistically accelerated relative to the other mouth while still keeping the distance between the wormhole mouths constant in hyperspace, then time as perceived within the wormhole will be the same at both mouths, but perceived differently from the outside, at each mouth. The

134 The Physics and Astronomy of Science Fiction

Amy Pond (Karen Gillan) and the Doctor (Matt Smith) inside the TARDIS. Clearly, it's bigger on the inside than on the outside. BBC/Photofest.

consequence of this is that if the wormholes' mouths are close together, then one could jump through the wormhole, and be back close to the starting point, but at a time before the original departure. As a concrete example given by Thorne, if, say Mouth A were to be moving much faster than B, so that B perceived one day while A perceived 10 days, then someone could look through the mouth at A, and potentially see a calendar through B that has a time that is nine days earlier. Thus, a traveler at A could jump through to B and go back in time (Thorne 1994).

Though Kip Thorne's wormhole time machines are interesting, and are among the most seriously considered theoretical time travel concepts in physics, there is not yet any practical way to create a wormhole (and there may or may not be astrophysical wormholes of this type) and any stable wormhole would need large amounts of exotic matter, in addition to a means to relativistically accelerate one of the mouths. This exotic matter is so "exotic" because it needs to be negative matter or energy. As yet, we have not discovered any negative matter and there are only two potential ways to get "negative" energy; the amount we could get from either of these is currently extremely limited. It was predicted in 1933 that the quantum effect of virtual particles and anti-particles popping in and out of existence would create a net pressure on two parallel plates (this is known as the Casimir Effect). Between the plates, the energy of these particles would be limited to energies related to the size of the plate spacing. This pressure and associated energy would be very small, as dictated by the Heisenberg Uncertainty principle (Kaku, *The Physics of the Impossible* 2008). Also, Dark Energy discussed in Chapter 2 could fit the bill, but as yet, we have no way of harnessing this (Clegg 2011). In fact, there have been a number of allowable time travel solutions that do not involve exotic matter. One of these was developed by Amos Ori of the Israel Institute of Technology (Technion). Using normal matter, space-time is configured in a loop pattern. For every lap around the loop (you must go around at speed close to the speed of light), you can begin to go backward in time. What is perhaps most interesting about Ori's model is that it is more likely to arise naturally, such as via particles being accelerated near a neutron star. If such a naturally occurring time machine is close enough to the Earth, and also has existed for 100 million years or more it may be possible to achieve what only characters in pulps have been able to do for decades: visit the time when dinosaurs dominated Earth, ancient Rome, etc.

Ron Mallett at the University of Connecticut may have a model for time travel that is the most tenable, as it does not require a large mass or an extremely dense state of matter that is impossible to find on Earth. In fact, he outlines an idea for a potential experiment that could be done in a modest physics lab (though it would require an initial investment in millions of dollars for special laser equipment). The underlying concept is that just as mass can effect space, so can energy in the form of laser light. In fact, laser light sent around in a ring can create a distortion in space and time similar to a vortex. In this sense, the Mallett model is quite similar to Tipler's rotating cylinder, but making use of light instead of mass. The effect of this is that any particle that finds itself in the vortex can be transported backward in time. This concept is very intriguing, since it is one of the only time-travel concepts that is clearly testable (at least currently), though it may be the least tenable for actually transporting humans across time. However, if successful, just the notion that we can possibly travel back in time would be a great revolution (Mallett 2006). We should note that this particular model has received some criticism in recent physics journal articles, as summarized in *Time Travel and Warp Drives* (Everett and Roman 2012). One problem is that this model (and also those of Ori and Tipler) violates the Hawking theorem, which states that time machines can only be created using exotic matter unless the object is of infinite extent (and no real objects can be infinite). Though there have also been some criticisms of the Hawking theorem itself, most physicists in this field (not unexpectedly) side with Hawking. Even ignoring Hawking though, there are some additional problems with the Mallett time machine. The main additional problem is that the distance out to the region where "closed time like curves" (i.e., the time machine) would be created would be much larger than the size of the observable Universe. Furthermore, this is not a number that can be mitigated much by using more powerful lasers (even if you assume, rather generously, that they have the power of the Sun!). However, it may yet be worth investigating this sort of time machine, as its construction could teach us about frame-dragging or even the validity of the Hawking theorem. Even without time travel, Mallett predicts "frame-dragging" in this type of experiment, a type of distortion of space-time caused by rotating mass-energy. If frame-dragging were to be detected by a Mallett-like device, it might point in the direction of this being a valid avenue to explore for time travel. Astrophysicists first detected frame-dragging indirectly in 1997 via X-ray signals coming from accretion disks precessing around black holes. Since then, the satellite Gravity Probe-B has detected frame dragging due to its orbit around the rotating Earth, though not to the high accuracy originally hoped for before launch. So, though we now know that frame dragging exists, the breakthrough would now be the ability to control the effect, and Mallett may have found a way to do that, even without time travel capabilities.

An additional model of this type is that of J.R. Gott (Gott 2002). He supposes that two cosmic strings moving at very high velocity towards each other could create a time machine. Cosmic strings are extremely thin (possibly less than one atomic nucleus in diameter) strands of matter that are extremely long (many light years, potentially) and have extremely high density. However, it's usually theorized that these cosmic strings most likely were only created in the early moments of the Universe, and perhaps none have ever formed. So, though the model is valid, it depends on the existence of cosmic strings, the existence of which has not been proven. In addition, we would not be able to manipulate these strings due to their vastness, so though we might be able to witness time travel, it's doubtful that we'd be able to make a workable time machine for our own use in this manner.

Furthermore there are works of science fiction which suggest that the time travel is caused by the mind or body of the individual. For instance, in Kurt Vonnegut's *Slaughterhouse-Five*, the protagonist, Billy Pilgrim, becomes "unstuck in time," and travels about, uncontrollably, to his past during World War II (especially connecting to becoming a prisoner of war at the hand of the Germans and surviving the bombing of Dresden and its aftermath), back to the present, and even the future. Perhaps the time travel in this instance is completely metaphorical for some form of flashbacks related to post-traumatic stress disorder, but taken literally there is some form of time travel that rests with the man, Billy Pilgrim. Another example comes from the novel *The Time Traveler's Wife*. Here, the time travel is related to a genetic condition. Though neither of these seem possible without some form of outside interference involving an immense energy source (the time-traveling Tralfamdorans may have something to do with this in *Slaughterhouse-Five*), they do give some interesting perspectives on time travel that could relate to the more physical models as well. In *Farscape's* "Back and Back and Back to the Future," Crichton has become "unstuck" in time (mentally feeling that he has been transported to the future without his body physically being transported there), however, in this case, it is suggested that this is caused by experiments being conducted by visiting alien Varell on quantum singularities (mini–black holes).

Messages to the Past

Sending messages back to the past without actually traveling to the past may be possible if a special kind of particle, a tachyon, actually exists. In 1967 Gerald Feinberg of Columbia University proposed the existence of tachyons that could (and always must) travel at speeds greater than the speed of light. Upon examining the equations for special relativity, Feinberg interpreted them to mean that the true ban is not on objects going faster than light, but just on objects moving at the speed of light (or that have to accelerate from

The time machine from H.G. Wells' *Time Machine*, here adapted in the 2002 film. Warner Brothers/Photofest.

low speed through the speed of light up to faster than light speeds), at which point the equations relating mass, speed, energy and so forth are rendered meaningless. One consequence of faster than light travel in special relativity theory is the possibility for the tachyon to go backward in time. Since no object we could fathom could be made of tachyons or become tachyons (perhaps it's possible that tachyonic beings with tachyonic spaceships and so forth could exist somewhere, but we do not know of them or really know how tachyonic atoms or molecules would remain bonded) we could not send a solid object of normal (subluminal) matter back in time this way. But we could send individual tachyons into the past in a pattern, and thus send messages to the past. In fact, this exact method was used in Gregory Benford's novel *Timescape*, in which physicists use tachyons to send warnings to the past about the oncoming ecological doom faced by the Earth. Tachyons were used in the final *ST:TNG* episode, "All Good Things," in order to explain a temporal rift that was larger in the past, and in fact so large in the past that it was said that the rift would not have allowed life to form on Earth (this plot element is a bit muddled, but at least it relates tachyons to time and time travel). It's soon revealed that the rift was greatly increased because in the future a much smaller version of the rift was bombarded by tachyons by the *Enterprise* and others that came to investigate the anomaly. To date, in real life no tachyons have been found (Everett and Roman 2012). Though no experiments can be designed to directly detect tachyons, since we don't really know their specific nature, we can look for indirect evidence of their existence. For instance, if it were possible for protons to decay into tachyons, we could possibly see this as the protons recoil. Since many archival pictures of proton trails exist, we could examine them for evidence of proton recoil from decay into a proton and a tachyon (there could be more complicated decays as well). The tachyon can be thought of as having negative energy and moving backward in time, so when released from the proton, the proton will recoil with that same amount of energy. Even indirect evidence of this sort has yet to be discovered after about 45 years of trying, so most researchers have long ago given up on the tachyon. I have to add here a humorous story involving Gerald Feinberg from 1987 (he died five years later in 1992). My fellow physics students at Columbia and I enjoyed occasionally playing pranks on each other and our instructors. We knew that Dr. Feinberg (whom we all had as instructor for our senior quantum mechanics class) liked to wear bow ties. So, for one class, we decided to all wear bow ties ourselves (and this was the era of physics majors wearing flannel shirts, so bow ties definitely would be out of place). It took some time for him to notice (and I think he only figured something was up once we started to giggle), but we did get a bit of a smile from him. I hope now that he did not think we were being disrespectful.

Another, similar technique for sending messages to the past may be possible. Dr. John Cramer of the University of Washington is investigating a technique that could potentially send messages to the past. Experimentally, the set-up looks much like any optical bench with lasers, lenses, etc. However, the point of the experiment hinges on a controversial interpretation of quantum mechanics. Essentially, it allows for communication via the EPR experiment, including communication to the past, which as we have seen before, is not allowed in most quantum mechanical interpretations.

As Everett and Roman note, paradoxes are still possible with tachyons, even though only transmissions of information are possible. For instance, if a tachyon signal causes another slightly faster tachyon signal to be sent back, it can potentially cancel out the original tachyon (before it reaches the original destination). The paradox is that the second tachyon should only exist in the first place if the first tachyon was received. Yet, if the process is successful, then the second tachyon should destroy the first tachyon before the second one got sent out!

Though it may be impossible to send people and other solid objects back in time this way, it might be possible to do the next best thing. For instance, if information can be sent, why not send back all the information needed to construct a new version of you in the past (essentially, a time traveling teleporter, though as we see in Chapter 7, teleportation introduces a number of other problems)?

Manipulating Time

In science fiction other manipulations of time are presented besides time travel. For example, in the *Twilight Zone* episode "A Kind of Stopwatch," a man had the ability to stop time for everybody but himself with just what seems to be an ordinary pocket stopwatch. However, he is able to use this newfound ability to his advantage by robbing banks with impunity. However, in the end, he breaks the watch in the middle of a "freeze" and is unable to get back to normally flowing time. A similar example is the "Timelash" episode of the television series *UFO*, in which the mysterious aliens "freeze" time on Earth to better accommodate the destruction of the earthbound headquarters of SHADO, the organization with the responsibility of stopping the inevitable alien invasion. The villain of this episode (an aggrieved worker for SHADO) declares that the aliens have allowed him to live outside of time (presumably meaning normal time for everyone else on Earth). The protagonists take a drug that speeds up their metabolism by many times, allowing them to visualize the villain and the aliens. This episode appears to have borrowed generously from the "The Premonition" episode of *The Outer Limits* from six years earlier. In "The Premonition," an experimental flight leaves a pilot, and mysteriously his wife who was watching the plane from the side of the runway, in a limbo state in which they are advanced in time, but everyone else appears to be frozen. They come to learn that though everybody appears to be frozen at first, they are moving, but just at an imperceptibly slow rate from their perspective. A similar plot device is seen as well in the *ST:TOS* episode "In the Wink of an Eye." In this episode, the Scalosians operate at a speed that is many times faster than human speed. This allows them to take over the *Enterprise* without being noticed.

In *The Outer Limits* episode "The Form of Things Unknown," Tone Hobart is an eccentric inventor who constructs a "time tilting" device (represented fantastically as a closed-off room filled with loudly ticking clocks, connected by a web of strings) that he claims is able to reverse the cycles of time. Though it can't be used to travel in time per se, it can reverse the effects of time on a particular individual, and, say, bring back someone from the dead, as is done as part of the core plot for this episode.

Chapter 6

Computers, Robots, Androids and Cyborgs

The History of Computing

An early predecessor of the modern computer (1820s) was the proposed difference engine of Babbage (he never actually had one built). The idea was to mechanically keep track of the approximations needed in tabulating certain functions, such as logarithms, in order to limit the large number of errors introduced when only manual calculations were performed (Swedin and Ferro 2005). More recently, in the 1920s, the differential analyzer was invented by Vannevar Bush (no relation to the American political family). Though this device was mostly mechanical, it allowed for solutions to differential equations a few times more quickly than what a competent person could calculate manually, particularly important for calculating artillery trajectories in a timely fashion (Luokkala 2014). The first electronic computers trace back to the era just before World War II when John Atanasoff at Iowa State built the first digital computer using binary numbers for calculations. Though different from modern computers in some critical ways (it was not programmable), it was the first to be fully electronic in its components, using vacuum tubes as the switches that controlled calculations. Binary numbers are a perfect match for digital computers. The binary system puts all numbers in a form in which they are represented by a string of 1's and 0's (see Chapter 6 endnotes for details).[1] Practically speaking, a digital computer can control a current to be "on" (1) or "off" (0). During World War II this computer, known to only a few, was dismantled and forgotten. Thus, the credit for being the first computer, for some time, went to ENIAC, created by Mauchly and Eckert as part of the Army effort during World War II to more accurately determine missile trajectories (and with considerably greater speed). It did not take much time at all for a commercially available version, UNIVAC, to be developed. However, as important as these developments were, computer technology was highly limited by the sheer bulk of the equipment, mainly due to the use of bulky (and hot!) vacuum tube technology. Interestingly, science fiction writers of the day found it difficult to extrapolate beyond what was the available for computation and the computers of the future as pictured even as late at the 1960s and 1970s in *Star Trek, Lost in Space, Space: 1999* and others have more resemblance to ENIAC than anything in use today (Pak 2011). It's worth a short diversion to note that one of Isaac Asimov's star recurring characters was the sentient yet often neurotic Multivac computer, clearly playing on the tendency to give computers names with the "-ac" suffix (standing for "automatic computer"). Fortunately, shortly after the development of UNIVAC, a breakthrough was made in electronics with the invention of the transistor (which won Bardeen and Shockley the Nobel Prize in 1956), drastically reducing the sizes of computers. Transistors are small electronic components made of layers of silicon. These layers can be treated with other elements that either promote or stop flow of electrons, and thus currents. The layers can be put together in a way that will help a small current coming in to induce a current in another direction, or completely turn off a current. In this way, the transistor can act similarly to the vacuum tubes of old. Next came the microprocessor (miniature electronic circuits), which made even more dramatic progress, essentially giving almost anybody computing power equal to supercomputing power of decades ago.

Parallel to the development of computer hardware there has been a discussion of the limits of the capabilities of computers. For instance, would a computer be able to think in the same way that a human does? If not, then how could a computer think? These considerations have opened up the entire field of artificial intelligence, starting in the 1950s and going on until the present day, which we will discuss below.

The Future of Computing

In 1965 Intel co-founder Gordon Moore published his famous eponymous "law" regarding integrated circuits. In short, Moore saw that the density of transistors on these circuits was rapidly increasing, and would double every three years (though he later adjusted this to every two years). The author of the 1999 book *The Age of Spiritual Machines*, Ray Kurzweil, notes that in terms of computer processing speed per unit cost (in his case, for every $1,000), Moore's Law can even be extended back in time to earlier than the vacuum tube era, and, in fact, includes hand cranked machines of the 19th century (Kurzweil 1999). If it were to increase at that rate, soon (possibly by as early as 2020) circuits would have their components so close together that they would have several problems. One issue is that of heat. If circuit

6. Computers, Robots, Androids and Cyborgs 143

components are too close together, they will begin to emit enough heat to melt the circuit. Another is that circuit components would begin to be about one atom apart and unwanted quantum effects would take over the electronic function of the circuit (a limitation that Moore himself has realized). In particular, at the subatomic level, electrons couldn't be depended upon to follow the expected route on a circuit. They'd always have a probability of being slightly outside of the circuit, thus leading to current leakage. As of this writing, the "law" is slowing down a bit, perhaps to doubling every three years. Industry leaders say that they can partly mitigate these problems by making circuit components smaller (possibly with X-ray lithography). Though this may slow the problem for a while, it guarantees we will bump up against the quantum limit soon enough. However, taking a less literal view of Moore's Law and applying it to any technology, once the industry goes beyond the integrated circuit, Lawrence Krauss and others determine that the ultimate limitation on computer power will be the accessibility to matter in the Universe as the Universe expands and accelerates its expansion. This limit is predicted to be exceeded in about 600 years (Krauss and Starkman, arXiv.org 2004). Interestingly enough, this fate bears some resemblance to the computer of the Isaac Asimov tale "The Last Question," which we will address a little bit later.

There is some hope that the computer can be saved from demise (or at least, lack of further growth) by developments in quantum computing. In this way, computers can use information from the states of atoms themselves. Just as a conventional computer uses bits, a quantum computer uses quantum bits, or qubits. The qubits are the spin states of the electrons in these atoms (or ions, etc.). The superposition of these states allows qubits to be more efficient in calculations than conventional bits. Some simple experiments show that previously intractable problems, such as factoring very large numbers, can be solved relatively easily with a quantum computer. One such early version of this type of computer in action uses nuclear magnetic resonance techniques acting on chloroform molecules. The spins associated with the molecules are the qubits and the magnetic fields and radio waves interacting with the spins can act as the software that determines what operation will be performed. The problem with this sort of computer will likely be in implementation because keeping these spin states stable from decoherence is difficult. That is, even small disturbances can keep these atoms from being in the proper spin states necessary for performing these calculations. The most recent quantum computers have all focused on proof of concept with the emphasis on showing that the theory can be implemented with a real quantum computer. However, actually factoring large numbers with most of these will be some time off. It has been possible with alternate techniques, such as ion traps, to get to somewhat higher numbers of qubits (Darling 2005). Also, the first attempt at a commercially available quantum computer, D–Wave, is using super-conducting quantum dots and now has 439 operational qubits. A quantum dot is a very small collection of up to 100 or so semi-conducting atoms that can have controlled spin by applying small voltages to the dot. All previous developments of the computer over the last few decades have led to increased computing power with decreased size and cost and although neither is likely to happen (dramatically) with quantum computing any time soon, they are likely to happen eventually, and with perhaps D–Wave as the UNIVAC of the 21st century.

Artificial Intelligence

Another avenue of research is in developing artificial intelligence (AI), that is, computers that can learn and make independent decisions (the term artificial intelligence was coined by Marvin Minsky and collaborators in 1956). There have been several routes to understanding AI. One general method, referred to as symbolic AI, focuses on viewing the brain as we would a computer. An early approach was to determine the rules for how humans solve problems (heuristics) and have computers follow those rules. Such a list of rules could potentially be applied to figuring out how to play chess (the first intention of researchers in this area), or how to prove a geometric theorem (the first success in 1955). At the same time others were working on computer languages that would mimic the way the brain processes information, as it was known at the time (Nocks 2007). One of the earliest languages developed for these purposes was LISP, still in use, and now most famously used in the robotic vacuum cleaner Roomba. As Chris Pak quips (Pak 2011), this is perhaps not the grand dream of AI researchers, but perhaps the familiarity and mundaneness of AI is one sign of its success (a point Rodney Brooks makes, as quoted by Ray Kurzweil in *The Singularity Is Near*). A general problem in the development of AI, though, has been difficulty in assuring that a computer could understand subtleties behind instructions or in understanding language, not just in abiding by official grammatical rules, but understanding the common, yet "incorrect" ways in which people communicate. This had been battled by working on programs that allow computers to use "common sense" that humans only learn from experience, for instance, allowing computers to make adjustments to initial setting in situ depending on desired outcome. This methodology has been used in such diverse systems as Mars probes and washing machines (Kurzweil, *The Singularity Is Near* 2005).

Another line of approach is modeling the function of the human brain (to date, the only independent learner we know of) by setting up neural networks on a computer. Though they are simplified versions of actual neurons in the brain, the hope is that they will effectively mimic the way the brain learns, and then can be adopted by certain computers in their functioning (Hinton 2002). These networks operate by accepting inputs (say, a number of some sort), and then eventually get to an output, just like any other computer. However, each modeled neuron in the network receives an added signal from every other neuron. How these signals get to each neuron is controlled by "weights" (adjustable values of some control number). The adjustment of these values is analogous to learning within the brain. An example, such as that given by Hinton, would be the task of recognizing a digit (0 through 9) written by hand. Sensors can be used to detect the presence or absence of ink in a particular area that would indicate a particular digit. The data from the sensors is then sent on to the "neurons." The network can be trained by showing the sensors representations of some of the digits, calculating the differences between the actual representations and what the network is determining, and going through this cycle until the errors are reduced. A concept that grew out of this was fuzzy logic, and the ability for a computer, in simulating the human brain, being able to deal with uncertain data sets that didn't fit into neat categories (Swedin and Ferro 2005). However, there are also those who think imitation of the human brain is perhaps as wrongheaded as trying to achieve human flight by imitating a bird. That is, it may lead to only limited knowledge of the true processes involved, and not at all lead to a truly working example. Perhaps this motivated AI research with robots that focused on ability to move, see, sense, and otherwise confront situations and solve problems (Nocks 2007).

Computer Anxiety in Science Fiction

In science fiction, an uncomfortable and even paranoid or suspicious view of the computer is often presented. In general, we all understand how the rapid calculation speed and vast memory of computers have positively affected our lives but there has always remained an anxiety over how much control computers have or may grow to have or how "human" they may become (and not in a good way!). These feelings have revealed themselves in many classic "computer run amok" plots. In one early example from the 1954 film *Gog*, a control computer (Nuclear Operative Variable Automatic Computer or NOVAC) is essentially hacked by an enemy spy plane causing various robots (such as the one named Gog, and another, Magog) to go out of control, committing murder, and trying to destroy the secret base where a space station is being built. In the Isaac Asimov short story, "Sally," positronic brains are used to control cars and it is implied that they have at

The "eye" of the HAL 9000 control computer for the *Discovery* spacecraft in the 1968 film *2001: A Space Odyssey*. MGM/Photofest.

least a rudimentary intelligence. When someone tries to steal and dismantle some cars that have been collected on a farm and use their brains for other purposes, he is surrounded by a group of cars and forced away, apparently in an act of self-defense. The story ends with the cars' owner wondering if perhaps all cars will rebel against humans at some time in the future. The most heinous computer in science fiction is likely Harlan Ellison's AM computer from the nightmarish 1967 short story, "I Have No Mouth, and I Must Scream" (even the title instigates night terrors). In this tale, a set of computers (each major world power had one) was created to control the battles of World War III, but then, as the war progressed the computers merged into one entity, destroyed humanity, and took over the world. For reasons only fully known to the AM, five humans were saved by the computer, apparently for the sole purpose of giving them a greatly extended lifespan so that AM can torture them in a creatively sadistic manner. Perhaps this is the ultimate commentary on disgust with humanity being taken to the brink of nuclear war: a machine was so disgusted that it killed most people, but was sure to leave enough humans so it could show its disgust through torturing some of them. The AM was a sociopath, but it knew what it was doing. A more recent spin on this kind of tale was *ST:V's* episode "The Thaw," in which a group of scientists who took refuge in suspended animation to ride out an intense stellar flare, relied on a computer and its simulation software to keep their brains active while their bodies were in stasis (an idea that may have partly inspired the film *Vanilla Sky* and the Spanish film on which it was based, *Abre Los Ojos*). However, as part of the computer's role to stay adaptive, the control software created a sadistic clown (played wonderfully by Michael McKeon) to torture and even to kill some of the scientists. The Michael Shaara short story "2066: Election Day" features the computer S.A.M., and though it's not quite so psychopathic as AM, it is left with the ultimate responsibility of routinely picking the president of the United States from among the most qualified men (the word "men" is used by this 1950s author). Eventually the computer determines that there are no more qualified men. Though a group of presidential advisers of the previous president are able to fool the computer into picking a proxy for their group, the fear is that inevitably S.A.M. will decide that only he is able to be the president. Similarly, in the *Twilight Zone* episode "The Brain Center at Whipples," the factory owner Whipple oversees the automation of his work force by bringing in a top of the line computer. This ultimately eliminates many jobs, and infuriating the men whose jobs were eliminated. However, once Whipple eliminates all of his employees, the computer determines that Whipple himself is obsolete, and replaces him with a robot. Another maniacal computer appears in the 1973 *Doctor Who* serial, "The Green Death," in which the B.O.S.S. (Bimorphic Organizational Systems Supervisor) supercomputer is implicated in controlling and killing employees of a chemical company (Global Chemicals), and severely polluting the environment in its demented attempt to develop new efficient fuels and gain control of the world through economic dominance. *Space: 1999* actually had two episodes featuring psychotic computers. In the first-season episode "The Infernal Machine," Moonbase Alpha encounters a sentient spaceship, *Gwent*. Within the ship is a humanoid only identified as "Companion." As we eventually learn, Companion created *Gwent*, but *Gwent* took on Companion's worst qualities and amplified them. When Companion dies, *Gwent* goes into mourning and acts erratically. He takes several Alphans hostage, and kills those who try to come after them. Eventually he's thwarted and the hostages go back to the moonbase. However, realizing what he had done, and that he can't have true companionship again (if he ever had it), *Gwent* drives himself into a crater rim, essentially killing himself in the resulting explosion. The *Space: 1999* episode "Brian the Brain" features a computer, apparently accidentally created with murderous tendencies (he kills his creators, and then attempts to kill several inhabitants of Moonbase Alpha who later encounter him). Isaac Asimov's short story "All the Troubles of the World" features Multivac, a supercomputer that is tasked with regulating the entire world. However, Multivac has become neurotic and suicidal and then plans out steps that will lead to it being disabled. Perhaps the most famous of these terrible computer tales in film is *2001: A Space Odyssey* and the eerie murderous HAL who monitors and controls the life functions of the crew of the spacecraft *Discovery* on its way to

Jupiter. Eventually, HAL was able to kill all but one crewmember (who eventually was able to disable him). From the same time period, we have the *ST:TOS* episode "The Ultimate Computer," in which the M5 computer is supposedly a superior computer, designed to make many crew members of the starship obsolete (including, to large extent, the captain). However, ultimately, the computer's slavish devotion to efficiency, in the words of the episode, violates the laws of man and God by destroying another ship during a war game and killing its crew. In a poignant moment at the climax of the episode, the computer decides it must terminate itself as punishment for this unforgivable crime. On a more humorous note, in the *Twilight Zone* episode "From Agnes—with Love" an emotional computer, Agnes, falls in love with its (invariably male) programmers, and sabotages all of their lives. As the computer becomes more obsessed, "her" attention is driven away from her normal tasks (such as controlling a probe to Venus). The programmers, in turn, then become obsessed with fixing her programming, and, one by one, go insane doing so as they come to recognize the truth about Agnes.

In a 1973 episode of *The Starlost* entitled "The Gallery of Fear," an intelligent computer holds our regular protagonists hostage by tricking them with various illusions (some of these plot elements appeared a few years earlier in *Lost in Space* episode "Flight into the Future" and *Doctor Who* episode "The Mindrobber"). We also see advanced computers used to chilling effect in *ST:TOS* in "A Taste of Armageddon," in which two planet-wide societies at war feel that it is more civilized to let computers fight battles for them, and that any designated casualties have to report to special stations to be vaporized. Similarly, in the 1983 film *War Games*, a defense department computer (WOPR) is given control of nuclear weapons launching. When a hacker (David Lightman) inadvertently activates a war game sequence on WOPR, the military is led to believe that the nuclear attack is real. A retaliatory strike is then initiated, but after it is realized that the Soviet attack was simulated by the computer, an attempt is made to abort the response. However, the computer will not relinquish control, thinking it should still carry out the retaliatory strike. David and the inventor of the WOPR, Stephen Falken, are now aligned in attempting to cancel the strike. They realize they must teach the computer to realize it must stop the strike. First through replaying tic tac toe, and then by playing through simulated nuclear launches, WOPR realizes that nuclear war is unwinnable, and thus the best option is not to start the "game" in the first place. The strike is then successfully aborted by the computer. Perhaps the ultimate criticism of the computer's effect on society is in *Space: 1999's* "The Guardian of Piri." Here, a technological society has long ago created a seemingly omnipotent computer, the Guardian, which has suspended time in order to keep people in a blissful state. However, the original Pirians became obsolete and then extinct. The people of Moonbase Alpha,

6. Computers, Robots, Androids and Cyborgs

captured by the Guardian, are ostensibly saved from their fate of drifting through space endlessly. However, their suspended state essentially keeps them vegetative. Perhaps this work was somewhat inspired by the 1909 E. M. Forster short story "The Machine Stops." Though this story predates any kind of digital computer by at least three decades, it does speak to how a completely automated society can be drained of its ambition, and to such a great extent that they can no longer even maintain the Machine that controls them, and which they worship as a deity. Though society gains its freedom from the Machine, they must pay with their lives.

However, an underlying theme in many similar television episodes is that man can ultimately beat out the computer, and in fact, we sometimes see that a computer can be overtly tricked via logical deduction into destroying itself or letting itself be destroyed, such as in *ST:TOS*'s "Return of the Archons," "The Changeling," and "The Ultimate Computer." Alternatively, sometimes Captain Kirk and others tricked the computer using contradictions, as in "I, Mudd" in which the *Enterprise* crew purposely confused individual androids who are linked together via a master computer. The goal was to then overload the master computer. Kirk and Harry Mudd finally accomplish this by stating to Norman (the master computer): "Everything Harry tells you is a lie." Harry then adds, "I am lying." The computer cannot handle this contradiction, and after mandatorily smoking a bit (as did other confused computers in previous episodes), shuts down (Barad and Robertson 2001).

In contrast, during this same period, we see computers portrayed as being able to solve almost any problem. For instance, in the *Science Fiction Theater* episode "Doctor Robot," a computer scientist surreptitiously uses a top-notch secret government computer to figure out how to best treat his wife's illness. Furthermore, we see computers going well beyond problem solving and portrayed as divine or nearly divine (or mistakenly seen as divine by ignorant subjects). In Isaac Asimov's short story "The Last Question," when a computer is queried about how one could reduce the entropy of the Universe (a seeming impossibility), the computer ultimately accumulates enough power in ostensibly trying to answer this question that it gains the ability to create a new Universe (and thus, reducing the entropy of the Universe). *ST:TOS* features at least two episodes in which a computer is revered as a god-like power ("The Return of the Archons" and "The Apple"). In the *Twilight Zone* episode "The Old Man in the Cave," the survivors of a nuclear holocaust entrust themselves to a mysterious, seemingly omniscient Old Man in the Cave. As the story unfolds, it is revealed that the "Old Man" is actually a computer. Feeling deceived, the townspeople destroy the computer, and in defiance, ignore the computer's instructions not to eat contaminated food. At the very least, computers are seen as ultimately undefeatable. In Isaac

Asimov's short story "The Evitable Conflict," human society has evolved to the point where production and employment are carefully balanced by a control computer. Ultimately, when people try to subvert the computers, the computers anticipate the subversion by throwing a wrench into the works themselves (such as being sure that one man who wants to reduce the role of computers loses his job).

Still others respect the human brain as the ultimate computer, and in fact, their own standard electronic computers only function with the help of a humanoid brain. One example of this is the *Lost in Space* episode "Invaders from the 5th Dimension" in which the aliens can only use one of the human brains as the ultimate control computer. The computers on their spaceship and their robot, though superior in calculating ability, are seen as far too inferior by the aliens. *ST:TOS* episode "Spock's Brain" is another example in which a living brain is the only thing that can sufficiently control their society. In Phillip K. Dick's short story "Mr. Spaceship," a human brain is used to control a spaceship being used in a war against the natives of the Proxima Centauri star system. There may be a grain of reality to this. Some estimate that the human brain can handle quadrillions of calculations per second, much better than a supercomputer (Kurzweil, *The Singularity Is Near* 2005). However, the brain is best at certain types of "calculations," such as visualization of images, as compared to a typical computer, and it's not clear if this can easily be translated into the sorts of instructions that can control some specific external system. The storage capacity can also be seen as enormous, that is, about a million gigabytes, which certainly beats readily available desktop computers and storage devices (Reber 2010).

The History of Robots: Fact and Fiction

What can be more fundamental to speculative fiction than the mechanical man or robot? In fact the term "robot" itself was first used in the modern way in a play by Cupek in 1920s. Robots are often seen as the ultimate servants and the culmination of our technical skill in creating useful gadgetry. Whether we are speaking of the Klaatu's robot Gort (*The Day the Earth Stood Still*), the B9 robot of *Lost in Space*, Twiki and Crichton of *Buck Rogers*, K9 of *Doctor Who*, or C3PO of *Star Wars*, these robots exist primarily to serve, at least at first. The history of real robots traces to antiquity. The first "mechanical knights" were created by Gianello Torianno in the 16th century, probably inspired by some earlier work of Leonardo Da Vinci that never came to fruition. Though these automata were operated by pulleys and levers controlled by a system of weights, they did give a model of what to work toward in an independently powered and controlled robot. The next step in

6. Computers, Robots, Androids and Cyborgs 151

Originally this prop robot was Robby the Robot in the 1958 film *Forbidden Planet*. However, he later turned up, sometimes altered, in *Lost in Space* and *Twilight Zone* among others. MGM/Photofest.

history was going from showy devices that were really created mainly to impress wealthy backers to devices that were useful in automating important functions. During the early industrial revolution, crude programmable looms were created to make textile production more efficient. Similar automation progressed significantly with the industrial age, and led to the entire field of control engineering. Robots came into play because it was seen in the mid

20th century that automated robotic arms and such could be used in place of people on assembly lines, and increase efficiency and safety (Nocks 2007). Though hardly the robots of science fiction, we'll soon see how these developments led to increasingly more complex robots. Modern robotics has progressed from these robotic arms in factories to wider uses, including even humanoid robots developed in Japan. The last in particular has much overlap with the study of artificial intelligence since ideally we would want humanoid robots to be problem solvers. The first such robot was SHAKEY (although Beast, developed slightly earlier at Johns Hopkins' Applied Physics Lab, has some similar features) developed in the 1960s and 1970s at Stanford Research Institute. Though simple in appearance, SHAKEY was the first attempt at building a robot that could experience its environment and learn from it. SHAKEY had severe limitations (lack of speed in response) because such robots at the time had to process all information on a mainframe computer, and then radio back responses to the robot. Significant advances have been made gradually over the last several decades, primarily by focusing on some of the key problems in ultimately developing a humanoid robot. This can be as relatively simple as developing convincing faces that also possess human-like function, or more complicated, such as developing proper social skills. One group at Osaka University in Japan (led by Ishiguro) is focusing on very human-like robots in terms of appearance, but admits that getting them to respond in a human-like way is still a problem (Piore 2014). JPL's Telerobotics Research and Applications Group focuses on behavior-based approaches. In particular, they are working on getting robots to be more reactive to their environment. Still others have gone the route of simulating how the human body absorbs and distributes energy through its organs. Some famous humanoid robots have been developed for exhibition purposes, but we still seem a long way from having humanoid robot helpers in our homes. Robotics pioneer Hans Moravec points out that the hope in the early stages of this field has not borne the same fruit as the rapidly growing computer industry. In 1988, he predicted that there would soon be a "robot for the masses," depicted as having grasping claws for hands, wheels on legs that have ability to climb stairs, and video cameras for eyes, that bears some resemblance to "Number 5" from the 1986 film *Short Circuit*. Though progress has stalled at times, Moravec remains hopeful that true humanoid robots (with human capacity for thought) will come to pass by about 2030, and might surpass humans by 2050 (Moravec 1988). He sees this primarily as a matter of increasing processing speed to the point that such a robot can handle increasingly more complicated tasks that more accurately resemble what higher species have been able to accomplish. Of course, the details involve a variety of complex problems, such as pattern recognition and vision, dexterity, learning, et cetera. Since all of these require fast computing, we know that adequate solutions

6. Computers, Robots, Androids and Cyborgs 153

can only arise as computing capabilities increase (though that in itself is not necessarily a guarantee).

Within the scope of science fiction, robots began as useful helpers (and even surrogate grandmothers, as in Ray Bradbury's short story and *Twilight Zone* episode "I Sing the Body Electric") and as spelled out by Isaac Asimov, are constrained by internal laws (all robots are thus programmed) to never let harm come to humans or itself, unless this inaction would in turn, lead to harm of other humans. For example, Robby, the robot of Dr. Morbius, marooned on the planet Altair 4 in *Forbidden Planet*, also seems to be constrained by these laws. In a demonstration to Commander Adams, he orders Robby to kill Adams with a ray gun. Robby, though initially wanting to obey the order, is unable to carry out it out as it would lead to human injury. A very similar incident occurs in the *Doctor Who* episode "Robot" (the first with Tom Baker as the Doctor). Here, the Doctor's companion, Sarah Jane Smith, sneaks into the secret facilities of Think Tank, who, unknown to her, are developing a powerful robot. When she accidentally encounters the robot, the director of Think Tank orders the robot to kill her. After trying to obey and then hesitating, the robot states that he cannot harm humans. This basic idea is a commonly recurring science fiction meme, appearing again in the 2014 robot rebellion film *Automata*. This principle, though, is not universal. For instance, though the *Lost in Space* robot is generally depicted to be benevolent, he had originally been reprogrammed by Dr. Smith to kill off the Robinsons, and no mention was made at this point of a conflict with the robot's programming or Asimovian

The Lost in Space Model B19 environmental robot. The robot was played by Bobby May (the robot here was a costume, not a prop), voiced over by Dick Teufeld. Photofest.

laws. Though later in that series, in at least two separate episodes, "Sky Pirate" and "A Visit to Hades," the robot explicitly mentions that it is against his "prime directive" to cause harm to a human or let harm come to a human (*Lost in Space* played fast and loose with the robot's abilities and programming). In the first of these episodes, the robot refused to kill Alonzo P. Tucker, a human rogue who haplessly ends up on the same planet as the Robinsons. In the second of these episodes, the robot explains that it will not be dangerous for him to send others into the "dimension" where the alien Morbus has been exiled and has kidnapped Judy Robinson, for if it would potentially be dangerous, he would not be able to send anyone there. Soon after in science fiction we see the creation of robots that might be equal to men, entitled to rights of their own (see for instance, Isaac Asimov's "The Positronic Man," various incarnations of his "I, Robot," and the *ST:TNG* episodes "The Measure of a Man" and "The Quality of Life"). Even in *Lost in Space*, we see a basic, functional robot turn into a true companion, capable of emotions, as well as human thought. But acquisition of emotions also is often depicted as being too much for robots and androids to handle. An early example is in the 1932 short story by John Wyndham, "The Lost Machine," in which the robot character, a native of Mars, travels to Earth. Overcome by being out of place in a primitive society that doesn't understand what he is, he commits suicide. Another early example of this from television is in the *Tales of Tomorrow* episode "Read to Me Herr Doktor." A retired professor creates a robot as a companion. However, as time goes on, the robot becomes capable of independent action, and eventually forces his creator to teach him everything in all of the books he owns. Following this, the robot falls in love with the professor's daughter, and, in an attempt to follow the romantic notions of the books he has read, even sends away a potential suitor and also fights off the professor in an attempt to gain favor with his daughter. However, the daughter rejects the robot, and tells him that "the books are wrong" in their romantic notions. The robot, unable to comprehend that the books could be incorrect, ceases to function. In the *Twilight Zone* episode "The Lonely," a man (played by Jack Morgan) sentenced to exile on an asteroid is given a robot as a companion. At first, he resists treating her as if she were a person. However, by the end of his sentence, he has fallen in love with her (and she with him, apparently). When a team comes to retrieve him, they tell him that the robot must stay behind. After he pleads for them to take the robot (they can't, due to weight limits), they destroy the robot. The 1969 *ST:TOS* episode "Requiem for Methuselah" has a similar story line in which an android created by the savant, Flint, falls in love with Captain Kirk, who does not know that she is an android. Conflicted over her feelings for both Flint and Kirk, and disturbed that they are both fighting over her, she also "dies." A bit earlier, in the *Lost in Space* episode "The Revolt of the Androids," the android IDAK becomes disabled when his growing love for another android, Verda, conflicts with his original mission to destroy her. In Tom Baker's first episode (1974) as the Doctor in *Doctor Who* ("Robot," which we discussed above), a robot becomes conflicted when ordered to kill in clear violation of its original programming to not harm humans. In particular, the robot appears to be very upset when it finally kills his creator. The robot then temporarily deactivates after this outburst. In 1976, *Space: 1999* also had such a tale. In this episode, "One Moment of Humanity," two of our usual protagonists are kidnapped by two androids, Zamara and Zarl. The goal of these androids is to get the humans to show them how to kill by replicating the necessary emotional process (why they would actually need to be emotional in order to kill is not really explained). However, as Zarl begins to mimic these emotions, he becomes more and more human. In fact, he begins to fall in love with Helena, and just as he does so he achieves one final moment of humanity, but dies (why love in particular is more commonly a problem than jealousy, hatred, etc., is not usually explained in such tales). In 1992 we saw a similar plot return to *ST:TNG*, in which Data creates an android daughter. Unfortunately, as she begins to feel emotion, something her "father" was never able to master, she begins to break down and die. In the reboot *Outer Limits* episode, "Valerie 23," a female robot is developed to be a companion to handicapped individuals. On an experimental basis, Valerie is loaned out to one of the workers at the robotics company who had been in a debilitating accident some years before. Eventually, she develops feelings for him, though he becomes very reluctant to reciprocate (save for one night of passion), and instead concentrates on building a relationship with his physical therapist. Not knowing how to proportionately control her jealousy, Valerie stalks the "other woman" and attempts to kill her.

Similar to the "Kirk beats the Computer" episodes of *ST:TOS*, we see a number of science fiction texts focusing on man's attempts to triumph over robots, and for humans to hold on to their humanity in such a society. The *Twilight Zone* episode "Steel" is set in the near future and boxing between people has been banned; however, boxing is allowed between robots. When one of the managers of a boxing robot, Maxo, realizes that his robot won't be able to function in the next match, he disguises himself as Maxo and fights the other robot. Though he does not last long in the ring, he is able to collect the money to help him fix Maxo. In a similarly themed *Twilight Zone* episode, "The Mighty Casey," a baseball coach decides to use a robot on his team when he sees how well the robot can pitch. When "Casey" is injured, he gets found out as a robot, and it's ordered that Casey be banned from playing. However, it is decided that if he were to get an artificial heart, he'd be ruled to be sufficiently human that he could play (that is where fantasy creeps in). Unfortunately for the team, after getting the artificial heart, he becomes too human,

Lt. Commander Data (Brent Spiner) of *Star Trek: The Next Generation*. He's an android with a "positronic brain" and longs to be human. Photofest.

becoming so compassionate that he no longer wants to strike out players, for fear that he'll damage their careers. "Steel" shows that though a human can't literally triumph over a machine, the human spirit can still persevere and achieve some of humanity's goals. In "The Mighty Casey" a robot can beat humans at their games until he's given some elements of humanity. At that point, though the robot can no longer beat humans, he can better serve them with his newfound compassion.

In addition, we can also see robots diverted for devious purposes, as in the *Fireball XL5* episode "Trial by Robot," in which the robot expert, Dr. Himbler, steals the best robots of settled planets for the purpose of building his own planet dominated by robots (which he renames Robotvia). In the end, after Himbler and the robots were vanquished, it was concluded, in the words of the characters, that robots will "never be able to replace people."

In still other texts we see robots as the only remnant of mankind. In Roger Zelazny's short story "For a Breath I Tarry," several robotic probes continue to take data for centuries after all men have died off. One probe named Frost takes on the "hobby" of examining and interpreting the artifacts of man. The probes contemplate their differences with man, but in doing so, ironically, seem very human.

Cyborgs and the Singularity

The term "cyborg," a shortened version of the term "cybernetic organism," traces to a 1960 article by Clynes and Kline calling for research into enhancing normal biological organisms with mechanisms such as those that automatically dispense drugs to regulate blood pressure. The intent of this research was to be able to enhance man as he explores space so that he may better deal with the harsh environment. They proposed some far-reaching ideas, such as eliminating the need for breathing by breaking up carbon dioxide (into oxygen and carbon) as it is produced by the body, and recirculating the oxygen (Clynes and Kline 1960). Experimentation in this field has made great strides since the time of that original article. Kevin Warwick at University of Reading implanted a chip in his body that allowed him to do such simple tasks as turn on lights as he passed them. He eventually was able to step up this experiment by linking this chip to his nervous system so that he was able to control a computer screen in front of him by making motions with his hand (Parsons 2010). Ray Kurzweil has gone so far as to predict that rapid developments in both AI and nanotechnology will allow for humans to become less and less truly biological with time, essentially reaching a point in time, called "the singularity," at which humans will transition to becoming androids with intelligence that will exceed human intelligence of today. Kurzweil is clearly optimistic concerning this outcome. Elon Musk, CEO of Tesla Motors and Space-X, provides an alternate opinion. He believes we should be more cautious regarding developments in AI, lest we lurch toward a doomsday Terminator-like scenario. Among the achievements that are likely to occur in nanotechnology is the addition of machines into the bloodstream to directly attack or aid certain cells and may even be able to circumvent the need for lungs by bringing oxygen directly to the blood. Kurzweil estimates that the singularity will occur in 2045, but even if some of the assumptions that go into calculating this number are relaxed, the singularity will likely only be put off for decades, and not centuries (Kurzweil, *The Singularity Is Near* 2005). Particularly compelling is that at the point of the singularity and thereafter, it will be possible to transfer the data and software of the mind, potentially to an android, so that this "mind" may live a greatly extended physical life, and may essentially be immortal. The *Twilight Zone* episode "Uncle Simon" shows a crude form of the singularity when the curmudgeonly Simon programs a robot to take on his characteristics and torment his niece after he has died. It's a matter of some debate whether this event would be a net positive or negative for humanity. In *ST:TOS* episode "What Are Little Girls Made Of?" we find out that archaeologist Roger Korby, at a time before the happenings of the episode and near his death, transferred his essence (we're not really told how much of the original person really is copied, or how this is done) to an android. As the plot unfolds, we see Korby taking actions that are supposedly uncharacteristic of him (such as holding Captain Kirk prisoner), slowly revealing what we are to learn in the end: that he has lost his humanity both figuratively as well as literally. Perhaps the writer's thoughts on this subject are best summed up best by Captain Kirk's words to Mr. Spock as he departs the planet: "Roger Korby was never here." This topic was similarly broached earlier in the *Twilight Zone* episode "In His Image." Here, a man, Alan, begins to question his identity when none of his memories of his hometown seem to be consistent with the people who actually live there. On top of this, he has auditory hallucinations that include electronic noises and voices that urge him to kill. Eventually he injures himself, exposing his arm, which he sees actually to be a robotic arm. He is eventually led to his creator, Walter, who is a man identical to him. He asks Walter, "Who am I?" Walter answers with, "Well, who is this watch I'm wearing, ask me that. Who is the refrigerator in the kitchen?" Clearly he feels that Alan has no separate identity. In *The Outer Limits* episode "Demon with a Glass Hand," Trent finds out that he is not really a man, but a robot sent from the future with the digital remains of the rest of human society. He has been sent to the past so that these human survivors will be protected from their enemy, the Kyben, but also from a plague that the humans released themselves in an effort to kill the Kyben. Just a few moments before finding out the truth of his identity he had fallen in love, but now his only role of importance is protector of the human race, at least for the next 1,200 years.

The topic of the singularity itself has now been broached in science fiction with the 2014 film *Transcendance* (with the roboticist, William Caster, a Kurzweil-type figure, played by Johnny Depp). Many science fiction texts touch on the subject of cyborgs, and not surprisingly, they are often depicted as menacing. *Doctor Who* perhaps did this most relentlessly (with the Cybermen and the Daleks), and *ST:TNG* came up with the ultimate (and terrifying) cyborg society, the Borg. The Cybermen began as a purely organic race, similar to humans, and then over time enhanced themselves with metal plating and electronic parts. In the series, it's often stated that it is this process of mechanization itself that has led to the Cybermen being calculating and emotionless. The Daleks are genetically engineered creatures that became enhanced by using artificial outer metallic shells that also have features such as turret guns. They were purposely engineered by Davros of Kaled to gain an advantage in a long-standing interplanetary war. Two different Irwin Allen television productions had episodes that concentrated on cyborgs. The first was the *Voyage to the Bottom of the Sea* episode "Cyborg" and was the more serious attempt. In this episode, Dr. Tabor Urlich (Victor Buono) plots to have a supercomputer and an army of subservient cyborgs trick the U.S. into starting an apocalyptic nuclear war with the Soviet Union. The intention is then to take over during the chaos of the war's aftermath. *Lost in Space's* attempt at introducing cyborgs ("The Space Destructors") falls a bit flat, since the cyborgs appear to be moaning monsters made of dough, rather than a truly challenging menace (though they are controlled by a computer, "The Master Mechanism"). It does not help that many of the cyborg costumes and props are borrowed from the earlier serious production.

Chapter 7

Teleportation and Replication

Though we first see the concept of teleportation in some early science fiction short stories and novels, teleportation first made it into the realm of science fiction television in the 1950s with *Science Fiction Theatre*'s episode "Strange Lodger" in which an alien living among humans on Earth uses radio transmissions to teleport himself to a mother ship in high orbit. The concept here (though not the exact technology) is a foretelling of what we'd see in the *Star Trek* television series about a decade later, when the transporter was used primarily to "beam" people down to planets. Of course, this device was originally employed as a cost savings device by the producers of the show, so they wouldn't have to invest in setting up complicated shots of a model ship landing on a planet, but it soon became an iconic technology (Whitefield and Rodenberry 1968). Slightly earlier, *Lost in Space* featured an alien race, the Taurons, who were capable of teleportation (and then later, some other aliens were also shown to have a very similar technology in, for instance, the episode "Prisoners in Space"). In addition, aliens as well as future humans were depicted as capable of teleportation in other Irwin Allen productions, including *Voyage to the Bottom of the Sea* (in the episode "Time Lock") and *The Time Tunnel* ("Chase Through Time"). The ramifications of employing such technologies were frighteningly presented in the 1958 film *The Fly*, in which a teleportation accident leads to a scientist's atoms being mixed with a fly that was carelessly left in the teleportation chamber. The results of grisly teleportation accidents were also seen in various *Star Trek* films and episodes, as well as satirized in the 1999 film *Galaxy Quest*, when the "giant pig-lizard" chasing Jason Nesmith/Commander Taggart is transported aboard the ship, but turns inside out and then explodes. In other instances, such as in the 2008 film *Jumper*, teleportation is presented more as a superhuman ability (without explanation) rather than assisted by any technology. Furthermore, in the *Doctor Who* episode "The Planet of the Spiders," we see an example of

7. Teleportation and Replication

teleportation aided by meditation (though they seem to also have the aid of a powerful crystal from the planet Metebelus). In *Space: 1999* ("The Guardian of Piri"), the Guardian is able to teleport both the Alphans and his own servant at will, though the technology used goes unexplained. Also in *Space: 1999*, the androids of Vega and those they control are able to teleport by means of "positronic transport," activated simply by wishing to be transported to a particular target. An unexplained teleportation technology (the "transbeamer") is also seen in the *Space: 1999* episode "Devil's Planet," though it seems to be limited to beaming to a companion planet. In the finale of *Space: 1999* ("The Dorcons") the Dorcons were able to use a transport beam called a "meson converter." Though this technology goes unexplained, it is physically possible to convert normal matter into mesons (a type of subatomic particle) by bombardment with high-energy protons (this process occurs naturally in space when cosmic rays from distant galaxies bombard cold hydrogen gas clouds in the Galaxy). The mesons then decay into gamma rays. And though this would be a light beam of sorts, it wouldn't be visible, and it would be extremely dangerous for humanoids to go anywhere near it. Phillip K. Dick's short story "Prominent Author" features a teleportation technology called the Jiffi-Scuttler, and though its technology goes unexplained in detail, does work by cutting through extra dimensions. We also face some additional philosophical and ethical issues. For instance, can our personality, and what some would call the soul, really be transported along with all of the molecules? Can all of the information relating to the precise state of these molecules be transported? Can "personality" then be totally accounted for by this information? Is the transported individual fundamentally different from the original person? Can there be a crime committed if a "copy" of the original person is made, and we either dispose of the original or the copy? In humorous fashion, some of these dilemmas were addressed by meth addicts Badger and Skinny Pete in the *Breaking Bad* episode "Blood Money":

> SKINNY PETE: "What do you think all those sparkles and shit are? Transporters are breaking you apart right down to your molecules and bones. They're makin' a copy. That dude who comes out on the other side? He's not you. He's a color Xerox."
> BADGER: "So you're telling me every time Kirk went into the transporter he was killing himself? So, over the whole series, there was, like 147 Kirks?"
> SKINNY PETE: "At least. Dude, no, why do you think McCoy never liked to beam nowhere? 'Cause he's a doctor, bitch! Look it up, it's science!"

I could not have said it better myself.

As Lawrence Krauss discusses in *The Physics of Star Trek*, there has been some debate in the past both regarding how teleportation is supposed to occur in the *Star Trek* universe, and also how we'd best accomplish this in reality. Do we actually wish to transport matter, or is it easier or better to just transport the exact information about an object (or person) needed to properly transport someone to some other location? It turns out that either has severe obstacles, which we will discuss, but in the last few years there has been growing promise for teleporting information. Furthermore, going back to the *Star Trek* episodes themselves shows some inconsistencies with matter transport (at least for reconstructing the transported person only from his original matter). For instance, as Richard Hanley points out in *Is Data Human?: The Metaphysics of Star Trek*, in the classic *ST:TOS* episode "The Enemy Within" in which a transporter malfunction creates two Kirks, one animalistic and "evil," the other, kind, calm and cerebral. The matter for two Kirks clearly would have to come from somewhere else besides the original Kirk (Hanley 1997). The reverse happens in *ST:V* when Tuvok and Neelix are mixed and become an amalgam person "Tuvix." Clearly, this wouldn't have taken the same amount of matter.

There are a number of problems regarding the actual teleportation of

Crew members of the *Enterprise* transporting down to a planet in the *Star Trek: The Original Series* episode "Where No Man Has Gone Before." From left to right: Spock (Leonard Nimoy), Gary Mitchell (Gary Lockwood), Elizabeth Dehner (Sally Kellerman), Captain James Kirk (William Shatner) and Dr. Mark Piper (Paul Fix). NBC/Photofest.

atoms that make up a person. One of them is the enormous energy requirements needed to disassemble someone down to the atomic level or lower (nuclei, quarks).[1] Breaking down matter to the level of protons and neutrons requires millions of times more energy than breaking apart atoms bonded in molecules. Further breaking down matter to the level of quarks takes millions of times more energy than breaking down to protons and neutrons. If we wanted to accelerate these constituent particles in a beam to be sent down to a planet, we'd need even more energy. Still another problem would be reassembling the matter that would be precisely equivalent to the person or object we originally disassembled. Doing this would almost certainly require transferring all or most of the information anyway, so it would seem like transporting matter couldn't really be done independently from transferring the information (Krauss, *The Physics of Star Trek* 1995).

We could decide that we want to just transport the information and not the matter itself in the first place. However, again, we reach unfathomable numbers, many powers of ten beyond what our best computers can hold in memory to even hold the information held in one human's atoms. For similar reasons it would then also be a challenge for Trent (the man who finds out he is a robot from the future in "Demon with the Glass Hand") to really have stored on a wire the essences of every human on Earth. Similarly, from "The Chameleon" episode of *The Outer Limits* it would really not be possible to store all of Louis Mace's genetic information on one magnetic tape.

Complicating these issues further are the rules of quantum mechanics which tell us that we can't know every parameter of a system of particles arbitrarily well (see Chapter 1). Therefore, if we are inherently prevented from copying, say, a human, with complete accuracy, does that mean we can't really transport an object or person with the precision we want?

Quantum Teleportation

Fortunately, the problem is somewhat ameliorated by the newly discovered technique of quantum teleportation. This fundamentally depends on the concept of quantum entanglement which we discussed earlier in Chapter 1. In this form of teleportation what we are teleporting is a particular state associated with a particle and then sending that state over to some other similar particle, thus making this new particle indistinguishable from the original. This second particle need not be physically distant from the original in any way; however, some of the experiments being worked on now involve teleporting states to more distant particles. The core idea is that we can start with two entangled photons, A and B (we could potentially do this with particles as well with no significant change in the general conclusions). We then let one photon in the pair (A) interact with third photon (X), say, of a particular created state. This is the state (X) we wish to eventually teleport. As strange as it may seem, a measurement of the second photon (B) in the entangled pair would then have to reveal something about the state of the interacting photon, X. Furthermore, if a scientist monitoring the A and X Bell state measurement communicates the results to a scientist monitoring B, the second scientist can make small changes to B to make it identical to X (note that there are only a small number of ways to change the B photon to the correct state, and all would have required knowing what the final state of the A and X combination was). At this point, when the changes have been made, the state of X has been teleported to B. In a Bell state measurement we can know the polarization of a photon, A, along one direction, thus also determining that same value for the entangled photon, B. However, in the way these measurements are made, the original photon, X, is lost. Zellinger and Zoller in 1993 were the first to conduct just this sort of teleportation by sending an ultraviolet laser beam through a barium borate crystal. The nature of such a crystal is such that an ultraviolet photon can react with it to create two infrared photons. In this way, you can create an entangled pair, such as that described above. The trick then is to make the Bell state measurement and teleport "photon X." This is done with mirrors that are aligned in a way that can, in some cases (not all, due to the probabilistic nature of the quantum mechanical measurements), lead to the combining of the two photons that are then received at a detector. However, only this one single Bell state measurement can be made, in a way that makes it difficult to distinguish whether the state of X had really been teleported in all cases. This has been one of the primary criticisms of this initial groundbreaking experiment.

In the months and years immediately following this type of teleportation, there were other accomplishments in this field. Not surprisingly, each claimed to be, in a manner, the first to achieve true teleportation, some meaning this in the sense it was conceived by physicists some years before in Montreal, and others meaning this more in the sense of the original science fiction concept, particularly as popularized by *Star Trek*. In particular, a group from Rome adopted a method similar to Zellinger and Zoller, yet eliminated the "messenger photon," X, from the experiment. That is, the teleported state was included with the original photon "A." The point of doing this was to allow all Bell state measurements to be made, and thus be sure that this was the proper quantum mechanical effect they were observing. The first such experiment involving matter instead of photons occurred in 2004 with a small number of beryllium atoms. The states of these atoms were teleported over 600 meters. Later experiments, such as one in Copenhagen in 2006 involved entanglement with an immense group of cesium atoms, and transmitted the information regarding the states of the atoms across macroscopic distances, in this case, a bit over one foot (Darling 2005).

Teleportation Without Entanglement

Furthermore, there have been some teleportation techniques that don't involve entanglement at all. One of these used light along a fiber optic cable to transmit information (states) from rubidium atoms to recover them at a distant location, and, of course, they claim that their achievement is most in spirit with the science fiction concepts of teleportation. The real issue is whether it's promising in terms of implementation. However, this method of teleportation involves using Bose-Einstein condensates, which need to be cooled to just barely above "absolute zero" degrees Kelvin. This sort of cooling is very cumbersome, and cannot be achieved for every kind of atom. The process involves a matter beam interacting with the Bose-Einstein condensate (BEC). A BEC can shed excess energy in terms of a light beam that can contain information about the states of the original matter beam (Kaku, *The Physics of the Impossible* 2008). This technique has some resemblance to a means of teleportation described in the *Lost in Space* episode "Return from Outer Space." Here John Robinson says that teleportation occurs by maser, the microwave version of a laser. As we see in the episode, a cone of light shines on the subject of teleportation. They are then transported to their destination. Though masers wouldn't be visible by eye, and all of the subjects shown in the episode would be well above BEC temperatures, it's interesting to see how some types of actual teleportation can resemble classic science fiction depictions.

Darling further speculates that developments in teleportation, especially those that may lead to teleportation of macroscopic objects (including humans!), will probably focus on classical techniques and not quantum techniques, as outlined above. The reasons end up being ones of feasibility and practicality. For one, quantum teleportation techniques all require destruction of the original states. For all intents and purposes, the original "you" in all of its original states has been destroyed (and must be), if it is to be teleported elsewhere. However, such a classical copy could not be the perfect copy that quantum teleportation provides. This is the cost of "classical" vs. "quantum" teleportation. So what would this classical technique look like? The thought is that this would work something like a medical scanner that records detailed information about your body without physically copying it. This would not record states perfectly as in the case of quantum teleportation, but it might be good enough, at least good enough for non-human subjects. However, since developments in quantum teleportation, even those involving entanglement, are accelerating, practical technological developments such as transportation of humans, may occur faster than we now expect.

Replication

Another possibility made famous by *Star Trek* is that of the replicator. With the touch of a button, or even a voice command, one can instantly get their favorite tea, or hot chocolate, or a full meal. Perhaps more usefully, replicators are shown to craft tools as well. For instance, in the *ST:TNG* episode "The Quality of Life," the exocomps (small intelligent robots that are used in dangerous operations) are equipped with micro-replicators that can help them craft the right tool for the job which with they are presented. As usually presented, this is another take on teleportation, though with atoms re-arranged in a somewhat different form (that is, whatever food or other item a crew member might request). Michio Kaku mentions in *Physics of the Future* that this may be possible using nanobots, small molecule sized robots. These nanobots would disassemble a supply of atoms and then put them back together in the requested form (Kaku, *Physics of the Future* 2011). However, there is some debate as to whether nanobots could really be effective on such small scales.

However, perhaps a more realistic version of this that we may see sooner is likely to work more like a 3D scanner and printer. A 3D scanner can scan a particular object (say, a broken part) you are interested in replicating or repairing using a laser, build a data matrix that corresponds to 3D information on what exactly the outside of the part looks like (it can't gain information on the internals of the part), then, using a 3D printer, you can construct the outside of the part using materials on hand. With technology available today (such as X-ray devices), it might also be possible to create a 3D scanner and printer that more thoroughly re-created the original object (including the internal part) (Darling 2005).

Chapter 8

Weaponry

In the 1968 campy utopian science fiction film *Barbarella*, the title character (played by Jane Fonda) is asked to help in tracking down the scientist Durand Durand, who is known to be working on a secret weapon. Barbarella innocently and quizzically asks her superior, "A weapon? Why would anyone need a weapon?" Though this scripting was likely to have been more of a commentary on the events of that time in the outside world (the film came out during the peak of U.S. involvement in the Vietnam War) than on the utopian society depicted in the film, it does force us to think of why weapons would ever be necessary, especially in a highly advanced society. Much of the rest of science fiction amply answers that question, but usually under the assumption that conflict will be one of the problems that man and other intelligent societies will struggle to avoid. Many science fiction texts deal with conflict and war, and, of course, involve some highly destructive weapons. These weapons include simple souped-up versions of common lasers to the phasers and photon torpedoes of *Star Trek*. Some of these weapons seem reasonable, whereas others are far beyond what we can realistically even imagine. We'll see that weapons fall into a number of general categories: kinetic weapons, explosives, chemical weapons, nuclear weapons, biological weapons, photonic (light-based) and other weapons.

Kinetic Weapons

Kinetic weapons are the oldest, as they simply involve propelling objects and giving them enough kinetic energy (see Chapter 1) so that they could potentially harm people and property. This is the basic concept behind throwing stones, David knocking down Goliath with a slingshot, or the shooting of cannonballs and bullets. However, on the largest scales, it might be more efficient to divert a large asteroid, and let the impact do most of the damage to an enemy planet. In fact, this could release even more energy than what we can expect a photonic weapon to release (even though the photon weapons are often sexier in science fiction movies). The energy released by an asteroid on impact would be related to its kinetic energy. For a large "dinosaur killer" asteroid (about 10 km across), the kinetic energy would likely have been about 10 billion times the energy of a Hiroshima atomic weapon.[1] Though it might take some effort to divert an asteroid; most intelligent societies would have figured out a way to do this anyway to prevent natural disaster from chance collision. In addition, it is clearly an efficient way of inflicting damage on an enemy planet, though it would take some advance planning, and might be counteracted by the victim society.

Explosives

In addition to kinetic energy, we can exploit the chemical energy inherent in atoms and molecules. Here the energy is in the bonds between atoms. When these bonds are broken, energy is released. Effective chemical-based explosives started to be used in the middle ages when the Chinese began to use gunpowder. Though fancier weapons have been developed since, and probably even more will be in the future, we even see such simple chemical explosives featured in *Star Trek*. In the *ST:TOS* episode "Arena," Captain Kirk, forced to fight the lizard-like alien, the Gorn, seeks anything on the "arena" asteroid that he could use as a weapon. Slowly but surely, he realizes that some of the mineral deposits he finds can be made into the components of gunpowder: sulfur, charcoal, and saltpeter (although in reality he probably would have had to at least crudely refine these minerals to make effective gunpowder, it at least made an interesting problem for Kirk to solve).

Chemical Weapons

Certain chemical weapons can simply be used as an effective poison, such as chlorine, phosgene and mustard gas used during World War I, and sarin gas and other nerve agents used in terrorist attacks (such as the Uhm subway attack in Japan) and acts of repression by ruling governments, such as Iraq and Syria, for nearly 100 years afterward (Spiers 2010). These types of weapons have the advantage of not generally destroying property. Of course a disadvantage (and unfortunately, for some, an advantage) is that the death toll can be comparatively high for little sacrifice of military personnel. From a military perspective, these weapons never progressed to be an important factor in the outcome of a war. However, since such gases have been used against civilians to much greater effect, there has been some valid trepidation over revival of their use in warfare and terrorism.

In science fiction, one common form of chemical weaponry is the use of a planet's poisonous atmosphere (or lack of atmosphere) against an enemy. For instance, in the *ST:TOS* episode "Whom Gods Destroy," a mental institution, the only outpost on planet Elba II, is taken over by one of the inmates, Garth of Izar, a former Starfleet captain who has become criminally insane. He partners with the other inmates, including Marta. He eventually punishes her for perceived disloyalty by taking her out from the protective dome of the mental institution and into the poisonous atmosphere (it's depicted as a greenish gas, but is never specifically named). She begins to choke and gestures wildly to be brought back into the dome. In this moment, Garth kills her by remotely detonating a powerful explosive he has placed on her person. Again, in the *ST:TOS* episode "The Squire of Gothos," Trelane, a powerful alien who has captured some of the *Enterprise* crew, briefly sends Kirk into the deadly atmosphere of Gothos to give him a taste of his authority. Similarly in the "AB Chrysalis" episode of *Space: 1999*, pilot Alan Carter accidentally breaks the chamber that holds the alien leader in stasis with a chlorine atmosphere. Quickly trying to save the leader's life, the control computer on this planet fills the entire room with chlorine gas. Alan Carter, being exposed to this chlorine, is nearly killed. In another *Space: 1999* episode, "Brian the Brain," the psychotic computer, Brian, captures Commander Koenig and Doctor Russell onboard his spacecraft. Brian then uses threats of letting atmosphere out of the passenger cabin (and occasionally just letting out a bit, just to show he means it) as a method of keeping his captives in line.

Nuclear Weapons

As described in chapters 1 and 3, it is possible to utilize the binding energy in the nuclei of atoms through fission or fusion. Early on in the development of the science, it was realized that the potentially large amounts of energy involved could be harnessed as a weapon. However, it certainly took some time (decades, and a high-stakes war effort) to first discover these processes in nature and then for practical nuclear weapons to be developed based on these concepts. A breakthrough came when in 1939 Otto Frisch discovered that neutrons can be used to artificially cause fission of atoms (Bernstein 2008). After this discovery, the rest became an engineering feat under Enrico Fermi's urging. Inside of the nuclear weapons ultimately used in World War II were two separate pieces of a radioactive element such as uranium or plutonium. These two elements were (and are) important, as certain isotopes can naturally release neutrons, which can then sustain a fission reaction by breaking apart more atoms. These elements also occur in high enough abundance naturally to be a useful supply. When forced together by a conventional explosive, the two pieces would reach a critical mass from which a chain reaction could begin, causing a sudden release of tremendous amounts of energy in the form of a bomb. More powerful hydrogen bombs used the concept of fusing hydrogen atoms and releasing energy in the process. We should note that nuclear weapons are not 100% efficient and can yield significantly less energy than theory would suggest, thus leading to bombs that are significantly more than critical mass. Around this same period of time, it was also realized that this same source of energy was responsible for energy generation in stars, including the Sun. Though extremely powerful, nuclear reactions use less than 1% of the energy available via $E=mc^2$. Thus, we can imagine even more powerful weapons. Perhaps this is why we see in *Star Trek*, that the *Enterprise* is occasionally confronted by "primitive" societies (ones that are more or less like 20th century Earth or just beyond) that try to hold them off with nuclear weapons, which can be effective, up to a point. In the previously mentioned film *The Doomsday Machine*, the Earth is destroyed by a nuclear weapon that starts a chain reaction that completely destroys the planet. As discussed in the Chapter 1 endnotes, the binding energy of the Moon is, trillions of times greater than even the most powerful nuclear weapons. Thus, it is unlikely that a conventional nuclear weapon (or even all of the nuclear weapons on Earth) could lead to the complete destruction (explosion) of a planet.

Biological Weapons

Biological warfare has its roots about 650 years ago when combatants in European struggles of the time began to purposely try to spread disease to enemies with the corpses of their own plague-infected soldiers. Most recently, the 2001 anthrax attacks in the United States showed the world that biological terrorist attacks were real and could be effective. Even though, thankfully, the number of casualties was low, we know that the potency of these biological agents could have killed many more people. In addition, there have been growing fears that anything from virulent strains of flu, or stored smallpox can be used as a weapon. A number of science fiction short stories and novels focus on a post-apocalyptic civilization after either a natural plague or biological war, such as in Steven King's *The Stand*, in which weaponized influenza is accidentally released from an army base, causing a global biological holocaust. A similar circumstance was seen in Orson Scott Card's series of short stories, *The Folk of the Fringe*. In Ray Bradbury's "The

City," the city of Toalla on a distant world has become desolate after all life was killed off by an infection said to have been brought 20,000 years in the past by a previous civilization from Earth. The city, however, somehow remains alive and exacts its revenge on new visiting astronauts from Earth by infecting them and sending them back to destroy all life back home. In other stories we see weapons that can change the DNA of the victim, even to the extent of turning them into an alien life-form (as in the film *District 9*). In the original *Planet of the Apes* film series, the ascendancy of apes is initiated when a plague affects household pets such as dogs and cats, and the typical family replaces them with ape servants who eventually rebel against their masters. In the reboot version of *Planet of the Apes* (an origin story under the title *Rise of the Planet of the Apes,* 2011), the chain of events that led to ape rule are the release of an experimental drug that was meant primarily to reverse the degeneration of cognitive function in Alzheimer's patients (the protagonist purposely exposes his elderly father, who suffers from dementia, to the drug). A chimp who has already been exposed to the drug and becomes more intelligent, releases the drug first in a pen of exotic apes, which then leads to a rebellion of all apes.

Light-based Weapons

Light-based weapons found their way into early science fiction with H.G. Wells' 1898 novel, *War of the Worlds*. The invading Martians are described by the narrator as using a "heat-ray," which is a form of unseen light, amplified by a parabolic mirror. The way this is described, it's probably meant to be focused infrared light, which probably could do significant damage, as described in the novel. A fundamental early result of quantum mechanics is that all light has an associated energy. In fact, this energy, in the case of X-rays or gamma rays, can be very high. We know X-rays can pass through our skin and some organs, which in small amounts and at low enough photon energies is helpful in medical diagnostics, but in greater intensities and higher energies, can start to be destructive. So, one type of weapon might be to create X-rays and gamma rays at high intensity and high photon energy. However, due to their high energy, it is very difficult to focus high energy X-rays or gamma rays into a concentrated beam (which is also why it's difficult to construct telescopes that detect light at these energies and focus into a sharp image, especially at gamma ray energies). Although one possibility that was mentioned earlier in Chapter 3 is that the drive of a spaceship that would emit gamma rays as its exhaust could also be used as a weapon, since gamma rays are so destructive to life. Michio Kaku (in *The Physics of the Impossible* 2008) has suggested that this could potentially be

172   The Physics and Astronomy of Science Fiction

taken to the point where a highly advanced civilization could control a dying star emitting copious gamma rays and somehow aim it at an unsuspecting enemy. A similar weapon can be accomplished with accelerated subatomic particles (such as protons, neutrons, etc.), though we still face the problem of getting those particles up to high enough energies. As we discussed before, charged particles can be accelerated in magnetic fields, but it would be difficult to get to high energies without a huge (and very expensive) device, such as the LHC particle accelerator in Switzerland.

A more popular form of light weapon that we see repeatedly in science fiction is the laser or some sort of souped-up variant (such as *Star Trek's* phaser). So, why are lasers so commonly appealed to as effective weapons? The term "laser" was created initially as an acronym for "light amplification of the stimulated emission of radiation" (and maser just substitutes "microwave" for "light," though microwaves are just a form of low energy light). In a laser, atoms can be stimulated to release large amounts of energy all at one wavelength. For various applications in the study of atoms and molecules, we would like to be able to fire a very precise beam of light at a precise wavelength. In the application of a weapon, we could potentially create a beam that has a wavelength corresponding to a much higher energy, such as

Captain Kirk (William Shatner) and Spock (Leonard Nimoy) use their phaser sidearms against the Horta in the "Devil in the Dark" episode of *Star Trek: The Original Series.* NBC/Photofest.

an X-ray laser. The most common type of laser is of the Helium-Neon variety and emits visible light. These are not powerful enough to be used as a weapon (though can do some damage if aimed directly into someone's eye, hence the warning printed on most of these).

Lost in Space consistently used the laser, then freshly invented in the lab and also discovered as a phenomenon in space, as weapons (both in the form of sidearms and rifles) in multiple episodes starting from the early episodes (used to kill a giant in one of the early episodes on the first planet they've landed on and then as late as the third season), and even mentioned the maser in reference to a possible mode for teleportation. Lasers also make their appearance in other Irwin Allen productions, such as *Voyage to the Bottom of the Sea*. *Space: 1999* went from just carrying small sidearms to producing a moon-wide laser defense system by the beginning of the second season. Films such as *Forbidden Planet* use a laser as stasis field for stabilizing the crew during atmospheric entry; however how or why this is done is not entirely explained. *The Day the Earth Stood Still* is one of the first major films to use a laser-like weapon (though an intense pencil beam of light is used as a weapon, the word "laser" is not used since the scientific concept was not to be published for a few more years). Of course now, the most famous example is the use of the laser on the Death Star of *Star Wars* fame. Could we even create enough energy to blow up an entire moon or planet? Generally speaking, as we've discussed before in another context (see Chapter 2), to break apart a planet, you'd need about as much energy as the gravitational binding energy of the object.[2] For a small moon or asteroid (say, about 20 km across) this would be about 6×10^{18} joules and for the Earth, much larger, about 2×10^{32} joules. The latter number is many orders of magnitude beyond what we are now able to create for the entire power supply of the Earth, though the former is a similar order of magnitude, if we consider that the Earth is currently using power at the rate of about one trillion watts and will thus use about 10^{19} joules in a third of a year (Cavelos 2000). As Cavelos points out, perhaps this indicates that our goals for destruction would be more attainable if they were more modest. That is, perhaps if we just distorted a planet by drilling down to its core, it would be enough to cause devastation to the planet without totally obliterating it.

Can we possibly use such lasers in reality? Megawatt lasers have been in use and are powerful enough to burn holes in airplanes from miles away or be deployed in Earth orbit to destroy satellites or incoming missiles (Cavelos 2000). The U.S. Navy is now deploying somewhat less powerful (tens of kilowatts) lasers on board transports and is looking to deploy lasers that are about five times more powerful (over 100 kilowatts) within the next few years (Kramer, "Lasers Will Shine in Future Warfare" 2014). Historically, lasers mainly generated their power through chemical reactions, as was the case

The Death Star of *Star Wars* using its planet-busting laser. Lucasfilm Ltd./20th Century-Fox/Photofest.

with the megawatt lasers developed in the past. However, more recently, as in the case of the lasers now developed by the U.S. Navy, there has been increased development of solid state lasers, which are more compact and less hazardous (Kramer, "Lasers Will Shine in Future Warfare" 2014). The main difference between these lasers and those of science fiction is that in reality they must be much bulkier mainly because of the need for generating sufficient power. The power source, since energy may be needed, say, to destroy an invading airplane, is much higher than what we can place in a portable pack for now. This would even be the case for something smaller scale, such as a hand laser used to kill one individual. As of now, the only feasible power source for such lasers would be a nuclear power plant. As explained in Chapter 3, a fusion plant would be even better than a fission plant, but we have not yet achieved sustainable fusion. Furthermore, nuclear power plants are gigantic and there is no real hope of getting them to portable size in the near future. In the future, innovations in battery power could help out with this. There have been some interesting developments in this area, especially for smaller scale batteries, but perhaps the same technology can be scaled up. Though this leaves some hope for portable lasers (or at least, more portable than now), it does not leave very much hope for lasers that can destroy planets (Death Star), which would take more energy than a megawatt laser could supply during one million times the known lifetime of the Universe.

Set Phasers to Stun!

Especially during and after the run of ST:TOS, it became popular to also use photonic weapons as stun weapons. Though it's certainly possible to hit someone with two possible bursts of energy, one that would likely kill them and one that likely wouldn't, it seems possible that the second choice would likely cause other permanent injuries (burning, blinding, etc.). If stunning is the goal, then we already have that sort of weapon (though they weren't developed in the 60s and 70s when photonic stun weapons were popular in science fiction). Though there is some variety, the current brand of stun guns use electrical impulses to disrupt the normal signals our brains send to muscles, mainly for use in disabling an attacker at close range. The U.S. military has also developed various forms of what is called an "active denial system" which is essentially a truck mounted stun weapon that can be used for crowd control. In particular, the intention is not to cause lasting injury to the victims of this particular weapon (Kramer, "Lasers Will Shine in Future Warfare" 2014).

Photon Torpedoes

The photon torpedoes of *Star Trek* are meant to be contained anti-matter that is set to combine and detonate in a destructive light pulse. Considering the release of pure energy in such a reaction, this can be quite an effective weapon. However, a real problem is as we mentioned before in chapters 2 and 3, and that is the distinct lack of anti-matter for much of any use.

Plasma Weapons

Another weapon, at first seeming like a photon weapon, is the light saber of *Star Wars*. However, though it seems a bit like a laser at first, some properties, at least as depicted in the films, suggest that we must be dealing with something else. A laser should more or less continue in a beam until it hits an object. It should not "stop dead" after just a meter or so. Also, a light beam would simply pass through another light beam when they cross (and not appear to repel or make a loud noise). Jeanne Cavelos suggests that these are likely to be plasma beams (Cavelos 2000). In a plasma electrons are separated from the atoms to which they are normally attached, and then can act collectively, often flowing along magnetic fields. We can potentially create our own plasma trapped in a magnetic field, and depending on the temperature, it could emit light and possess some of the other properties seen in the films. However, a new discovery uncovers another possibility. In studying quantum properties of photons (for potential use in a quantum computer) scientists have discovered that photons may have a property of "stickiness" in certain situations that allows them to bind in a way analogous to the way atoms bind in molecules. If this is so, then light can potentially behave in a collective way, as seen in a light saber (R. Staff 2013).

Freeze Guns

In the 1960 film *Angry Red Planet* we see another type of weapon altogether, a freeze gun. As presented in the film, this weapon seems to be using something like liquid nitrogen (which is usually kept under pressure at a temperature of lower than -321 F/77 K) to flash freeze various items, especially in attacking the various monsters that threaten the first crew to land on Mars (unfortunately, it does not always turn out to be effective). A similar weapon is used a few years later in the television series *Batman*, by the villain Mr. Freeze. In addition, in the film *Terminator 2*, the "terminator" played by Arnold Schwarzengger uses liquid nitrogen to freeze the morphing, liquid metal "terminator" (the T-1000 model) who has come after him. In reality such a weapon would likely have to come with a large tank to hold a significant amount of liquid nitrogen under pressure and at low temperature. Also, though such a weapon could be effective against pesky fauna or flytrap-like flora, or android assassins sent from the future, if you already have laser sidearms, there probably isn't much value added with this kind of weapon.

Sonic Weapons

Most people realize that if sound is loud enough, it can transition from being irritating to being harmful to your hearing (and, in fact, hearing loss due to excess sound exposure through life is affecting a greater number of people, including the author, and at decreasingly younger ages). An early occurrence of a sonic weapon is in the 1954 film *Gog*, in which a sonic weapon is demonstrated at the space station test area featured in this film. Soon afterward in the *Science Fiction Theater* episode "Sound that Kills," it is revealed that an important government weapons researcher had been murdered with an ultrasonic device (Grams 2011). Not only are ear-busting sonic weapons used in *Doctor Who* ("The Ice Warriors"), *Lost in Space* ("The Colonists") and *ST:TOS* ("The Way to Eden"), in reality such weapons have been used by the United States Navy in fending off small boats approaching larger ships (in the hopes of preventing terrorism and piracy). In fact, loud enough sound can be deadly (Parsons 2010). Both *Star Trek* ("This Side of Paradise") and *Space: 1999* ("Bringers of Wonder") use another kind of sonic weapon that is used in both cases to dislodge people from mind control by alien forces. Furthermore in the *Space: 1999* episode "Seed of Destruction," a sonic weapon is used to shatter the giant crystal that an alien force has used to drain energy from Moonbase Alpha.

We should keep in mind that sound waves are pressure waves and can occur just about anywhere where there is matter, even very tenuous matter. For instance, earthquakes create sound waves that travel through the earth. Shockwaves created by supernova explosions send intense sound waves through the interstellar medium.

Giant Mirrors

We discussed previously in Chapter 2 how large mirrors could be used in terraforming to focus sunlight and melt the polar caps of Mars. A similar concept could be used for a space-based weapon as well. The principle is essentially the same as a child focusing sunlight with a magnifying glass onto leaves or ants in order to burn them. However, mirrors are used in all of these cases instead of lenses because large ones can be made with much less material. The film *Gog* that we mentioned before shows how a giant mirror used for solar power on a space station can also be used for a weapon. The demonstration in the film shows a small version of the mirror burning a model of a number of buildings in a section of a city.

Defense: Shields, Force Fields, Cloaking Devices and Tractor Beams

In many episodes of the *Star Trek* franchise, the captain or other bridge officer commanded a lowly ensign to "raise the shields" in order to protect the ship from the sorts of weapons we have already discussed. But what are these shields and what could they possibly be doing? Though we can't really know the exact engineering of such a device, we can get the sense of roughly which principles are involved. In order to deflect light, it can operate under principles similar to the engines themselves by warping space through the manipulation of gravity. In other earlier television shows (such as *Lost in Space*) and films such as *Forbidden Planet* we see the use of "force fields" that keep out intruders and deflect weapons. Since these tend to be much smaller scale than the "shields" of the *Enterprise*, they realistically couldn't involve the same sort of manipulation of mass and energy. However, a smaller scale forcefield could use magnetic and electric fields to at least deflect some types of charged particles (Parsons 2010). It may also be possible to quickly bombard a target with charged particles in order to make it more susceptible to electromagnetic fields.

Just as mass can attract other masses, and even warp space enough to distort orbit or even bend light, tremendous amounts of energy can be used in the same way. Thus, we can imagine a "cloaking device." The cloaking devices were made famous in *ST:TOS* episodes featuring the Romulans (such as in "The Balance of Terror"), whose ships had the ability to remain completely invisible after engaging this special device. That is, if we can deflect mass, we can also deflect light, and potentially in a way so as to make a target seem invisible (though it would have to be invisible at every wavelength). But as Lawrence Krauss suggests in *The Physics of Star Trek*, bending light on this scale takes stellar type masses (or the equivalent energy) and stellar scale masses and energies put into the volume of something like a starship (we can refer to energy per unit volume as energy density), which means something on the same scale of energy density as a neutron star or black hole. Under such conditions, the gravity would be extreme, and humans would certainly be crushed and unable to survive. Potentially, even a tractor beam (seen as part of the regular complement of tools in *Star Trek* and in other series such as *Lost in Space* and *Space: 1999* as an alien technology) can work on similar principles. Certainly, rearrangement of mass or energy can be used to attract other mass or energy. The main problem then becomes how to manipulate something like this, especially if the mass and speed are similar to the spaceship with the tractor beam. As Newton's Laws show, in such a case, it's hard to then point out what is doing the pulling! That is, if you try to pull on a fast-moving asteroid, it can pull you too. So, realistically, such a system could only be effective for relatively small objects (objects that are much less massive than the spacecraft).

On smaller scales, it may be possible to create something similar to, say, Harry Potter's invisibility cloak by bending light with special materials called meta-materials that use embedded copper within a material rendering anything shrouded by the material essentially invisible to microwaves (Kaku, *The Physics of the Impossible* 2008). In principle, similar techniques using different materials could be used to render an object invisible to light at all wavelengths. However, one of the biggest obstacles is that the embedded materials that do the refracting (create the invisibility effect) must be about the same size as the wavelength of the radiation itself. This means that for visible light, we have to create microscopic implants less than one millionth of a meter across. They must be 1,000 times smaller to render an object invisible to X-rays. It's thought that perhaps the same lithographic techniques that have been used to print tiny circuits of these sizes may be successful in creating these types of meta-materials.

Exosuits

The *Iron Man* series of films features a superhero whose powers mainly come from an external metallic suit. The suit is able to become properly pressurized at high altitude, has rocket power able to match speed of military jets, and has a hard enough exterior to withstand bullets and other weaponry. Similar suits were seen in the *Edge of Tomorrow* although these were used primarily as fighting machines and had no rocketry. In *Elysium*, Max is equipped with a more rudimentary exosuit. Having been weakened after radiation exposure, he is unable to get up to the space colony, Elysium, unassisted. However, he is equipped with an exoskeleton that gives him added strength and helps him move faster. Other characters are also seen with exosuits of varying degrees of sophistication.

Chapter 9

Extraterrestrial Life

The Search for Extraterrestrial Life and Intelligence

Another natural ramification of considering the formation of planets and discovery of potential Earth-like planets around solar-type stars as we did in Chapter 3 is to go further and ask whether or not life exists on any of these planets (or potentially, any others). Before we look into this in more detail it would help us to come up with a working definition of "life." Though it's possible that no definition we use will be applicable to all actual beings we might encounter in the Universe, we can come up with a working definition that applies to all life we encounter here on Earth. Should we encounter a being out there that does not correspond to this definition, we'd have to then make a decision as to whether we should reject it as being a true lifeform, or whether to change our definition. All forms of life (though not necessarily any one individual being at a given moment) must be able to use energy by absorbing materials or energy from the outside and use it for movement, growth and other functions. Since any kind of normal functioning requires energy, we can easily see how this would be mandatory more or less as a result of conservation of energy. It must reproduce itself in order to thrive past the lifespan of the individual organism. It must be able to react to the outside environment (though this can be limited in some cases, such as for most plants) or else run the risk of being fried, frozen, eaten or meet any other untimely demise. Life must also be able to evolve over time to be able to survive in changing environments (Bennett and Shostak 2012). These concepts are considered in a first-season *ST:TNG* episode, "Home Soil," in which Dr. Beverly Crusher goes through a similar checklist for what can be considered to be life, and then concludes that an inorganic source of light flashes discovered on the planet below is really an intelligent life-form. In a later episode, "The Quality of Life," Data examines the possibility of whether robotic devices called "exocomps" could possibly be considered to be life,

9. Extraterrestrial Life

and also consults with Dr. Crusher, who again goes through a similar checklist. Further questions regarding the nexus of artificial and natural life were also considered in Chapter 6.

Before we investigate life in the Universe, we should reflect on how life likely came to be here on Earth. The prevailing model for the early Earth is an atmosphere with a high content of carbon dioxide due to venting from volcanoes. Bombardment from comets would supply most of the Earth's water as well as some of the compounds (such as methane) that could be broken down and then re-form into complex molecules. We think these events most likely occurred between 3.5 and 4 billion years ago. At 3.5 billion years we have fossil evidence of life, so we know that the most primitive life-forms must have developed prior to this point. At 4 billion years, we know from determining the age of lunar craters that there was an era of heavy bombardment. During this era we believe water was supplied to Earth from crashing comets, but likely left too hostile of an environment for life to have actually formed and developed at that moment. Oxygen would have primarily come as a by-product of life much later on. In 1952 Urey and Miller famously conducted their experiment modeling the early Earth in the laboratory. Essentially, they exposed a closed flask of water, ammonia, methane and hydrogen to electricity and ultraviolet light. The primary result was the production of

Dr. Ellie Arroway (Jodie Foster) detecting a radio signal from an alien civilization, from the film *Contact*, based on the novel by Carl Sagan. Warner Brothers/Photofest.

more than half of the amino acids that are the building blocks of complex compounds such as RNA and DNA that are essential to life here on Earth. Many years later, similar experiments were conducted with the addition of carbon dioxide and hydrogen sulfide (the components from volcanoes), and even more amino acids were produced (Kay et al. 2013). The *Science Fiction Theater* episode "Before the Beginning" delves into the topic of how life can form. A scientist more or less conducting an experiment similar to that of Urey and Miller is looking to go the extra step to look for the beginning of life. Though he does not succeed in this, he does succeed in producing a self-replicating crystal (sort of a proto-life) that helps his wife overcome a debilitating disease.

Next, we have to think about where we might be able to find life. Though we can't say for certain that life could not exist on another type of world besides one like our own, it's probably reasonable to eventually look for life on worlds that are most similar to our own. By "similar," we mean both in composition (a terrestrial planet) and location in parent star system. We know that if the Earth was at the distance of Mars much of the water would freeze. At the distance of Venus, it could boil. Thus we know that every star has a zone around it that describes the region where a planet could potentially have most water be in liquid form on the surface. This is called the habitable zone of the star (or sometimes the "Goldilocks Zone," after the children's fairy tale in which Goldilocks finally finds porridge that's at the "just right" temperature). Though some life could potentially exist without water, and it may even be that life on Earth was initiated outside of water, we know for sure that life now on Earth requires water, so our first hope at finding life is to follow the water trail. That is, we concentrate on planets where water can exist. This has been the primary strategy for the exploration of Mars. Though, as we have said, there can be no liquid water currently on the surface, there is mounting evidence that water once flowed on some section of the planet about 3.5 billion years ago, but not lasting long (save for sporadic changes in flow). One compelling piece of evidence is the ratio of deuterium to hydrogen in the atmosphere of Mars. Over time, ultraviolet radiation from the Sun would have broken down the bonds between hydrogen and oxygen in water covering the surface. A small fraction of this water would be composed of deuterium (heavy hydrogen) and oxygen. Because deuterium is heavier than normal hydrogen, less of it will escape the atmosphere over time and this will lead to an enrichment of deuterium relative to hydrogen in the atmosphere. If this ratio is much higher on Mars than it is on Earth, it would suggest that on Mars, there would be an additional source of this deuterium. The clearest answer is that a source of water has evaporated from the surface and risen up to the atmosphere (Wilson 2015). If so, it is possible that conditions were conducive for the evolution of life for a short, though "long enough" period of time (Encrenaz 2013). However, as yet, there have been no conclusive signs of past or present life in Mars.

Currently, we do not have the means for visiting such planets outside of our own Solar System, but as mentioned above there are future plans for Earth-orbiting telescopes allowing for spectroscopy of exoplanets. A primary goal of such a spectrograph would be to look for signatures of life. In fact, we can suppose that when *ST:TOS* off-handedly mentioned scanning for "life signs" in many episodes that this would be one part of making such discoveries (and this even makes its way into *Space: 1999*, which wouldn't be so bad if it weren't putting this miraculous jump in technology into more or less the present day). Such telescopes must have the ability to detect radiation from infrared into ultraviolet in order to cover the known wavebands of these features. These will, for example, be able to detect atmospheric absorption features of the same variety that can readily be detected in spectra of the Earth's atmosphere, such as water vapor. We can also potentially observe absorption features of chlorophyll. It turns out that chlorophyll absorbs much of the visible spectrum until about 0.7 microns at which point this effect cuts off, and plants become much more reflective. This shows up as the so-called "red edge" in the Earth's spectrum (Jayawardhana 2011). In the previously mentioned novel *Proxima*, the fictional planet Peradua, in the Proxima Centauri system, is first discovered to have life based on the discovery of the "red edge." This same effect is discussed in Michael O'Brien's *Voyage to Alpha Centuari*. Jayawardhana notes that the red edge might be shifted depending on what pigment may have become dominant after plants adapted to the light of their parent star. For instance, if plants adapted to primarily absorb blue light (either because more blue light was available from the parent star, or because of absorption in the atmosphere), then there would be a blue edge in the spectrum rather than a red edge. Another possibility is to look for spectral signatures of by-products of life, such as CO_2 (Jenkins and Jenkins 1998). However, we should note that these are all the collective signs of life on an entire planet. Though we might eventually be able to resolve this a bit into sections of a planet, going down to the level of tracking the signs of life from one particular individual, especially on the scale of millions and up to trillions of miles, is well beyond what we would even expect decades into the future.

In addition, life might be possible on some "exo-Moons," that is, the moons of some of the giant exoplanets within the habitable zone of the parent star. Rene Heller and Jorge Zuluaga have shown that large habitable moons (larger than Mars) probably cannot form, and that the smaller ones (analogues to Europa) are not yet observable with current techniques. Since smaller moons would not be able to generate their own substantial magnetic fields, they would have to rely on the magnetosphere of a giant planet they orbit to ward off radiation from the parent star. Unfortunately, there seems to be no "sweet spot" (location of Moon around planet or location of planet around star) for such a Moon to be conducive to habitability (Heller and Zuluaga 2013).

On another separate path, first initiated by Frank Drake in the 1950s, there has long been a search for extraterrestrial life that has gone in the direction of looking for intelligent life in particular. This avenue has been seeking evidence of communication from other planets by focusing on radio signals that might be emitted by an intelligent civilization. It's thought that most intelligent civilizations would focus on sending radio signals because radio signals do not require as much energy as sending out signals at higher frequencies. In addition, radio signals are not as efficiently absorbed or scattered by interstellar gas and dust as much as visible light or high energy light such as x-rays or gamma rays. Also, intelligent civilizations that are advanced enough to contemplate sending signals across the galaxy would also surely be well aware that hydrogen naturally emits light in radio waves (1.4 GHz in particular). Thus, it might be a particularly good choice to send signals at a frequency similar to this one, as it is one that all intelligent species would think to check (though, not long after, all species, like us, would probably attain the ability to scan all of frequency space, so this may not be as important as once thought). Most searches for extra- terrestrial intelligence have looked across the electromagnetic spectrum with very high spectral resolution (but near just one isolated frequency), and thus much of "frequency space" as well as physical space has not been covered in looking for signals. Though some signals have been detected, all have either later been dismissed as some sort of Earth-bound interference, such as the 1997 signal that ended up being an accidental detection of the SOHO research satellite (Shostak 2009) or have not repeated. A promising way of detecting such signals in the future would be with the Allen Array, an array of radio antennas now beginning to come online (and funded by Microsoft co-founder Paul Allen). This array will allow for dedicated time toward SETI, examination of large chunks of the radio spectrum, but with high spectral resolution, all simultaneously. Thus, if there are signals to be found, our chances of detecting them would increase by a large factor, and as Shostak estimates, by 2030 or so we'd have looked across the spectrum at millions of star systems. Thus, we should start to see whether the most generous estimates based on the Drake equation (discussed in detail below) are even close to being correct. Of course, if they are not, it may mean the end of SETI (Shostak 2009). Another possibility is to try to detect optical laser signals from other civilizations. Though optical light generally takes more energy to emit than radio light (per photon), a laser signal can still be thought of as fairly efficient because its sent out at a single energy, and also suffers minimal attenuation and there is likely to be little cosmic background at the particular energy being looked at it (where we know that there is a lot of background radio hiss).

Communicating with Intelligent Civilizations

The flipside of searching for signals is sending out signals ourselves. For a long time it was generally thought that we shouldn't bother to send out signals until we received a signal ourselves. But if we are searching for someone else's first message, it certainly might make sense to send out some ourselves (assuming it doesn't matter who finds out about whom first). The first such signal was sent out in 1974 and was directed toward the M13 globular cluster (and will get there in about 25,000 years) and more recently one was sent out in 2008. For reasons of technology at the time, these messages had to be short, and there was some debate over what should be included in such a brief message. Shostak makes the point that we no longer need be concerned about figuring out appropriate content to send to a civilization, so we simply can send them the entire content of the internet! Though much of the content would be in particular languages, the redundancy of the content could help in translation, much like the Rosetta Stone's effect for translating hieroglyphics (Shostak 2009).

The Drake Equation

As part of Frank Drake's initial work on studying potential communications from intelligent species in the Galaxy, he came up with his famous eponymous equation to estimate how many intelligent technological civilizations (capable of sending out a radio signal) there are in the Galaxy. The exact equation and some example calculations are given in the chapter endnotes,[1] but the main idea is that he'd start with the total number of stars in the Galaxy. This can be thought of as a rough maximum number of civilizations (though it's possible each star could have multiple planets). However, for a number of reasons, the estimate would be considerably lower than this. For instance, we now know that many stars do not have planets, and that many others that have not yet been observed probably do not either. So, depending on whose estimates you use, anywhere between 50% and 90% of all stars are out. Of these remaining stars, some may have more than one habitable planet (or moon) in the system, so we have to take that into account. However, the really depressing news comes from how many of these planets may actually have (or have had) any kind of life evolve at all, and what fraction of those led to intelligent life. We simply do not have a good handle on these numbers, though its likely reasonable to assume that many planets that get to the point of microbial life probably do not reach the point of having a technological situation. Though the range of numbers can be anything from one (just us) to many millions, reasonable assumptions can lead to at least thousands of civilization in our Galaxy. One overall interpretation that we can derive from our Drake Equation results is the average distance we'd expect to see out to in order to detect an intelligent civilization. This calculation is also in the chapter endnotes, but we can gather that if N is large, then the number density of civilizations in the Galaxy is also large, meaning we wouldn't have to see out very far in order to detect a technological civilization. If N is small, then you may have to see clear to the other side of the Galaxy (or maybe to another galaxy) in order to find another civilization. Some readers might be bothered by the inexactness of the results of this equation. But we have to keep in mind that the Drake Equation was devised to approximate a range of numbers that would likely be greater than one (just us) and not bigger than hundreds of billions (every star in the Galaxy).

Is Intelligent Life Rare in the Galaxy?

However, Ward and Brownlee in *Rare Earth* give a number of reasons to suggest that we should not lean towards being so optimistic. Their argument centers on the development of life on Earth as having likely been highly dependent on a set of conditions that would likely be rare (at least all of them together for one planet) in the Galaxy (Ward and Brownlee 2000). For instance, both the Earth's tilt and the stability of this tilt have led to consistent seasonal variations that are favorable to life. In particular, the existence of a large Moon in close proximity to its parent planet has been a major factor in stabilizing the tilt of the Earth's rotation axis. In addition, the Earth's magnetic field has protected life against harmful energetic cosmic rays, the most dangerous ones being from the Sun during relatively common solar flares. Even the configuration of our particular Solar System favors life. That is, the existence of a large planet such as Jupiter, an average of about 400 million miles from us, helps to deflect comets away from the Earth that could lead to devastating events (we know the Earth has experienced mass extinctions, with probably some being caused by collisions with asteroids or comets, but the number of these events would have been much higher without Jupiter to protect us). Another important factor is location in the Galaxy. That is, it's likely that billions of stars near the center of the Galaxy are exposed to too much radiation both from the stars themselves and accretion onto a central black

9. Extraterrestrial Life 187

hole, and no life as we know it would be able to thrive. The fundamental conclusion made by Ward and Brownlee is that though basic conditions might exist for a time on some exoplanets (or in the Solar System), they likely do not exist long enough for intelligent life to evolve, making Earth-like planets in the full sense (with intelligent life), very rare indeed. The ramifications of the Rare Earth hypothesis are part of the underpinning of a set of novellas by Peter Cawdron, *Galactic Exploration*. For instance, the novella *Serengeti* focuses on an intergalactic quest for intelligent life (as it is already known that life can't be found in the Galaxy). In the afterword of this book Cawdron suggests that the Rare Earth hypothesis violates the Copernican principle and gives Earth a special place in the Universe. I believe that to be a misinterpretation. The hypothesis, based on sound scientific analysis, states that the probability of life in our galaxy (and maybe the Universe as a whole), especially intelligent life, could be quite low, but is not zero. So, Earth might be unique, or not. However, in adopting this hypothesis, we might have sound reason not to expect intelligent life on any of the planets we have been able to observe telescopically (most within about 150 light years). Rare Earth is also central to Dror Burstein's novel of personal reflection, *Netanya*. Burstein uses the theory itself as well as other details from Ward and Brownlee's book as a framing structure to show the uniqueness and preciousness of our current lives.

In addition, Ray Kurzweil gives a different explanation for why intelligent life in the Galaxy (and perhaps, much of the Universe) is very rare. He argues, as he does for Earth, that within just 300 years from achieving the technology for radio communication, a civilization should be able to harness the energy of its parent star, and thus be able to easily achieve interstellar travel. In addition, under this paradigm, some societies should even be well beyond this point, and have been able to colonize the Galaxy. At this high level of technological development, any such society might likely also leave some evidence of a signal, whether in radio waves or some other band of the electromagnetic spectrum. However, such an advanced society may also have ways of communicating without radiating or hiding the radiation from others. Believing in his own assumptions about the acceleration of technological achievement on Earth, he concludes that if we see no evidence of alien civilizations having reached these points, then there must be no alien civilizations. However, this conclusion is completely dependent on the assumption that human technology really will accelerate as quickly as he predicts (Kurzweil, *The Singularity Is Near* 2005). It may be that Kurzweil is incorrect in at least some of his assumptions. Only time will tell which is correct. Others though have reached similar conclusions (Armstrong and Sandberg 2013). They argue that with relatively modest uses of energy, a technological civilization should eventually be able to colonize the Galaxy and even the visible

Universe using spacefaring techniques that were discussed in Chapter 3. That no other civilizations have reached the Earth (or been detected otherwise) could perhaps suggest that perhaps someone did reach Earth, but in the deep past (and may have seeded it with present life) or, perhaps more realistically, they do not exist or do not exist yet (though Armstrong and Sandberg only weakly support that as a way out of the problem). Max Tegmark has also reached similar conclusions (Tegmark, *Our Mathematical Universe* 2014).

There are some valid counterarguments to the "Rare Earth" hypothesis. For instance, we now know that life can live in some fairly extreme environments here on Earth that had previously been ignored. It may be that similar life can exist in similar conditions on exoplanets. Also, we now know, for instance, that water is likely to exist on Europa underneath a thick (many miles) layer of ice. However, to reach underneath these layers of ice to search for life would mean developing new drilling techniques. The deepest drilled hole on Earth so far is just over 12 km (Umino, Nealson and Wood 2013). The bottom line may be that though certain conditions may make it much easier for life to persist, it may also be the case that there are more environments where life can take a foothold (and perhaps survive and evolve) than we originally thought. In addition, astronomers now believe that certain star systems once thought to be too hostile for life may be more amenable than once thought. For instance, red dwarf stars, the most common type in the Galaxy, are thought to put out so much less light than the Sun that any potentially habitable planet would have to be so close to the star that it would become tidally locked with one side always facing the star, this leading to temperature extremes that are inhospitable to life. In addition, red dwarfs are known to have particularly strong flares that could lead to damaging radiation that would dash any hopes for life. However, there may be some mitigating factors, such as cloud formation on tidally locked planets, which could help to even out the temperature on these planets. Also, since there are expected to be many red dwarf stars in the Galaxy (hundreds of billions), the overall chances of finding a planet that happens to have the right temperature conditions for life will be relatively large. One potential planet of this type has been discovered orbiting the relatively nearby (about 20 light years distant) red dwarf star Gleise 581 (Vogt et al. 2010). Though there has been some controversy regarding the detailed results for the Gliese 581 system, astronomers generally agree that the system has at least one, and maybe two potentially habitable planets (Stevenson 2013). The previously mentioned novel, *Proxima*, takes place on one such world, though as yet, no planets have actually been detected around Proxima Centauri.

The possibility of communication with other alien civilizations and the impact has been approached in science fiction for some time. The first detection of an alien radio signal was the focus of Carl Sagan's *Contact* (both the book and film). In the first episode of *The Outer Limits* from 1963 ("The Galaxy Being"), a radio station owner using his transmitter for SETI experiments, accidentally stumbles upon communications from a civilization in the Andromeda Galaxy. In the initial episode of *Space: 1999*, the motivation for covering up the brain damage astronauts were getting due to increased magnetic field activity from increasing atomic waste, was the desire to explore the planet Meta from which the Earth was receiving indecipherable signals.

Alternatively, some works of science fiction suggest the possibility of telepathic communication from alien intelligences, and this started at least as early as the 1954 *Science Fiction Theater* episode "Y.O.R.D." (Grams 2011), and continued for many years, including in the *ST:TOS* episode "The Menagerie," in which the Talosians use telepathy to draw in several spaceships to their planet, including two different incarnations of the *Enterprise*. Later, in multiple *Space: 1999* episodes, such as "Ring Around the Moon," "Space Brain," and "The Lambda Factor," mysterious nebulae and other space phenomena telepathically influence the residents of Moonbase Alpha (Muir, *Exploring Space: 1999* 1997). Though there have been some developments in crudely determining moods and emotions of patients using MRI scans (Kaku, *The Physics of the Impossible* 2008), this is a long way from tracking or transmitting exact thoughts. Since there have been no scientific confirmations of telepathy, this remains primarily an element of highly speculative fiction. We discuss these issues in more detail in Chapter 10.

What Would Life Look Like?

Often aliens are depicted as being enlarged versions of Earth insects. Perhaps the most famous example of this was the giant mutant ants of the 1954 film *Them!* (I've cheated a bit here. The giant ants in this film are not of extraterrestrial origin, but the principles would the same for extraterrestrial giant bugs) but have recurred in many forms, such as in the battles against giant insects in the film *Starship Troopers*, giant bees of the "The Beehive" episode of *The Starlost* or the giant spiders of *Doctor Who*'s "Planet of the Spiders." However, we know this can't work, originating with a physical law that was noticed as early as Galileo in the 1600s (Galilei 1914). The primary reason is that though the mass of the giant insect will increase as the scale length cubed (that is, if we increase the height and width by 10 times, the volume will increase by a factor of 1,000, and so will the mass if the density of the object is constant). The support strength of a giant insect (or giant anything) will depend on the cross sectional area of the limbs that support it. The cross sectional area depends on the scale length squared, so if we increase the width and length of limbs by 10 times, the strength of the animal will only go up by 100 times. Therefore, if we just scale up the size, the giant bug will collapse under its own weight. The situation would be made even worse for insects with relatively heavy exoskeletons. Once scaled up, these exoskeletons would add even more to the crushing weight (Sofge 2014). The same would go for scaled up gorillas such as King Kong or giant people as in the television series *Land of the Giants*. That doesn't mean that very large creatures aren't possible, however, they would need very different bone structure that could support their mass, or need something else to support their immense size and mass (such as water, which makes it possible to have large whales).

We also have reason to be skeptical of aliens such as in *The Outer Limits* episode "Zanti Misfits" in which we see intelligent ant-like beings (pictured to about as large as a rat) but with humanoid facial features! A similar "mutant ant" was featured in *The Outer Limits* episode "The Mutant." Our facial features (and those of practically all mammals) have developed over millions of years to accommodate our eyes, brains, respiratory system (mouth and nose) and digestive system. It's very unlikely that any creature that did not develop these same systems would develop a similar face.

Silicon-Based Life

We might also consider what kind of life we'd expect to encounter. Most science fiction considers humanoid life (especially for television and film, this may be primarily a budgetary concern). However, we could encounter intelligent life that differs dramatically from our own. Arthur C. Clarke addresses this possibility in his 1945 short story "The Fires Within," in which scientists discover evidence of an intelligent species that has been able to live inside solid rock at the core of the Earth. This topic was brought up more poignantly in *ST:TOS* episode "Devil in the Dark" in which a silicon-based creature (which we later learn is a species called Horta, and is highly intelligent) is able to move through solid rock and kills a number of people (by naturally emitting an acid) who have accidentally destroyed her eggs. A bit earlier, *The Outer Limits* episode "Corpus Earthling" featured living rocks that could take over the bodies of people, though no mention is made of how this form of life came to be. Later, a living rock was featured in an episode of *Space: 1999* in "All that Glisters" (featuring miscommunications with a rock creature that appears as more or less just a normal rock that glows) and in *Doctor Who's* 1978 serial, "The Hand of Fear," in which a fossilized hand of a silicon-based creature is found on Earth in the modern day. Eventually the hand gains enough energy to regenerate itself into a full-blown organism, and forces the Doctor to take it back to its home planet. Another creature

9. Extraterrestrial Life 191

A giant ant from the 1954 film *Them!* Warner Bros./Photofest.

forming out of volcanic rock is featured in the *ST:TOS* episode "The Savage Curtain." Also, a crystallized inorganic life-form appears in *ST:TNG*'s "Home Soil." More comically, *Lost in Space* introduced "rock monsters" from time to time, such as in "Cave of the Wizards" and a similar menacing rock monster, Gorignak, was featured in *Galaxy Quest*.

But is silicon-based life even possible? Probably not, there being several reasons. The first problem is that there is much more carbon in the Universe, and thus bound up in planets and available for life than silicon. Also, though theoretically silicon has some of the same bonding chemistry as carbon, in reality, silicon-based molecules are unstable and reactive. This would make, say, silicon-based DNA-like molecules a poor substitute for the carbon-based chains we are used to. Alternatively, *Doctor Who* proposes that the Slitheen are a calcium-based life-form. However, this is even more problematic than silicon. Calcium only has two electrons available for covalent bonding, which is not complex enough to allow for chain molecules similar to DNA (Parsons 2010).

Energy Beings

Another completely different sort of intelligent life-form commonly portrayed in science fiction is the "pure energy being," that is, a being with no corporeal form, just somehow cohering energy only. Some examples from *ST:TOS* are the beings from "The Lights of Zetar" (represented as blinking stellar-like objects), Ambassador Kollos of Medusa from "In Truth Is There No Beauty?" ("he" is confined to a box, and those who look in at his formless existence are driven insane), and the inhabitants of Organia (in the episode "Errand of Mercy"), who disguise themselves as normal corporeal beings. Yet another example is the true forms of the creatures of Gothos. Though Trelane, who we discussed in the previous chapter, presents himself as humanoid, at the end we learn his true origins. His parents are presented as pulsing green lights. An apparent energy being is central to the "Immunity Syndrome" episode of *Space: 1999*. Here, this being controls the entire planet to react against the "invading" Alphans. As they begin to test the environment, they are tricked into drinking what they think is safe water, but then those who drank the water die from it. In addition, their spacecraft disintegrates. With help from a found video journal of a previous alien leader who had attempted to colonize the planet, they realize that there is a controlling intelligence, and that they must communicate with it. Eventually, they are successful. Another example of energy beings is in Isaac Asimov's short story "Eyes Do More than See." Here there are two energy beings, Ames and Brock, now trillions of years old and dispersed across space, who recall their days when they were corporeal.

As Lawrence Krauss points out in *The Physics of Star Trek*, "pure energy beings" seem unlikely, especially in the way they are portrayed on screen. Anything that "consists of pure energy" would have to be traveling at the speed of light. If so, such a being would not be able to "hover" or move around at less than the speed of light. Another similar sort of being is that of *The Outer Limits* episode "The Bellero Shield." In this episode a laser-testing device accidentally captures an alien being who claims to be made up of light.

When asked why the laser didn't kill him, the alien answers, "Does fire quench fire?" He then goes on to explain that everything in his world is made up of the same constituents as the laser beam that captured him. A being made of light, but taking on corporeal form that can stay stationary, or travel at any speed less than the speed of light is contrary to the laws of physics, and goes back to the same problem we had with pure energy beings.

Intelligent Plant Life

The thought of intelligent plant life is very intriguing because we usually treat plants in a very passive manner, thinking of them as completely inanimate. It's very jarring to see the tables turned and have plants suddenly acting either malevolently or benevolently, or really just acting out at all! This was seen in an early short story by Murray Leinster, "Proxima Centauri." As Isaac Asimov writes concerning this short story, "It is almost an unfailing recipe for a startling science fiction story to begin by inverting some thoroughly accepted situation, some so ordinary as to be almost disregarded. Of course animals eat plants, and of course, animals are quick and more or less intelligent, while plants are motionless and utterly passive (except for a few insect-eating plants, which can be disregarded). But what if intelligent and carnivorous plants fed on animals, eh?" Ostensibly about the travels of a generational space ark, the *Adastra*, to the nearest star system, the mission ends when the crew is first contacted by, and then is attacked unexpectedly by a race of intelligent, yet hostile, plant creatures. Additionally, Harry Harrison's *Deathworld Trilogy* features carnivorous plants.

In the later Ursula LeGuin short story "Vaster than Empires and More Slow," a scouting group is sent down to explore a planet that appears to be dominated by plant life. One of the crew, Osden, has empathic abilities, and has been added to the crew to acts as a "human sensor" of sentient life. Through him, it's revealed that the plant life on the planet act as one intelligent organism through a network. The 2008 film *Avatar* uses this same concept. The plant life of Pandora has a collective brain via contact through their roots. The indigenous humanoids, the Na'vi, are able to make direct contact with this plant brain and are thought to be able to receive data directly from it. In the film *Guardians of the Galaxy*, one of the companions of Peter Quill is Groot, an intelligent, motile tree creature (despite only speaking the phrase "I am Groot"). We see many times in the film that Groot can greatly extend his limbs, and most spectacularly, in the end, when we think he has died, he can totally regenerate if a small branch from his body is replanted. One of the alien races featured in the television series *Farscape* are the Delvians, introduced primarily through the character, Zhaan. They look human, but

194   The Physics and Astronomy of Science Fiction

A Na'vi from the moon Pandora featured in the 2009 film *Avatar*. 20th Century-Fox/Photofest.

are actually motile plants. For instance, their skin has chloroplasts to absorb sunlight.

An invasive and apparently intelligent flower was the focus of a short story by John Wyndham and later, a television mini-series, *The Day of Triffids*. There have been at least two similar examples: the apparently semi-sentient flowers and spores in the *The Outer Limits* episode "Specimen: Unknown" and similarly in the "This Side of Paradise" episode of *ST:TOS* in which the invasive "spores" coming from a flowering plant that may have originated from another star system, takes over the minds of, first, the colonists of Omicron Ceti III, and then the crew of the *Enterprise*.

Intelligent plants have made their way into many additional science fiction television episodes. Unfortunately, some of these were often the least serious of the episodes of these particular series. The "Dark Planet" episode of *Space Patrol* features an intelligent plant found on Uranus. The *Fireball XL5* episode "The Plant Man from Space" features a mad scientist who, after becoming enamored of the planet Hedera (another name for ivy), dominated by plant life, creates a sentient plant creature that he calls a "chloroform." Another of these episodes was "The Great Vegetable Rebellion" of *Lost in Space*. Here, Tybo, an intelligent giant carrot (yes, you read that correctly) seeks to punish the Robinsons for landing on his planet and killing plants during their initial explorations. This series additionally features intelligent plant life in the episode "Flaming Planet," in which a mutated normal tree becomes both ambulatory and apparently intelligent (though servile). Earlier, this series in its episode "Attack of the Monster Plants" also featured a cyclamen plant that would duplicate anything it could trap, including people (the core of this idea is similar to John Campbell's 1936 short story, "The Brain Stealers of Mars," in which plant-like creatures can change form and take on the features and personalities of people). At around this time another Irwin Allen production, "The Plant Man" episode of *Voyage to the Bottom of the Sea*, featured a plant creature that was able to replicate itself and threaten the submarine. Another story similar to that in "The Great Vegetable Rebellion" made it into *Space: 1999* with "The Rules of Luton" in which Commander Koening and Maya are put on trial for picking flowers and eating berries on a planet that has been taken over by sentient plants (their judges in the trial are trees). Fortunately, *Space: 1999* had a more serious entry on this subject with "The Troubled Spirit." Due to the timing (filmed in 1974 and broadcast in 1976), it seems likely that this was inspired by two popular books from 1973, *The Sound of Music and Plants* by Dorothy Retallack, which summarized her experiments exposing plants to different types of music, and *The Secret Life of Plants* which focused on the possibility of sentient (and telepathic!) plants (Tompkins and Bird 1973). In a critique and history of the *Space: 1999* television series, *Destination Moonbase Alpha*, Johnny Byrne, the writer of this episode, does mention that he was influenced by research on plants that was announced in the media at that time, but doesn't mention a particular experiment or book (Wood 2010). Furthermore, Retallack mentions that plants responded particularly well to Indian music, a fact that seems to have made it into "The Troubled Spirit" (the episode starts with a recital featuring Eastern music). In the more controversial sections of her book, she further conjectures that her experiments may be related to previous investigations by Cleve Backster that claim to have shown that plants have a form of extrasensory perception (E.S.P.) (Retallack 1973). In "The Troubled Spirit," Dan Mateo, a botanist on Moonbase Alpha, believes that humans and plants have an affinity, and through this affinity can potentially communicate. He and his colleagues use a séance as the means of communication with the plants. In a slightly different take on this theme, *Doctor Who's* "Seeds of Doom" features a krynoid plant that can spread seeds through space. The seeds can infect animals and transform them into plants. Similarly the Doctor stops the germination of a race of plant people in "Terror of the Vervoids" (Muir, *A Critical History of Doctor Who* 1999). *Star Trek's* entry into this arena is in the animated series episode "The Infinite Vulcan," in which a planetary exploratory team encounters a species of intelligent and motile plants.

196   The Physics and Astronomy of Science Fiction

Groot, the tree creature from the 2014 film *Guardians of the Galaxy*. Walt Disney Studios Motion Pictures/Photofest.

In reality, on Earth, plants have not developed this way. Unlike animal life, they do not have cells that have differentiated into, say, nerve cells, that would (as far as we know) be necessary for an animate let alone intelligent creature. Plants do however transmit chemicals that are similar to those in animal nervous systems (ionotropic glutamate receptors), and it is thought they play a similar role. Plants have not developed complex nervous systems, brains and consciousness because, over the course of evolution on Earth, these "features" have not been needed since plants don't engage in very complex activities (Parsons 2010). However, that doesn't necessarily prevent something that resembles a plant (in that it absorbs sunlight for energy and has a chemical such as chlorophyll in its cells, etc.), yet has developed the ability to move or even to think.

Cloud Creatures

We have already discussed the possibility of pure energy beings and understand that such entities could not exist as usually presented. In addition, it is common to present menacing amorphous gas clouds that turn out later to be alien life-forms. One such case is from *ST:TOS* ("Obsession") and here, the gas creature goes from being about the size of a person on the planet's surface to chasing the *Enterprise* at faster than light speed and apparently larger than the starship. As Captain Kirk says, "It's something that can't possibly exist, but does." They eventually vanquish the creature with a tremendous matter–anti-matter burst. Another cloud creature, "the companion" of the "Metamorphisis" episode of *ST:TOS*, is said to be made of hydrogen gas and "erratic electrical impulses." It becomes very clear that this creature is sentient and emotional. A similar creature is encountered in the *ST:V* episode "The Cloud," in which a life-form is mistaken for a common nebula. Here, rather than fight the creature, they heal it, after realizing that their entry into what they thought was the nebula actually injured the creature. *Lost in Space* had its own cloud entity in "Space Creature," in which the creature was part of a blue mist that made up the otherwise methane-laden atmosphere of the planet the *Jupiter 2* was orbiting.

Space Amoebas, Space Brains and Crystalline Entities

In the *ST:TOS* episode "Immunity Syndrome," the *Enterprise* encounters a giant space amoeba. Similar creatures were featured in the short story "Mr. Spaceship," discussed earlier. The Yucconae, the natives of the Proxima Centauri star system, use giant amoeba-like life-forms in battling human spaceships and weapons. This is but one of the giant space born creatures to be encountered in *Star Trek* and elsewhere. In the *Space: 1999* episode "Space Brain," the Moon encounters what looks at first to be a giant colorful amorphous amoeba-like creature (although it's compared to an anemone in the episode), but is actually a highly intelligent and benevolent creature that is able to try to help the Moon avoid a catastrophic collision with it. The *ST:TNG* episode "Datalore" introduces us to the Crystalline Entity, which as the name suggests, is a giant space-born sentient crystal, capable of faster-than-light travel ("warp speed"). They also come to learn that it is the entity that has killed all of the colonists on Omicron Theta (the planet they were investigating at the time) many years earlier and that this creature appears to "feed" on all forms of life. In the *ST:TNG* episode "Silicon Avatar," Dr. Marr, a visiting scientist on the *Enterprise* and mother to one of the murdered colonists, destroyed the crystalline entity with a continuous signal of gravitons. The original plan was to use pulsed gravitons as a means of communication. When Marr noticed that a more continuous signal irritated the entity, she kept up the continuous signal until the entity shattered. This is somewhat analogous to shattering a glass by bombarding it with sound at a very particular resonant frequency leading to high amplitude oscillations in the glass that will eventually shatter it. Gravitons are the particles that have been theorized to mediate gravity. Though they have yet to be discovered directly, many observations are consistent with their existence. Since the *Enterprise* is otherwise shown to be able to warp space as a means of travel, deflect or tow massive objects, it is clearly able to manipulate gravity on a large scale (see Chapter 3 for further discussion). If this is so, it seems plausible that gravitons could be manipulated in a way that could destroy a massive object such as the crystalline entity.

One potential problem, though, with all such creatures is their immense size. On one hand we'd expect organisms to be arbitrarily large in space. This is because the size of creatures we are familiar with on Earth are restricted by limitations in having to constantly work against gravity. If you get too big, then anything from moving around to ingesting food and circulating blood becomes more and more difficult if you are on a planet with significant gravity (Jenkins and Jenkins 1998). These restrictions would be lifted in deep space, far from any sources of gravity. In addition such a creature would need some source of energy, whether it be particles or light, but in such a rarefied medium as space, the creature would have to have a big collecting surface area to get enough "food," but not so massive as to need more nourishment than it could possibly collect. As the creature gets bigger and bigger, another problem arises. To act as a cohesive organism, there must be some form of communication across the organism. However, for such immense organisms, communication across could take anything from minutes to years. The former would make the creature sluggish, and the latter would be unacceptable for a living organism that would have to react to its surroundings. In the "Immunity Syndrome" the amoeba was said to be 11,000 miles by 2,000 miles. Thus, it would take any signal a minimum of a bit under 0.1 seconds to travel across the amoeba. This isn't too bad. Such a creature, limited in energy supply, would likely have to be extremely cold and sluggish. I'm afraid that "warp speed" would be out of the question (Jenkins and Jenkins 1998). Also related to immense size is that we'd expect such a large object to eventually be observable with our best telescopes, even if it was very cold (it would then possibly be a detectable source of microwaves).

Intelligent Planets

Perhaps most intriguing is the possibility that even an entire planet can be intelligent. In some sense the possibility was adopted by serious scientists in accepting the Gaia hypothesis. Though in that case, it's not argued that the Earth acts as an intelligent organism it certainly has been argued that the earth is acting as a unified organism. An early example of this type of collective intelligence is Isaac Asimov's 1950 short story "Green Patches." Here a ship from Earth lands on a lush planet. They come to find out that the plant and animal life all act as one organism. The organism makes various benevolent attempts (from its point of view) to absorb humans into its collective consciousness. Another similar example of this is the planet Pandora in *Avatar*, already mentioned in the context of its intelligent plant life and its interacting ecosystem. In Stanislaw Lem's *Solaris* the planet is covered by a sentient ocean. In Peter Cawdron's novel *Little Green Men*, a group of deuterium miners (as we learned earlier in chapters 2 and 3, deuterium can be used as fuel for nuclear fusion) encounter a living and probably sentient planet that reacts to their landing on and "attacking" the planet by creating carnivorous "little green men" who attack the miners. In other texts, Isaac Asimov writes of sentient planets twice, first with a planet Gaia (not intended to be the Earth) in *Foundation's Edge* and then Erythro (actually a moon of the planet Megas, orbiting a nearby red dwarf star) in *Nemesis*. To some extent, Mr. Nobody, in the like-named episode of *Lost in Space*, seems to have been some sort of planet intelligence, or at least a great non-corporeal intelligence trapped inside of the planet. At the end of the episode "he" morphs into a galaxy (or at least, that's how he appears as he goes off into space). He is simply described as "pure cosmic force," but none of the other characters are able to really describe what that is exactly.

Living and Sentient Spaceships

In the television series *Farscape*, the primary spaceship in which the featured space travelers all live and travel is a type of creature called a "leviathan" and is named Moya. Though Moya is a living organism, she also has mechanical parts integrated with her fundamental biological structure. Chief among her abilities is the ability to achieve faster than light speeds in space by undergoing a process called "starburst," which appears to be similar to the hyperspace jumps of Isaac Asimov novels and *Star Wars* films. The *ST:TNG* episode "Tin Man" features a living ship, Gomtuu (nicknamed "Tin Man" by the *Enterprise* crew), that is thousands of years old and may have originated in another galaxy. Gomtuu is also capable of faster than light travel and creating destructive blast waves as a type of defensive weapon. Clearly, Gomtuu is also sentient and feels emotions, though (within the confines of this episode) can only communicate this telepathically to Tam Elbrun, a telepathic humanoid who is on board the *Enterprise* during their mission to intercept Tin Man/Gomtuu. In the *Space: 1999* novel, *Survival*, Susura is a living ship, capable of feelings, including jealousy. Susura is native to the planet Leiram, which is inhabited by a humanoid species that lives symbiotically with both plant and animal life on the planet. Both animal and plant life on Leiram can be formed into their dwellings as well as spaceships. Living ships as depicted in these texts are interesting as a concept, but don't seem quite plausible. As we discussed in Chapter 3, the energies needed to even go near to the speed of light (let alone create something akin to *Star Trek's* warp drive that would exceed the speed of light) are exorbitant. This would be just as true for an organic ship as a mechanical one. Another problem would be adaptability to the extremes of outer space, though there is some evidence that certain microorganisms can survive under these conditions (Wickramasinghe, *A Journey with Fred Hoyle* 2014), so perhaps a macroscopic organism could evolve to be tolerant of space. "Space tolerant" creatures are also common elsewhere in science fiction. For instance, the shape-shifter Maya, in *Space: 1999*, in two different episodes ("Space Warp" and "Bringers of Wonder"), turns into creatures that can survive on the lunar surface for short periods by "storing oxygen like a camel stores water" and having "skin like a space suit," in the words of Maya and others.

Are UFOs Really Visiting Aliens?

We should add that there have been no confirmed encounters with extraterrestrial life of any kind. So, though some have claimed that unidentified flying objects (UFOs) are occupied by extraterrestrials (i.e., "aliens") and this has been the subject matter of a number of films and television shows (e.g., Gerry Anderson's 1970 television series *UFO*, regarding a secret organization, SHADO, based on both Earth and the Moon, intent on destroying invading spacecraft that seem to be coming from one particular unidentified alien civilization), there is no proof that UFOs have artificial or extraterrestrial origin. In fact, many UFOs turn out to be meteors, the planet Venus (especially when partially hidden by trees), flocks of birds, reflections off ice crystals in the atmosphere, or other mundane Earth-bound objects. The few incidents that seemed "interesting" at first, such as the crash at Roswell, New Mexico, have long ago been dismissed as hoaxes. In one case in Michigan in 1967, several witnesses reported sightings of zigzagging UFOs which couldn't possibly be explained by normal aircraft. However, these did end up being two military aircraft weaving around as they were testing ground radar (Klass 1974). In addition, some individuals have claimed to have been abducted by aliens. However, further analysis of these cases suggest that nearly all occurred upon falling asleep, waking, or in the middle of a long car drive at night. This would suggest that the "abductees" were in a dream or auto-hypnotic state when they had their experiences (Sagan, *The Demon-Haunted World* 1995) and that the experiences were probably not exactly as these people suggest (to say the least). Furthermore, there seemed to be consistent reports of the same thin, grey-skinned and wide-eyed aliens. This does leave some wiggle room for these to be alien spaceships, but there is currently no definitive evidence pointing to this (Plait 2002). It seems implausible that any technologically advanced civilization would expend the vast energies needed for interstellar travel just to come here and make quick appearances without serious attempt to contact civilizations here on Earth.

Was Life on Earth "Seeded" from Space?

This reasoning presented immediately above in this chapter hasn't kept some from speculating in fiction that we on Earth ultimately have an alien origin. This trend was made most famous by Erik von Daniken, passing off his work as reputable non-fiction (especially the 1968 book, *Chariots of the Gods?*), and famously claiming that the Egyptian pyramids were created by aliens. An even earlier example of similar thinking in science fiction was in the "Sun Gold" episode of *Science Fiction Theater*. Here, a group of scientists finds a type of glass in an Incan village that could have only been made with the sort of heat ray available to a technologically advanced society. They also hear of legends that the ancient Incans were able to fabricate gold. They then find a skull at an archaeological dig that looks as if it must belong to an alien, suggesting an ancient visit by aliens. Such a story was told in *Space: 1999*'s "Testament of Arkadia" (the name was likely picked to evoke the name Akkadia, related to ancient Mesopotamia) in which it was discovered that Earth had been settled thousands of years ago by the Arkadians (and again similar elements were placed in later episodes, "The Mark of Archanon" and "New Adam, New Eve"), and a similar story was told in the recent Arwen Elys Dayton novel *Resurrection*, in which an alien civilization infiltrates ancient Egypt. We already heard of the similar story in Dick's "Survey Team" in which Earth was originally settled by Martians abandoning their depleted planet. In the *Buck Rogers in the 25th Century* episode "Time of the Hawk," Hawk, a "bird man" (apparently, part eagle and part man) found on a planet in another star system, mentions that his people originated on Earth and then took to the stars when humans took over Earth and decimated his race. In addition, numerous references are made during this episode to statues of birdmen at Easter Island. The Easter Island figures and the bird men legends there are prominently discussed in Chapter 8 of *Chariots of the Gods?* As von Daniken relates, "An orally transmitted legend tells us that flying men landed and lighted fires in ancient times. The legend is confirmed by sculptures of flying creatures with big, staring eyes." An earlier version of a "bird man" alien appeared in *The Outer Limits* episode "A Second Chance," though in that case there is no reference to them having previously inhabited Earth. The *Twilight Zone* episode "Probe 7, Over and Out" suggests that Adam and Eve were astronauts who abandoned their doomed societies. In *ST:TOS* episode "Return to Tomorrow," the alien entity, Sargon, reveals that Adam and Eve may have been two of their earlier corporeal selves who traveled the Galaxy. Spock further hypothesizes that Sargon's race may have also settled Vulcan. In addition, the 2014 film *Radio Free Albemuth*, based on the much earlier Phillip K. Dick novel, suggests that the Albemuthans have been in touch with Earth secretly ever since they seeded Earth millennia ago. *Battlestar Galactica* (all versions) suggests that the opposite will happen: that Earth will seed distant planets by colonization (12 other planets), and then become mostly forgotten. Earlier, in the horror classic film *The Blob*, an alien creature (as the title suggests, an amorphous being, whose intentions are never known) falls to Earth inside of a meteorite. Stephen King tackled a similar subject in his short story "Weeds" (retitled as "The Lonesome Death of Jody Verril" in the film *Creepshow*). A concept related to this seeding that we see in science fiction but that's more scientifically tenable (yet remains extremely controversial) is the notion that life may have originated elsewhere in microbial form, but then eventually made it to Earth to evolve into an intelligent life-form. This hypothesis has taken on many forms, most famously, the "panspermia" concept that microbes formed in space all throughout the Galaxy, and then made it to various hospitable planets to grow from there. Though this theory has ancient roots and was discussed in the modern era by Arrhenius and Becquerel (who actually thought he had disproven the possibility), it's most well known in its recent form as discussed by Fred Hoyle (Wickramasinghe, "Panspermia According to Hoyle" 2003). In its last published form, he and collaborators suggested that bacterial life could form in comets (perhaps having originated in interstellar dust grains), survive interstellar space, and be dispersed onto planets via collisions. He even went so far as to say that certain epidemics may have originated with meteor showers related to specific comets (Wickramasinghe, *A Journey with Fred Hoyle* 2014). This last concept is also the basic idea behind Michael Crichton's *Andromeda Strain* (also a 1971 film). In addition Wickramasinghe and Hoyle have shown that some absorption features of interstellar dust are similar to those known for chlorophyll, a critical natural molecule for converting sunlight into usable food for plants. Some recent studies show that simple life (an algae called diatom) are found in the upper atmosphere during balloon experiments at about 15 miles altitude, but most scientists are unconvinced that their origin is extraterrestrial (Wall, "New Alien Life Claim Far from Convincing, Scientists Say" 2013). One way of perhaps proving so in the future would be to show that these diatoms are made of different types of amino acids than the type seen in all life on Earth.

In addition, it has been shown that similar life can survive high velocity collisions though that doesn't prove that life originated in this way, just that explosive impacts aren't a reason for dismissing the idea (Gannon 2013). A more recent study suggests that life could have begun much more easily in

9. Extraterrestrial Life 203

the early Mars environment than in the early Earth environment due to the relative presence of oxidized molybdenum or boron (in the form of the mineral borax) that are needed as catalysts in building sugars into RNA (Wall, "Earth Life Likely Came from Mars, Study Suggests" 2013). Furthermore, Benner (principal investigator on this study) argues that this process can only effectively occur in a dry environment (Webb 2013). However, the primary issue with this sort of hypothesis is how the life got to Earth, and the best bet would have to be a meteorite. We do know of Martian meteorites that have landed on Earth, and some have even suggested, though rather controversially, that there is some evidence for fossilized microbial life from Mars within these meteorites, in particular the Allan Hills meteor, ALH84001. Furthermore, these meteorites would have had to have left Mars during the small period during which life would likely have existed (only hundreds of millions of years, 3.6 to 4 billion years ago) and then make it to Earth around that same time to start the cycle of life here. The Allan Hills meteorite probably was blasted into space by a volcanic event about 16 million years ago, and then fell to Earth some 13,000 years ago, so this particular meteorite or others produced during the event that likely created it can't be the "seed" Benner is hypothesizing, but there could have been similar expulsions billions of years ago. This idea of a seeded Earth is part of the final revelation in Brian De Palma's 2000 film *Mission to Mars* (i.e., that intelligent Martians seeded the Earth with life). In the *ST:TNG* episode "The Chase," it is discovered that the DNA for species from twenty different planets, all in different star systems, is biologically compatible. Sequences programmed into the DNA itself form a computer program, that when run, tells the story of how a master species seeded the Galaxy four billion years ago with its own DNA. The final planet on which they discover the last piece of DNA that fits the puzzle is likely supposed to be analogous to Mars, a planet with little or no present life, but some fossilized life. Another type of "seeding" can be like that in the *Doctor Who* episode "City of Death" or *ST:TNG* episode "All Good Things," in which the beginning of life on Earth is affected by either humans or aliens invading from the future. Or perhaps some of the "seeded" life isn't biological life at after all, but artificial. The 1974 film (and later novelization) *The Questor Tapes* reveals that some apparent humans are actually androids planted by an alien master race some millennia ago.

However, generally speaking, even if we accept one of these "seeding" hypotheses, it doesn't explain how life formed in its original location. So, whether or not Earth's present life evolved from life that got itself started somewhere else, we need to find out how that first organism came to be.

Chapter 10

Super-Human Powers

Commonly, characters in science fiction are endowed with special powers. These can be powers of the mind (telepathy, psychokinesis, etc.) or of the body (flight, strength, etc.). These powers can vary from being central to the plot to just being a *deus ex machina* solution to escaping the difficult situation of the week in episodic television.

Telepathy

In the *ST:TOS* episode "Where No Man has Gone Before," two crew members gain extrasensory perception (ESP) and telepathic powers after crossing the a force-field barrier at the "edge" of the Galaxy (the concept of such a barrier is completely fictional). After a time, they gain extra strength and the ability of telekinesis as well. Here we also find usage of the term "esper" to refer to one who has extrasensory powers (another example of this usage being in the "Sky Pirate" episode of *Lost in Space*). In another *ST:TOS* episode, "The Menagerie," the Talosians are able to control prisoners by telepathically projecting illusions into their minds and have them believe they are conducting another life (usually constructed from their own fantasies). Similarly, in *Space: 1999*'s "Bringer's of Wonder," a band of hideous aliens are able to convince the residents of Moonbase Alpha (via telepathy) that they are actually compatriots from Earth who have come to rescue them (and then later almost manipulate them into creating a burst of energy that will feed the energy-starved aliens but destroy everyone else). In an additional *Space: 1999* episode, "Dorzak," we learn that one of the last surviving humanoids of the planet Psychon was the great philosopher, Dorzak. Unfortunately, he has become a criminal, using telepathic mind control to take over an alien spacecraft. Furthermore, in the "Dragon's Domain" episode of this series, it's clear that the monster that's encountered here draws in its prey by means of some sort of mind and body control from a distance, and then finishes them off

10. Super-Human Powers 205

with its own tentacles and maw. In the earlier Gerry Anderson production, the "Hypnotic Sphere" episode of *Fireball XL5*, an alien brain telepathically hypnotizes various crews in order to steal enough fuel so it can send out enough hypnotic spheres to "take over the Universe." In truth, here it would appear that the brain creature is telepathically controlling a satellite that then sends out conventional signals that use voice and light to hypnotize the crewmembers. Similarly, in the film *Journey to the 7th Planet*, another brain creature telepathically guides a crew from Earth (though why it doesn't just destroy them quickly if it wants them to go away isn't made clear). In *The Outer Limits* episode "The Mutant," Reese Fowler, a member of an interplanetary colonizing crew is exposed to particle radiation from the ever-present Sun their new home planet, Annex 1, orbits. One of the primary side effects is his newfound ability to read the minds of others. In a more fantasy-based episode of *Twilight Zone* ("Penny for Your Thoughts"), an unassuming bank clerk becomes telepathic when he tosses a penny while paying for a newspaper, and it accidentally stands on end. He's able to read the thoughts of bank customers and employees, and through this is able to become more self-confident and assertive, even after the penny falls down and he loses his telepathic powers. Sometimes a lower degree of telepathic power is presented, such as with the ability of Vulcans in *Star Trek* to undergo "mind melds" and unify their thoughts with others, but not to be generally telepathic. Perhaps the most interesting example of this is when Spock is able to meld with the silicon-based creature, the Horta, in *ST:TOS* episode "The Devil in the Dark." In other episodes he melds with a robotic probe (*ST:TOS*, "The Changeling"), and a formless intelligent creature called a Medusan (*ST:TOS*, "In Truth is There No Beauty?"). In the *ST:TNG* episode "Sarek," it is revealed that Spock's father, Sarek, is experiencing a form of Vulcan dementia called Bendi Syndrome. This is revealed before Sarek's final (yet critical) diplomatic mission. Captain Picard proposes a mind meld with Sarek in order to take on some of his knowledge, experience and abilities, and then assume Sarek's role at the negotiations. Though ultimately successful, Picard experiences much of the tumult of Sarek's mind as his thoughts and emotions become more turbulent as a result of his disease. Additionally we see the empathic powers of Counselor Troi in *ST:TNG* (the people of her home planet, Betazed, are shown to be fully telepathic, but she is half human and half Betazoid). She is also commonly portrayed as being more sensitive to the telepathy of others, without being telepathic herself (for example, in the episode "Night Terrors" during which a telepathic species sends clues to their existence as a recurring dream). Another earlier example from the same franchise is that of the empath, Gem, in the *ST:TOS* episode "The Empath." Here Gem's species is being tested by another species, the Vians, who want to see whether she and her people are worthy of saving from the demise of their star system. In addition,

Star Trek had examples of other telepathic species, such as the Yulians (*ST:TNG* episode "Violations") who were able to insert themselves into others' dreams.

By the 1950s, evidence for E.S.P. and telepathy seemed promising to some. Though such research was often met with a heavy dose of skepticism, some academics of the period, most notably Rhine at Duke and Soal in England, did find some examples of people who were able to guess symbols on cards at a statistically significantly higher rate than what would have been expected by chance (Soal and Bateman 1954). This isn't exactly either the fortune telling of psychics or the mind reading as usually depicted in science fiction, but it was a result worth reporting. However, over time, most of this earlier promising work has been discredited. First, problems with methodology were discovered. Then, some deliberate cheating was discovered (Hansel 1989). Even more damning is that the results haven't been confirmed by anyone (at least not in a repeatable and convincing manner). If telepathy had already been on shaky ground, it is now in quicksand. However, it remains a common science fiction trope, especially for aliens, but sometimes also for humans under special circumstances. Therefore, it's worth thinking of a potential model, even if it seems to strain possibility now. The most logical way in which we could possibly explain telepathy is if brain activity were to be transmitted via electromagnetic waves from one brain to another as discussed recently by Lawrence Krauss (Krauss, *Beyond Star Trek* 1997) and earlier by Milton Rothman (Rothman 1988). As told by the robot in the "Invaders of the 5th Dimension" episode of *Lost in Space* when asked if he could read minds he replies, "Minds emit waves. Waves may be captured and computed back into words." This is essentially the way in which we get radio or television broadcasts and now are becoming the more common ways of transmitting telephone calls, texts and internet in general. However, it's been known for decades that electrical activity in the brain is very weak, in the energy range of milliwatts (remember that even with newer compact florescent bulbs, the typical household light is tens of *watts*). Though this is discouraging news for those who hope for telepathy between humans, it leaves room open for alien telepathy (though even if an alien being were able to transmit more powerful waves, we have no known natural way to receive brain transmissions). Note that this does not mean that the author thinks that there is a physical explanation for claims of E.S.P., telepathy and the like, but it does leave an opening to explain such things as presented in science fiction.

Another form of telepathy is possession of one mind by another, such as in *ST:TNG* episode "The Turnabout Intruder" in which Dr. Janice Lester takes over Kirk's body with her mind (and transfers Kirk's mind into her body).

In *Physics of the Impossible*, Michio Kaku discusses whether it might be possible to achieve the goal of telepathy technologically, perhaps by enhancing medical devices that have already been developed. He uses the evidence that functional MRI (fMRI) scanners are able to indicate which sections of the brain are particularly active when the test subject reports to be in particular moods. This is a far cry from interpreting specific thoughts, though it may just be a matter of resolution. For instance, if such technology were able to improve to the point that it could track activity in ever smaller sections of the brain, it could potentially track something close to isolated thoughts.

Precognition

Precognition is difficult to reconcile with physics, though may remotely be possible if tachyons exist. If somehow messages can be sent backward in time using tachyons, then the people who were able to receive these (there probably wouldn't be a natural way to do this, but they might possess a means for detecting tachyons from someone else who wanted to intentionally let people in the past know what was going to happen). A prime example of precognition from science fiction is the film *Minority Report*, based on the Phillip K. Dick short story. Here the police are charged with capturing criminals before they commit crimes by using "precogs" (a few isolated clairvoyant individuals) to predict when and where crimes will happen.

Remote Viewing

Related to the ability of precognition is remote viewing. Essentially, this is the ability to see a distant event in real time, regardless of distance to the object, let alone absence of any known method for detecting these events from afar. If there is no distance related delay between the event happening in its own frame of reference, and an observer detecting it (neglecting further complications due to relativity) then this essentially is the same as precognition, since no observer could have possibly seen the light from this event yet under such circumstances. An early example of this is in the "Human Circuit" episode of *Science Fiction Theater*. Here a patient of a neurologist tells him that she has had visions of a strange event, a bomb explosion. After discussing this patient with a physicist colleague, the physicist, who witnessed an accidental explosion that day at a weapons test site in the Pacific, becomes convinced that this patient has paranormal abilities. Then, using physical principles (those of television), he is able "tune" her mind to various events. In particular, she is able to see a plane crash in what is assumed to be real time, and is able to report to authorities that she has seen a survivor. This survivor is then rescued.

Psychokinesis

Similarly characters go even farther than telepathy and use psychokinesis to move objects and most nefariously, commit murder. In *The Outer Limits* episode "The Man with the Power," physicist Harold Finley invented an implant (in front of the brain's frontal lobes) that focused "cosmic energy" to give him psychokinetic abilities. In the *ST:TOS* episode "Charlie X" a human boy is raised by a powerful telepathic alien race and begins to gain their abilities, which include being able to transform and even totally destroy individual people and starships at will. In the end, he becomes so destructive to his human hosts on the *Enterprise* that those who raised him come to take him back. *Space: 1999* introduced a similar character (though here influenced by an outside force in the form of a spiral cloud) in its episode "The Lambda Factor." In this episode, we can also see the anachronism of testing for E.S.P. with Zener cards (cards with special symbols, such as sets of wavy lines, developed by early researchers at Duke University for testing psychic powers). The cards were even anachronistic for researchers in the 1970s (the time of the filming of the episode), as computer programs were already being developed for this purpose. The "Twiki Is Missing" episode of *Buck Rogers in the 25th Century* featured a team of psychokinetic women who were enforcers for an entrepreneur attempting to steal the robot, Twiki, from Buck. The "Journey to Oasis" episode of the same series featured a blue-skinned dwarf alien, Odee-X, who was capable of psychokinesis. More recently, we see in *Looper* that a fraction of the population has a mutation that leads to telekinetic ability. In most cases the ability is mild, and as the film portrays, it's not good for much other than attempting to impress the opposite sex with floating quarters in the air. However, there is one overlord, the Rainmaker, who possesses much stronger abilities (and it is suggested that these powers that manifested themselves when he was a child probably led to his ability to become so powerful). In the previously mentioned mini-series, *Ascension*, a young girl onboard has extreme psychokinetic powers which appear to even be able to teleport people.

In general, the objections to psychokinesis are similar to those for telepathy, with even tighter restrictions. Somehow energy would have to make it from the transmitting person (that with the power of psychokinesis) to the receiving person or object. Or the person would have to be able to alter or counteract the local gravity field from the Earth near the receiving object. Altering gravity is very difficult, as it requires manipulating large masses or the equivalent amount of energy. It may be possible to counteract gravity over a small area by creating a magnetic field. However, then we would need a means for creating such a strong magnetic field.

Super-Intelligence

In some cases intelligence can be enhanced by a particular experience. An early example of this is the "Brain Unlimited" episode of *Science Fiction Theater*. Here a scientist develops a drug to enhance brain activity by a factor of a million. In the "Change of Space" episode of *Lost in Space*, the child prodigy Will Robinson experiences greatly increased intelligence after a spaceship he commandeers is able to go past the speed of light. The implication is that going through some sort of space-time warp had changed his brain structure. Two officers of the *Enterprise* had a similar experience in the "Where No Man Has Gone Before" episode of *ST:TOS*. Here they began to show increased intelligence and other powers after encountering an energetic barrier at the edge of the Galaxy (which, by the way, does not really exist). In addition, in the *ST:TOS* episode "Spock's Brain," the underground inhabitants of a planet are able to use a machine to increase their brain power and knowledge. In this particular episode, they need the knowledge of the machine to conduct brain surgery on Spock. In fact, they steal his brain to use as a controller for their underground colony. Dr. McCoy then later uses the same machine so that he can gain enough skill to know how to restore Spock's brain. In a later *ST:TNG* episode, "The Nth Degree," Barclay is temporarily granted greatly increased intelligence by the Cytherians. When Barclay is unable to access the computer quickly enough to affect changes to the endangered Argus array, he directly interfaces his brain with the *Enterprise* computer in order to more effectively and quickly accomplish the Cytherians' goals. In the original *The Outer Limits* episode "The Sixth Finger" (based on an earlier 1931 short story, "The Man Who Evolved," by Edmond Hamilton), a man who is caught inside a machine that claims to accelerate biological evolution via mutations, turns into a considerably more intelligent man (estimated to be 20,000 years ahead of his time) with an obviously immense head, presumably holding his larger and more efficiently utilized brain.

Extra Strength

We see evidence of superhuman strength among many aliens and superheroes. What may be the ultimate cause of relatively greater strength? In the case of the classic hero, Superman, Kakalios has proposed that his ability to leap over tall buildings is perhaps due to his home planet, Krypton, having stronger gravity. Thus, when coming to the Earth, he would find it considerably easier to, say, leap tall buildings in a single bound (Kakalios 2005). However, it's unlikely that this would lead to general overall strength since we know that muscle will atrophy over time when exposed to weaker gravity for long periods.

There may be more prosaic ways for an alien to gain relatively greater strength than considered normal for a human. For instance, here on Earth, various primates, such as chimpanzees and apes, can be significantly stronger for their size as compared to humans. However, at least on Earth, this greater strength is limited to a factor of several or so (depending on which sources you trust). This may be enough to account for the greater strength of Klingons and others.

Enhanced Vision and Hearing

The easiest way to enhance vision (for a person or a similar animal) in terms of the most fundamental physics would be to have larger eyes, and in particular, larger lenses and pupils. This would let more light into the eye (so that we could see under dimmer conditions) and increase resolution (ability to see fine details). Another way to improve vision is to improve the detector, which in the case of many animals are the specialized nerve cells, rods and cones, in the retina. The rods mainly are sensitive to the intensity of a broad spectrum of light, and the cones are sensitive to particular colors (Hecht and Zajac 1974). There's no *a priori* reason why another species couldn't have better vision in these ways. In fact, certain predatory animals, such as dogs and cats, have higher ratio of rods than humans, and are thus more sensitive to lower levels of light, as we would expect for an animal that might need to hunt (or escape being hunted) at night. We might then ask why humans do not have better vision than we have. In terms of human evolution, there are always trade-offs. Bigger eyes will mean either having a bigger head, or something else in the head (such as the rest of the brain) would have to be smaller. Thus, we have evolved to maximized brainpower while still keeping everything else good, though not necessarily the best it could be considering physics.

We should consider whether it's possible to see at other wavelengths of light besides the visible spectrum. It's worth discussing whether or not the X-ray vision discussed in science fiction really is referring to real world X-rays. In many cases it would seem that this is not so, such as being able to see through walls (and clothing) and see everything on the other side in full color. Here, we can be sure that the term "X-ray vision" is being used metaphorically to mean "looking through an opaque barrier." For true X-ray vision, it would be particularly difficult for animal eyes to be able to see at dramatically different wavelengths of light, as is the case with Superman and X-ray vision. Humans (and most animals) are slightly sensitive to ultraviolet and infrared light, and even marginally, to X-rays, but we would not be able to collect or focus X-rays very well. Though mathematical formulas for resolution would have us believe that we could possibly easily resolve X-rays with something the size of human eyes, the real problem is that X-rays are so energetic that organic materials in animal eyes would not be able to focus them. In addition, since there are no bright natural sources of X-rays, if our eyes were sensitive to X-rays, but not sensitive to light of the visible spectrum, then we'd have the problem of living in complete darkness. Perhaps having larger eyes in order to collect more light would be able help with this somewhat, but we already know the trade-offs that could involve. However, X-ray astronomers have been able to do this by building telescopes made out of concentric cylindrical mirrors lined with gold. Though we could perhaps imagine a robot created with eyes that could do this to a limited degree, it's hard to imagine an organic life-form that could naturally evolve this way, especially if they otherwise looked like humans. Furthermore, if we think that X-ray vision really means "seeing an object as it scatters or absorbs X-rays," as is the case with X-ray images of the human body, then Superman and others endowed with this type of vision would have to be emitting X-rays themselves in order to see the objects in shadow, essentially. Another method for achieving some of the same goals but with less energy would be in the use if microwaves, which is the method now employed by the TSA security screeners in the United States.

In *ST:TOS*, Vulcans are occasionally depicted as having particularly sensitive hearing relative to humans. For instance, in "The Way to Eden" Spock is intensely bothered by an ultrasonic weapon before Kirk and others can tell that it is being used.

Shape Shifting

An early example of a shape shifter from science fiction television is that of Garth of Izar in the *Star Trek: TOS* episode "Whom Gods Destroy." Born humanoid, he was shown the techniques of metamorphosis by the aliens of Antos when they found him injured on their planet. Though we are told that the Antosians had only intended to help Garth overcome his debilitating injuries, he had later used these powers to completely change his form, mostly for deceitful purposes. In this particular episode, as mentioned previously, he uses this technique to take over an insane asylum (by changing into Donald

Cory, the head of the asylum) where he has been committed and then later tries to take over the *Enterprise* (by first changing into Spock, and then changing into Kirk) by doing the same.

Shape shifting in science fiction has, at times, been a bit of a cheat. For instance, it's been a common means for escaping enemies at the last minute by means of turning into a bird, bug or mouse. In this sense it may seem like an easy out for writers and could have been easily dismissed as fantasy. At first we should consider that in a limited fashion, we could imagine shape shifting occurring in a manner similar, say, to plastic surgery. Minor changes would be possible with minor changes in mass and little expenditure of energy and practically no change at the molecular level. In fact, if the shape shifter didn't care about being an exact replica of the object he is changing into, but simply a convincing copy, this might be even easier. However, the more dramatically one changes form, the more difficult this becomes. For instance, when Maya in *Space: 1999*, a shape shifter they picked up from the planet Psychon as it exploded, changes into a mouse or an insect, where does the missing mass go? The same would apply to security officer Odo on *ST:DSN*, from a race of shape-shifters called Changelings. One possibility is that the mass goes nowhere, and if they turn into a mouse, they just become a very dense mouse. However, if the point is to become the creature they are transforming into, then much denser or lighter versions wouldn't be very convincing (imagine a 200-pound ant

Odo (René Auberjonois), the shape shifter from *Star Trek: Deep Space Nine*. Paramount Pictures/Photofest.

crawling on your foot). In case you are worried about Maya or Odo becoming a black hole: they would have to be concentrated into a radius of 10^{-25} m, which is many orders of magnitude smaller than any common animal or object they would turn into, even a virus. Transforming that amount of mass to energy would be enough to obliterate a large fraction of the Moon or whichever other planet or space station they happen to be on. This seems implausible, though the most advanced civilizations, able to manipulate enough energy to travel through the galaxy and travel through time may be able to handle the energy manipulation involved in these transformations. Some have suggested another way out. Perhaps if shape shifters were interdimensional beings, then they could, at will, "hide" some of their mass in a dimension or dimensions unseen to us.

Shape shifting has also made its way into several animated series, particular with the Wonder Twins, Zan (who can transform into different states of water) and Jayna (who could change into any kind of animal), of *Super Friends* , and then more recently with Beast Boy (who can change into any animal) of the *Teen Titans*.

Curiously, there was an extra limitation placed on Maya. It was revealed several episodes into the season during which she was introduced that she could only stay transformed for an hour. This restriction was likely introduced as an easy "trick" to allow for some dramatic tension on short timescales.

Shrinking and Growing

Though this can perhaps be seen as similar to shape shifting in general, the idea of being solely able to shrink or grow as an independent power (either as a natural power or aided by device) or pathology has been so popular in science fiction that it is worth exploring in and of itself. The details of "shrinkology" from a biological perspective are discussed in some detail in Mark Glassy's *The Biology of Science Fiction* (Glassy 2001), so I will mainly stick to the focus of physics. An early short story that shows a scientist shrinking after being exposed to a device that removes the space between atoms is "Submicroscopic" and the related story, "Uwlo of Ulm," both by S. P. Meeks. When shrunk, he experienced an entire sub-microscopic community with humanoids. This concept was later parodied in *The Simpsons* episode "The Genesis Tub," in which Lisa Simpson accidentally creates a microscopic society in a science fair project. Eventually the members of this society shrink her down to their size so they can ask her for help (they consider her to be a god). "The Genesis Tub" also parodies some elements of the *Twilight Zone* episode "The Little People," where astronauts from Earth land on a distant planet and encounter a microscopic civilization, though the miniature civilization here seems to have been the natural size of humanoids on that planet. A similarly themed early (1936) short story/novella was Henry Hasse's "He Who Shrank," in which a scientist subjects his assistant to a shrinking potion that makes him grow smaller and smaller until he is essentially comparable in size to atoms. When he is this small, he realizes that the molecules are like galaxies, and the individual atoms are much like stars and planets. As he approaches these planets, he realizes that they have civilizations, much like Earth. The story certainly shows that these worlds are recursive. That is, if he were to shrink even further, he'd again encounter atoms, but they realize that they too were inhabited planets (he goes through this cycle at least 30 times and then loses track). In the early sci-fi film *The Incredible Shrinking Man*, Scott Carey (Grant Williams) encounters a radioactive mist which causes him to shrink. First he shrinks to the size of a young boy, then to about the size of a mouse, and finally, without end, apparently, until he shrinks from view. In the 1966 film *Fantastic Voyage*, a team is temporarily shrunk down to microscopic size in order to the save the life of the only man who knows the secret of permanent miniaturization.

The shrinking man, Scott Carey (Grant Williams), and his normal-sized cat. From the 1957 film *The Incredible Shrinking Man*. Universal Pictures/Photofest.

10. Super-Human Powers

The closest nature comes to these effects of a shrink ray are the process of stellar evolution that work to make the core of star more compact. The overall effect is to remove most of the space between an electron and the nucleus, and then, for neutron stars, to make the entire star just as dense as the atomic nucleus by removing all of the space between the neutrons in the star. Indeed, the amount of shrinking we see in many of these tales suggests that, if the person is keeping all of his mass, then if he shrinks to be between about a millimeter and centimeter high, he'll reach white dwarf densities. If he shrinks to microscopic sizes, he'll eventually reach neutron star densities, and then become a black hole if he shrinks down to the size scale discussed above. At that point, he might be able to still exist, but nobody else would be able to see him, since no light would be able to escape from him, whether it is reflected light or light emitted due to the warmth of his body. Another type of miniaturization occurs in the *Starlost* episode "The Circuit of Death." Here, several characters become virtually miniaturized so they can repair microscopic circuits. Their bodies remain normal sized, hooked up to a computer. In the episode, this process is explained through a form of telekinesis in which their thoughts can be interpreted by the computer to make objects such as small wires move. This explanation is unfortunate since in today's terms, what we see in the episode could be more properly explained by a computer creating a virtual reality for the technicians (looking as if they have been miniaturized, so they can interact directly with the circuit, while also ensuring that the repairs to circuits are actually occurring).

In the *Lost in Space* episode "There Were Giants in the Earth," the Robinsons first notice that peas they planted in their garden on their new home planet, using native soil, grow to immense size and the large pods are invaded by a large parasitic organism. John Robinson hypothesizes that a number of creatures on the planet can undergo metamorphosis into giants, which they later witness. In another later *Lost in Space* episode, "Oasis," Dr. Smith (and the Robinsons' pet "bloop") grow to immense size after eating a native fruit. In the *Lost in Space* episode "Trip Through the Robot," the robot grows to immense size after being exposed to gases in an area they ominously name "Valley of the Shadows." Presumably these aren't the same types of gas that caused Scott Carey to shrink! In the *Voyage to the Bottom of the Sea* episode "Leviathan," geologist Tony Sterling grows to immense size after being exposed to "emissions" from an ocean floor fissure that goes down to the core of the Earth. Many of the sea creatures around him also grow to immense size. The entire television series *Land of the Giants*, another Irwin Allen production, features a space plane that accidentally passes through some sort of warp to a planet inhabited by giants (who in all other respects, seem very much like normal humans). Perhaps predictably, at least one episode is dedicated to the humans trying to grow to be the size of the giants ("Genius at

Work"), and another is dedicated to the giants trying to shrink down to the size of the humans in order to capture their spacecraft and its technology ("The Flight Plan").

Omnipotence

In some television episodes the protagonists are often confronted with an alien intelligence that at least at first seems omnipotent, and in fact, sometimes these antagonists introduced themselves as God. In the *ST:TOS* episode "Who Mourns for Adonais?," an alien introduces himself as the Roman god Apollo. In the *Space: 1999* episode "New Adam, New Eve," an alien who eventually admits he is really Magus first introduces himself as God. In *Lost in Space*, the imprisoned alien, Morbius, first introduces himself to Dr. Smith as the Devil. However, in each of these cases these divinities are shown to have significant limitations. Apollo needs a device (which is revealed to be in his temple) to help amplify his powers. Magus needs sunlight as a power source and an implant to help collect the energy from this light. Morbius is locked in his prison and needs others to get him out. In some other cases, the displayed powers of a particular species are so great that we may as well consider them to be omnipotent. One such case is the "Q" of *ST:TNG* (and then in later series). They can teleport at will without any technological aids (and teleport others, including an entire starship), travel in time and otherwise harness great amounts of energy in ways that seem unfathomable. We already know that interstellar travel and time travel (if possible) would both take tremendous amounts of energy, and if we were to encounter a civilization that has long been capable of such things, it may be that they seem to be omnipotent to us. However, Q, as presented in *ST:TNG* even goes beyond this level of energy manipulation, and at least implies he can change the gravitational constant of the Universe. This further implies that he can completely change the nature of the Universe he is in. Furthermore, he is even able to endow other mere mortals (such as Commander Riker) with similar powers (as in the "Hide and Q" episode of *ST:TNG*). However, this level of energy manipulation starts to strain credulity, and looks more to be a fantasy. Though, at least in the case of Q, he did appear to have some limitations. For instance, he could be limited in powers by other members of the Q continuum. More subtly, his own arrogance often hobbles him, even if it makes him more interesting for television.

Chapter Notes

Chapter 1

1. To get a sense for the strength of gravity over various scales of mass and distance, we can first compare the gravitational force between two people to that between one person and the Earth. In general, the formula for gravitational force is:

$$F_{grav} = \frac{GM_1M_2}{r^2}$$

Where here G is the universal gravitational constant, M_1 is the first gravitating mass, M_2 is the second gravitating mass and r refers to the distance between the two masses (for extended masses, it would refer to the distance between the centers of the two masses).

Substituting in the numbers for the first case (the gravity felt between two people):

$$F_1 = \frac{6.67 \times 10^{-11} \times 100 \times 100}{(1)^2} = 6.7 \times 10^{-7} \text{ Newtons}$$

And now the second (the gravity felt between a person and the Earth):

$$F_2 = \frac{(6.67 \times 10^{-11})(100) \times (6 \times 10^{24})}{(6.4 \times 10^6)^2} = 977 \text{ Newtons}$$

Now, taking the ratio between the two:

$$\frac{F_2}{F_1} = 1.5 \times 10^9$$

So, it's clear that the gravitational influence of the Earth on any person is billions of times greater than the gravitational influence of any two nearby people on each other. Generally speaking, gravity is very weak, unless you are close to a very massive object (a planet, star, etc.).

2. In thinking about whether the Moon could really escape Earth's orbit (or whether Earth could escape the Sun's, etc.), we have to consider what kinetic energy the Moon would have to have if it were to achieve escape velocity, and then compare this energy to the gravitational binding energy of the Moon. If the first is comparable to (or greater than) the second, then it isn't feasible for the Moon to escape, since that much energy applied to the Moon to get it to speed up would have obliterated it. The escape velocity of the Moon would be:

$$v = \sqrt{\frac{2GM}{R}}$$

Here, M is the mass of the central larger body, which in this case is the Earth. R stands for the radial distance between the center of mass of the system and the object which is escaping, which in this case is the Earth-Moon distance.

And substituting in the relevant numbers:

$$v = \sqrt{\frac{2 \times 6.67 \times 10^{-11} \times 6 \times 10^{24}}{3.8 \times 10^8}} =$$

1451 meters/sec (1.45 km/sec)
And the associated kinetic energy,

$$E = \frac{1}{2}mv^2$$

Where here the mass refers to the escaping object and in this case is the mass of the Moon, is:

$$E = \frac{1}{2} 7 \times 10^{22} \times 2.1 \times 10^6 = 7.4 \times 10^{28} \text{ joules}.$$

On the other hand, the gravitational binding energy is,

$$U = \frac{3GM^2}{5R} = 1.2 \times 10^{29} \text{ joules}$$

Thus it would take more than half of the binding energy of the Moon to get it to escape Earth's orbit, so, for the most part, (mostly) destroying it in order to free it. This is not a trivial amount of energy. It would take hundreds of millions times the energy released by the entire world's nuclear arsenal to come close to this level of energy.

Furthermore, the Moon, in the case of the 1970s television series, *Space: 1999*, would also have to escape the Sun's gravity, since we clearly see the Moon in that series traveling about the Galaxy.

In this case, using the mass of the Sun and the Earth-Sun distance:

$$v = \sqrt{\frac{2 \times 6.67 \times 10^{-11} \times 2 \times 10^{30}}{1.5 \times 10^{11}}} =$$

42,000m/sec (42 km/sec)

$$E = \frac{1}{2} 7 \times 10^{22} \times 1.8 \times 10^9 = 6.2 \times 10^{31} \text{ joules}$$

This is much greater than the binding energy of the Moon, and thus the Moon could never escape the solar system even if it could escape Earth's orbit (after having half of it obliterated!).

3. Next, we consider relativistic effects. Taking into account special relativity, we use the formula for time dilation:

$$t = t_0 \sqrt{\frac{1}{1-\beta^2}}$$

With $\beta=v/c=0.9$, where v is the speed and c is the speed of light, we can now substitute into the previous equation with $t_o=10$ years:

$$t = 10 \sqrt{\frac{1}{1-0.9^2}} = 23 \text{ years}$$

Chapter 3

1. We wish to see how the final velocity of a reaction rocket relates to the exhaust velocity and the mass used as fuel. In considering conservation of momentum involving a rocket that is losing mass via exhaust, we can arrive at an equation that relates the change in velocity to the change in mass. The precise details can be found in many advanced mechanics texts, such as *Classical Mechanics* (Taylor 2005). We start with:

$$dv = -v_{ex} \frac{dm}{m}$$

Here we note that the *dv* and the *dm* refer to very small (infinitesimal) changes in velocity and mass respectively, and v_{ex} refers to the exhaust velocity. Then if we integrate both sides with the limits that correspond to the initial (denoted by *0*) and final (denoted by *f*) values, we arrive at:

$$v_f - v_0 = v_{ex} \ln \left(\frac{m_0}{m_f}\right)$$

This result is often referred to as "The Rocket Equation." The "ln" refers to the natural log function, m_0 is the initial mass including all of the fuel, and m_f is the final mass after the fuel is expended. Now we can substitute in the numbers discussed in Chapter 3. If we assume a mass ratio of 5 and an exhaust velocity of 2 km/sec, we get a final velocity of 3.2 km/sec (we assume that the initial velocity is zero).

We can derive a similar result for a "relativistic" rocket equation, for which the exhaust velocity is an appreciable (at least 1%) fraction of the speed of light, following (Symon 1971):

$$\beta \gamma = \frac{1}{2} \left[\left(\frac{m_0}{m_f}\right)^B - \left(\frac{m_0}{m_f}\right)^{-B} \right]$$

Here the mass ratio has the same meaning as before. B refers to the ration of the exhaust velocity to the speed of light. β stands for the ratio of the final velocity to the speed of light, and γ is an additional factor that is dependent on the ratio β in the following way:

$$\gamma = \frac{1}{\sqrt{1-\beta^2}}$$

In many cases, it will be more instructive to solve the relativistic rocket equation for the mass ratio. In this way, we can see how much mass in fuel we need to get the rocket up to a particular velocity (and also based on a particular exhaust velocity). Solving for the mass ratio, we can derive the following expression (Goswami 1983):

$$\frac{m_0}{m} = \left(\frac{1+\beta}{1-\beta}\right)^{1/2B}$$

If we put in the numbers from the relativistic rocket example given in Chapter 3 (assuming that the exhaust velocity is about one tenth of the speed of light, we get:

$$\frac{m_0}{m_f} = \left(\frac{1+0.99}{1-0.99}\right)^{1/0.2}$$

And, calculating further:

$$\frac{m_0}{m_f} = \left(\frac{1.99}{0.01}\right)^5 = 3.12 \times 10^{11}$$

For comparison, we can substitute into the non-relativistic rocket equation, to get a sense for how "wrong" we would be in using it for this example.

$$\frac{m_0}{m_f} = e^{0.99/0.1} = 2\times 10^4$$

So, we would underestimate the fuel needed by a factor of more than 10 million if we had not used the relativistic rocket equation.

Chapter 6

1. Binary numbers are based on powers of 2, similar to the way that "base 10" numbers are based on powers of 10. They are then represented by the only two digits in the system, 0 and 1. For instance, 2 is represented by the digit 1, which is 2 raised to the zeroth power. Four is represented by 10, which is two raised to the first power. If we wanted to represent 3 in binary, that would be 2 to the zeroth power plus 2 to the first power, which is represented by 11.
Another way of think about this is as follows: In base-ten numbers, the number 271 is actually a sum of $2 \times 10^2 + 7 \times 10^1 + 1 \times 10^0$, that is, it's a sum of multiples of descending powers of ten. When thinking of binary numbers, they are a sum of multiples of descending powers of two. So, 111 in binary, "translated" into base 10 is $1 \times 2^2 + 1 \times 2^1 + 1 \times 2^0$, which is 7 (Hua, Weiland and Drummond 2014).

Chapter 7

1. If we want to completely turn a human being into energy in order to teleport him, the energy requirements would be determined by:

$E = mc^2 = (100)(3 \times 10^8)^2 = 9 \times 10^{18}$ Joules

This would be about the energy needed to run a large city for a year, so clearly enormous, for just taking apart one person.
However, to instead break apart a person into their constituent protons and neutrons, would take a fraction of that energy. Unfortunately though, as Lawrence Krauss points out in *The Physics of Star Trek,* if one wants to send these particles down to a planet's surface at close to the speed of light, relativistic mechanics dictates that you will need at least the rest mass energy of all the constituent particles up to many times more. Thus, in reality, you will likely lose all you save by avoiding turning all of the matter into energy in the first place.

Chapter 8

1. To consider the potential destructive energy of a colliding asteroid, the kinetic energy of an asteroid is dictated by the equation:

$$E = \frac{1}{2}Mv^2$$

Here, M is the mass, and in the case of a dinosaur killer asteroid that is about 10 km (10,000 m) in diameter (D), and density is about 3000 kg/m³, and using the formula for mass cast in terms of density, ρ:

$$M = \frac{1}{6}\rho \pi D^3$$

If we assume that the velocity is about 10 km/sec (10,000 m/sec), then the kinetic energy is about 8×10^{22} Joules. From what we presented in the Chapter 7 section of the endnotes, we know this would be enough energy for a large city for 10,000 years!

2. In order to blow up a planet, you will need to bombard it with energy that exceeds the gravitational binding energy of the planet. Using the equation from Chapter 2 section of the endnotes, and using the mass and radius of the Earth:

$$U = \frac{3GM^2}{5R} = \frac{0.6 \times 6.67 \times 10^{-11} \times 3.6 \times 10^{49}}{6 \times 10^6} =$$

2.4 10^{32} joules

Even a terrawatt laser, the most powerful now on Earth (Cavelos 2000) would need trillions of years to give off this amount of energy. This would imply that even the most powerful lasers are at least quadrillions of times less powerful than a Death Star would need to be.
For a small moon or asteroid:

$$U = \frac{3GM^2}{5R} = \frac{0.6 \times 6.67 \times 10^{-11} \times 1.6 \times 10^{33}}{10^4} =$$

6.4×10^{18} joules

This is still a tremendous amount of energy, but destroying an asteroid with a laser would only take about a factor of one million greater power than what we have access to today.

Chapter 9

1. Next we attempt to quantify the number of intelligent civilizations in the Galaxy. The Drake Equation has taken on several forms that are all more or less equivalent, but here we take the form that's more commonly seen in modern textbooks, and is a little bit easier

to understand conceptually (and the factors are described in the text):

$$N_{civ} = N_* n_p f_p f_l f_i f_*$$

We can substitute in some reasonable estimates for these terms to see what we get for a final number. The number of stars in our Galaxy is usually estimated to be about 300 billion. Though we can't yet even observe 1% of the stars in the Galaxy directly, we can infer from the mass of the Galaxy (calculated from following the orbits of stars and gas), and the light we observe, approximately how many total stars there should be. From reasoning already discussed in the text, n_p is about 3, f_p is about 0.1, f_l is possibly as high as one, but f_i is likely to be substantially less. We don't know how much less, but we can start with 0.01. f_* (fraction of star's lifetime the species can survive) can be pessimistically assumed to be just about 10,000 years or so if you think will kill ourselves off soon. However, some think we may even be able to survive at least as long as the Sun, or even longer, if we escape to another star system by then. Perhaps more realistically, or just as a compromise, we can assume that the human race and any other similar civilization would be no more than about 100 million years (making the fraction about 0.01). Multiplying these numbers together, we get a total of about 10 million. A very optimistic number! However, just dialing down the expected lifetimes of a species back to 10,000 years would be enough to make the expected number of civilizations closer to a paltry 1,000. Extending the same reasoning to the other fractions, we can easily see how we could get a number as low as one (just us). We can also calculate the number density of civilizations (civilizations within a given volume) in the Galaxy by dividing the previous number by the volume of the Galaxy, which is approximately 3.9×10^{13} ly^3:

$$n = \frac{1.0 \times 10^7}{3.9 \times 10^{13}} = 2.6 \times 10^{-7} \text{ civilizations ly}^{-3}$$

This last expression of units should be read as civilizations per cubic light year. And, we can calculate an average distance between civilizations to be (assuming the civilizations are evenly distributed in the volume):

$$d = \frac{1}{\sqrt[3]{n}} = 157 \text{ light years}$$

This is an important result, since it implies that if we even are likely to have a civilization within hundreds of light years of us, we'd have to have millions of civilizations over the entire Galaxy. In fact if much closer stars were discovered to have technological civilizations it would imply that nearly every star in the Galaxy has intelligent life. So, though it might fly in the face of some science fiction, the nearest star system, that of Alpha Centauri, is unlikely to harbor any intelligent life, otherwise, it would imply the virtually every star system in the Galaxy has intelligent life. Of course we can't be sure until we get a closer look.

Bibliography

Adler, Charles. *Wizards, Aliens, and Starships*. Princeton, NJ: Princeton University Press, 2014.
Alfven, Hannes. *Worlds-Antiworlds*. San Francisco, CA: W. H. Freeman & Company, 1966.
Armitage, Philip. *Astrophysics of Planet Formation*. Cambridge, UK: Cambridge University Press, 2010.
Armstrong, Stuart, and Anders Sandberg. "Eternity in Six Hours: Intergalactic Spreading of Intelligent Life and Sharpening of the Fermi Paradox." *Acta Astronautica*, 2013: 1–13.
Bago, E. Palle, and C. J. Butler. "The Influence of Cosmic Rays on Terrestrial Clouds and Global Warming." *Astronomy and Geophysics*, 2000: 18–22.
Bailey, M. E., S. V. M. Clube, and W. M. Napier. *The Origin of Comets*. Oxford, UK: Pergamon Press, 1990.
Barad, Judith, and Ed Robertson. *The Ethics of Star Trek*. New York: Perrenial/HarperCollins, 2001.
Barrow, John D. *The Book of Universes*. New York: W. W. Norton & Company, 2011.
Beech, Martin. *Alpha Centauri: Unveiling the Secrets of Our Nearest Neighbor*. New York: Springer, 2015.
Beiser, Arthur. *Concepts of Modern Physics*. Boston, MA: McGraw-Hill, 2003.
Benneke, Bjorn, and Sara Seager. "How to Distinguish Between Cloudy Mini-Neptunes and Water/Volatile-Dominated Super-Earths." *Astrophysical Journal*, 2013: 153–172.
Bennett, Jeffrey, and Seth Shostak. *Life in the Universe*. Boston, MA: Addison-Wesley, 2012.
Bernstein, Jeremy. *Nuclear Weapons*. Cambridge, England, UK: Cambridge University Press, 2008.
Blau, Steven. "Space-Station Experiment Measures Arriving Positrons with Unprecedented Precision." *Physics Today*, 2013: 66,6,12–13.
Brotherton, Michael. "Deja New." In *Fringe Science*, by K. Grazier, 81–96. Dallas, TX: Ben Bella Books, 2011.
Bullock, M. A., and D. H. Grinspoon. "Evolution of Venus' Climate and Implications for Terrestrial Exoplanets." *Comparative Climatology of Exoplanets*, 2012.
Caroll, B., and D. Ostlie. *Introduction to Modern Astrophysics*. San Francisco, CA: Addison-Wesley, 2007.
Caroti, Simone. *The Intergenerational Starship in Science Fiction: A Critical History, 1934–2001*. Jefferson, NC: McFarland, 2011.
Carroll, Sean. *From Eternity to Here*. New York: Plume, 2013.
———. *The Particle at the End of the Universe*. New York: Penguin Group, 2012.
Cavelos, Jeanne. *The Science of Star Wars*. New York: St. Martin's Griffin, 2000.
Clegg, Brian. *How to Build a Time Machine: The Real Science of Time Travel*. New York: St. Martin's Press, 2011.
Clery, Daniel. *A Piece of the Sun: The Quest for Fusion Energy*. New York: Overlook Duckworth, 2013.

Close, Frank. *Anti-matter.* Oxford, UK: Oxford University Press, 2009.
Clute, John, and Peter Nichols. *The Encyclopedia of Science Fiction.* New York: Saint Martin's Griffin, 1995.
Clynes, Mafred E., and Nathan S. Kline. "Cyborgs and Space." *Astronautics,* 1960: 26–27; 74–76.
Cooper, Keith. "New Model Could Help ID Potentiallly Habitable Alien Planets." *Yahoo News.* September 12, 2013. http://news.yahoo.com/model-coud-help-id-potenitally-habitable-alien-planets-184631265.html (accessed September 13, 2013).
Cox, Donald P., and Ronald J. Reynolds. "The Local Interstellar Medium." *Annual Reviews of Astronomy and Astrophysics,* 1987: 303–344.
Crowell, Lawrence. *Can Star Systems Be Explored?* Singapore: World Scientific, 2007.
Dainton, Barry. *Time and Space.* Montreal, Canada: McGill-Queen's University Press, 2010.
Darling, David. *Teleportation: The Impossible Leap.* Hoboken, NJ: John Wiley & Sons, 2005.
Davies, Paul. *Superforce.* New York: Simon & Schuster, 1984.
Davis, Marc, Piet Hut, and Richard A. Muller. "Extinction of Species by Periodic Comet Showers." *Nature,* 1984: 715–717.
Diehl, Roland, et al. "Radioactive 26Al and Massive Stars in the Galaxy." *Nature,* 2006: 45–47.
Draine, Bruce T. *The Physics of the Interstellar and Intergalactic Medium.* Princeton, NJ: Princeton University Press, 2011.
Dvali, Georgi. "Quantum Black Holes." *Physics Today,* 2015: 68, 1, 38–43.
Dyson, Freeman. "Interstellar Transport." *Physics Today,* 1968: 21, 10, 41–45.
Dyson, George. *Project Orion: The True Story of the Atomic Spaceship.* New York: Henry Holt and Company, 2002.
Encrenaz, Therese. *An Introduction to Planets: Ours and Others.* Singapore: World Scientific, 2013.
Engber, Daniel. "Bas Lansdorp has a Posse." *Popular Science,* November 1, 2014: 47–51.
Everett, Allen, and Thomas Roman. *Time Travel and Warp Drives.* Chicago, IL: University of Chicago Press, 2012.
Forward, Robert. "Probability of Interstellar Travel: A Review." *Acta Astronautica,* 1986: 243–252.
Freeman, Ken, and Geoff McNamara. *In Search of Dark Matter.* Chichester, UK: Praxis Publishing, 2006.
Galileo Galilei. *Dialogue Concerning Two New Sciences.* New York: Macmillan, 1914.
Gamble, David. *Skeptical Science.* July 17, 2015. http://www.skeptical-science.com/science/mini-ice-age-2030-nope/ (accessed July 24, 2015).
Gannon, Megan. "Did Earth Life Come from Space? Tough Algae Suggests Panspermia Possibility." *Yahoo News.* Sept. 26, 2013. http://news.yahoo.com/did-earth-life-come-space-tough-algae-suggests-193257118.html (accessed Sept. 26, 2013).
Gibbs, W. Wyatt. "Triple-Threat Method Sparks Hope for Fusion." *Nature,* 2014: 505, 1, 9–10.
Glassy, Mark C. *The Biology of Science Fiction Cinema.* Jefferson, NC: McFarland, 2001.
Gleick, James. *Chaos: The Making of a New Science.* New York: Viking Press, 1987.
Gooden, Brett. *Spacesuit: A History Through Fact and Fiction.* Sussex, UK: Tattered Flag Press, 2012.
Goswami, Amit. *The Cosmic Dancers: Exploring the Science of Science Fiction.* New York: McGraw Hill, 1983.
Gott, J. Richard. *Time Travel in Einstein's Universe.* New York: Mariner Books, 2002.
Grams, Martin. *Science Fiction Theater.* Albany, GA: Bear Manor Media, 2011.
Greene, Brian. *The Hidden Reality: Parallel Universes and the Deep Laws of the Cosmos.* New York: Knopf, 2011.
Hanley, Richard. *Is Data Human? The Metaphysics of Star Trek.* New York: Basic Books, 1997.
Hansel, C. E. M. *The Search for Psychic Power.* Buffalo, NY: Prometheus Books, 1989.
Harris, A. W., and G. E. Bromage. "The Abundance of Interstellar Chlorine in the Galaxy." *Monthly Notes of Royal Astronomical Society,* 1984: 941–953.

Bibliography 223

Hartle, James B. *Gravity: An Introduction to Einstein's Relativity.* San Francisco, CA: Addison-Wesley, 2003.
Hatch, Alden. *Buckminster Fuller at Home in the Universe.* New York: Crown Publishers, 1974.
Hawking, Stephen. "A Brief History of Relativity." *Time,* December 27, 1999.
Hecht, Eugene, and Alfred Zajac. *Optics.* Reading, MA: Addison-Wesley, 1974.
Heller, Rene, and Jorge I. Zuluaga. "Magnetic Shielding of Exomoons Beyond the Circumplanetary Habitable Edge." *Astrophysical Journal Letters,* 2013: 33-39.
Higgins, Paul A. T. "How to Deal with Climate Change." *Physics Today,* 2014: 67, 10, 32-37.
Hinton, Geoffrey E. "How Neural Networks Learn from Experiment." In *Understanding Artificial Intelligence,* by Editors of Scientific American, 42-58. New York: Warner Books, 2002.
Houghton, John. "Global Warming." *Reports on Progress in Physics,* 2005: 1343-1403.
Hua, David, Austin Weiland, and Scott Drummond. "Bits, Bites, and Binary: The Mathematics of Computers." *Tech Directions,* 2014: 18-23.
Huffman, Carl A. *Philolaus of Croton: Pythagorean and Presocratic.* Cambridge, UK: Cambridge University Press, 1993.
Huggett, Nick. *Space From Zeno to Einstein.* Cambridge, MA: The MIT Press, 1999.
Jayawardhana, Ray. *Stramge New Worlds: The Search for Alien Planets.* Princeton, NJ: Princeton University Press, 2011.
Jenkins, Susan, and Robert Jenkins. *The Biology of Star Trek.* New York: HarperCollins, 1998.
Johnson, John A. "Warm Planets Orbiting Cool Stars." *Physics Today,* 2014: 67, 3, 31-37.
Johnson, Richard, and Charles Hebrow. *Space Settlements: A Design Study.* Washington, D.C.: Scientific and Technical Office, NASA, 1977.
Kakalios, James. *The Physics of Superheroes.* New York: Penguin Group, 2005.
Kaku, Michio. *Hyperspace.* New York : Doubleday, 1994.
———. *Physics of the Future.* New York: Doubleday, 2011.
———. *The Physics of the Impossible.* New York: Doubleday, 2008.
Kanas, Nick. "From Earth's Orbit to the Outer Planets and Beyond: Psychological Issues in Space." *Acta Astronautica,* 2011: 576-581.
Karl, Thomas R., et al. "Possible Artifacts of Data Biases in the Recent Global Surface Hiatus." *Science,* 2015: 348: 1469-1472.
Kay, Laura, Stacy Palen, Brad Smith, and George Blumenthal. *21st Century Astronomy.* New York: W.W. Norton and Company, 2013.
Kite, Edwin, and Andrew Howard. "Let's Send the DOE to Alpha Centauri." *Physics Today,* 2013: 66, 9, 8-9.
Klass, Phillip J. *UFO's Explained.* New York: Random House, 1974.
Knutson, Heather A. "Exoplanet Atmospheres." *Physics Today,* 2013: 64-65.
Kondo, Y. *Interstellar Travel and Multi-generation Starships.* Toronto, Ontario, Canada: Apogee Books, 2003.
Kramer, David. "Lasers Will Shine in Future Warfare." *Physics Today,* 2014: 67, 7, 20-23.
———. "Taking The Next Steps in Fusion Ignition Quest." *Physics Today,* 2015: 68, 2, 24.
Krauss, Lawrence M. *Beyond Star Trek.* New York: Basic Books, 1997.
———. *The Physics of Star Trek.* New York: HarperCollins, 1995.
Krauss, Lawrence M., and Glenn D. Starkman. "arXiv.org." *arXiv:astro-ph/0404510v2.* May 10, 2004. arXiv:astro-ph/004510v2 (accessed Aug. 16, 2015).
Kring, David, and Mark Boslough. "Chelyabinsk: Portrait of an Asteroid Airburst." *Physics Today,* 2014: 67, 9, 32-37.
Kurzweil, Ray. *The Age of Spiritual Machines.* New York: Viking, 1999.
———. *The Singularity Is Near.* New York: Penguin Books, 2005.
Lean, Judith. "The Sun's Variable Radiation and Its Relevance for Earth." *Annual Review of Astronomy and Astrophysics,* 1997: 33-67.
Lecar, Myron, Fred A. Franklin, Matthew J. Holman, and Norman W. Murray. "Chaos in the Solar System." *Annual Reviews of Astronomy and Astrophysics,* 2001: 581-631.

Lehto, Steve. *The Great American Jet Pack: The Quest for the Ultimate Individual Lift Device*. Chicago, IL: Chicago Review Press, 2013.
Lewis, John S., and Ronald G. Prinn. *Planets and Their Atmospheres*. Orlando, FL: Academic Press, 1984.
Lovis, Cristophe, et al. "Neptune Mass Planets." *Nature*, 2006: 1–10.
Luhman, K. L. "A Search for a Distant Companion to the Sun with the Wide-field Infrared Survey Explorer." *Astrophysical Journal*, 2014.
Luokkala, Barry B. *Exploring Science Through Science Fiction*. New York: Springer, 2014.
Mallett, Ronald L. *Time Traveler: A Scientist's Personal Mission to Make Time Travel a Reality*. New York: Thunder's Mouth Press, 2006.
Manly, Steven. *Visions of the Multiverse*. Pompton Plains, NJ: Career Press, 2011.
Marschall, Laurence A. *The Supernova Story*. New York: Plenum Press, 1988.
Matloff, Gregory. "Fusion Starships." In *Going Interstellar*, by Les Johnson and Jack McDevitt, 197–217. Riverdale, NY: Baen, 2012.
Maudlin, Tim. *Philosophy of Physics: Space and Time*. Princeton, NJ: Princeton University Press, 2012.
Melia, Fulvio, and Heino Falcke. "The Supermassive Black Hole at the Galactic Center." *Annual Reviews of Astronomy and Astrophysics*, 2001: 309–352.
Mitchell, Flint, and William E. Anchors. *The Lost in Space Encyclopedia*. St. Louis, MO: LIS Fan Press, 2010.
Montandon, Mac. *JetPack Dreams: One Man's Up and Down (But Mostly Down) Search for the Greatest Invention that Never Was*. New York: Da Capo Press, 2008.
Moore, Patrick. *Space: The Story of the Greatest Feat of Exploration*. Garden City, NJ: The Natural History Press, 1969.
Moravec, Hans. *Mind Children: The Future of Robot and Human Intelligence*. Cambridge, MA: Harvard University Press, 1988.
Muir, John Kenneth. *A Critical History of Doctor Who*. Jefferson, NC: McFarland, 1999.
_____. *Exploring Space: 1999*. Jefferson, NC: McFarland, 1997.
Nahin, Paul J. *Time Machines: Time Travel in Physics, Metaphysics, and Science Fiction*. New York: AIP Press, 1999.
Neufeld, M. J. *Von Braun: Dreamer of Space, Engineer of War*. New York: Random House, 2007.
Nicolson, Iain. *Dark Side of the Universe: Dark Matter, Dark Energy, and the Fate of the Cosmos*. Baltimore, MD: The Johns Hopkins University Press, 2007.
Nocks, Lisa. *The Robot: The Life Story of a Technology*. Westport, CT: Greenwood Press, 2007.
Obousy, Richard. "Project Icarus: A Theoretical Design Study for an Interstellar Spacecraft." In *Going Interstellar*, by Les Johnson and Jack McDevitt, 219–232. Riverdale, NY: Baen, 2012.
Oldenburgh, G.J., A.T.J. de Laat, J. Luterbacher, W.J. Ingram, and T.J. Osborn. "Claim of Solar Influence Is on Thin Ice: Are 11-year Cycle Solar Minima Associated with Severe Winters in Europe?" *Evirnonmental Research Letters*, 2013: 1–7.
O'Neil, Gerard K. "The Colonization of Space." *Physics Today*, 1974: 32–40.
_____. *The High Frontier*. Princeton, NJ: Space Studies Institute Press, 1989.
Overbye, Dennis. "Astronaut and Writer at the Movies." *The New York Times*, October 1, 2013: D1.
_____. "Astronomers Find Biggest Black Holes Yet." *The New York Times*, December 5, 2011.
Pak, Chris. "Computers in Science Fiction: Anxiety and Anticipation." In *Science Fiction and Computing*, by David L. Ferro and Eric G. Swedin, 38–53. Jefferson, NC: McFarland, 2011.
Panek, Richard. *The 4% Universe*. Boston, MA: Mariner Books, 2011.
Parsons, P. *The Science of Doctor Who*. Baltimore, MD: The Johns Hopkins University Press, 2010.
Patterson, Joseph. "The Evolution of Cataclysmic and Low Mass X-ray Binaries." *The Astrophysical Journal*, 1984: 443–493.

Peebles, P. J. E. *Principles of Physical Cosmology*. Princeton, NJ: Princeton University Press, 1993.
Piore, Adam. "Friend for Life." *Popular Science*, November 1, 2014: 39–44; 83.
Plait, Philip. *Bad Astronomy*. New York: John Wiley & Sons, 2002.
Randall, Lisa. *Knocking at Heaven's Door*. New York: HarperCollins, 2011.
———. *Warped Passages*. New York: HarperCollins, 2005.
Reber, Paul. "What Is the Memory Capacity of the Human Brain?" *Scientific American*. April 10, 2010. http://www.scientificamerican.com/article.cfm?id=what-is-the-memory-capacity (accessed August 30, 2013).
Reed, B. Cameron. *The Physics of the Manhattan Project*. Berlin, Germany: Springer-Verlag, 2011.
Relaxnews Staff. "Scientists May Have Invented the Light Saber." *Yahoo News*. September 30, 2013. http://news.yahoo.com/scientists-may-invented-lightsaber-152606868.html (accessed September 30, 2013).
Retallack, Dorothy. *The Sounds of Music and Plants*. Marina del Rey, CA: DeVorss and Company Publishers, 1973.
Rogers, Lucy. *It's Only Rocket Science*. London, UK: Springer, 2008.
Rothman, Milton. *A Physicist's Guitde to Skepticism*. Buffalo, NY: Prometheus Books, 1988.
Sagan, Carl. *The Demon-Haunted World*. New York: Random House, 1995.
———. "Life in the Universe." In *All About Venus*, by Brian Aldiss, 141–147. New York: Dell Publishing Company, 1969.
Schmunk, Robert. "Science Briefs." *NASA GISS*. November 1, 1997. http:www.giss.nasa.gov/research/briefs/hansen_03/ (accessed Aug. 26, 2013).
Schroeder, Daniel V. *An Introduction to Thermal Physics*. San Francisco, CA: Addison Wesley Longman, 2000.
Schwarzschild, Bertram. "Earth-size Expolanets in Habitable Orbits are Common." *Physics Today*, 2014: 67, 1, 10–12.
———. "A Pulsar Reveals a Strong Magnetic Field Near Our Galaxy's Center." *Physics Today*, 2013: 66, 10, 12–14.
Seeds, Michael A. *Foundations of Astronomy*. Belmont, CA: Thomson Brooks/Cole, 2005.
Sharp, Z.D., and D.S. Draper. "The Chlorine Abundance of Earth: Implications for a Habitable Planet." *Earth and Planetary Science Letters*, 2012: 71–77.
Shaviv, Nir J., Giora Shaviv, and Rainer Wehrse. "The Maximal Runaway Temperature of Earth-like Planets." *Icarus*, 2011: 403–414.
Sheldrake, Rupert. *Science Set Free*. New York: Random House, 2012.
Shepherd, Simon J., Sergei I. Zharkov, and Valentina Zharkova. "Prediction of Solar Activity from Solar Background Magnetic Field Variations in Cycles 21–23." *The Astrophysical Journal*, 2014: 795:46–53.
Shostak, Seth. *Confessions of an Alien Hunter*. Washington, D.C.: National Geographic, 2009.
Shu, Frank H., Fred C. Adams, and Susana Lizano. "Star Formation in Molecular Clouds: Observations and Theory." *Annual Reviews of Astronomy and Astrophysics*, 1987: 23–81.
Silver, Brian. *The Ascent of Science*. New York: Solomon Books, 1998.
Sklar, Lawrence. *Philosophy of Physics*. Boulder, CO: Westview Books, 1992.
Smolin, Lee. *Time Reborn*. Boston, MA: Mariner Books, 2014.
———. *The Trouble with Physics*. New York: Houghton Mifflin Company, 2006.
Soal, S. G., and F. Bateman. *Modern Experiments in Telepathy*. New Haven, CT: Yale University Press, 1954.
Sofge, Erik. "When Inhumans Attack." *Popular Science*, July 14, 2014: 43–48.
Spiers, Edward M. *A History of Chemical and Biological Weapons*. London, UK: Reaktion Books, 2010.
Spitzer, Lyman. *Physical Processes in the Interstellar Medium*. New York: John Wiley & Sons, 1978.

Stevenson, David S. *Under a Crimson Sun: Prospects for Life in a Red Dwarf System*. New York: Springer, 2013.
Stocker, Thomas F., et al. *Climate Change 2013*. Cambridge, UK: Cambridge University Press, 2013.
Stuart, Sarah. *Into the Looking Glass: Exploring the Worlds of Fringe*. Toronto, Ontario, Canada: ECW Press, 2011.
Swedin, Eric G., and David L. Ferro. *Computers: The Life Story of a Technology*. Baltimore, MD: The Johns Hopkins University Press, 2005.
Symon, Keith. *Mechanics*. Reading, MA: Addison-Wesley, 1971.
Taylor, John R. *Classical Mechanics*. Sausalito, CA: University Sciences, 2005.
Tegmark, Max. *Our Mathematical Universe*. New York: Alfred A. Knopf, 2014.
____. "Parallel Universes." In *Fringe Science*, by K. Grazier, 53–80. Dallas, TX: Ben Bella Books, 2011.
Thomas, Kenneth S., and Harold J. McMann. *U.S. Spacesuits*. New York: Springer, 2006.
Thorne, Kip S. *Black Holes & Time Warps: Einstein's Outrageous Legacy*. New York: W. W. Norton & Company, 1994.
Tipler, Frank J. *The Physics of Immortality*. New York: Random House, 1994.
Tompkins, Peter, and Christopher Bird. *The Secret Life of Plants*. New York: Harper, 1973.
Trimble, Virginia. "Existence and Nature of Dark Matter in the Universe." *Annual Reviews of Astronomy and Astrophysics*, 1987: 425–472.
Tsonis, Anastasios. "Geoengineering Carries Unknown Consequences." *Physics Today*, 2013: 8–9.
Tyson, Neil DeGrasse. *Space Chronicles: Facing the Ultimate Frontier*. New York: W.W. Norton and Company, 2012.
Umino, Susumu, Kenneth Nealson, and Bernard Wood. "Drilling to Earth's Mantle." *Physics Today*, 2013: 66, 8, 36–41.
Van Riper, A. Bowdoin Van. *Rockets and Missles*. Westport, CT: Greenwood Press, 2004.
Vicsek, Tamas. *Fractal Growth Phenomena*. Singapore: World Scientific, 1989.
Vogt, Steven E., R. Paul Butler, E. J. Rivera, N. Haghighipour, Gregory W. Henry, and Michael H. Williamson. "The Lick-Carnegie Exoplanet Survey: A 3.1 Earth-mass Planet in the Habitable Zone of the Nearby M3V Star Gliese 581." *The Astrophysical Journal*, 2010: 723: 954–965.
Wall, Mike. "Earth Life Likely Came from Mars, Study Suggests." spacewww. August 29, 2013. http://news.yahoo.com/earth-life-likely-came-mars-study-suggests-221402608.html (accessed August 20, 2013).
____. "New Alien Life Claim Far from Convincing, Scientists Say." *Yahoo News*. Sept. 20, 2013. http://news.yahoo.com/alien-life-claim-far-convincing-scientists-163757104.html (accessed Sept. 20, 2013).
Ward, Peter D., and Donald Brownlee. *Rare Earth: Why Complex Life Is Uncommon in the Universe*. New York: Copernicus Books, 2000.
Weatherall, James Owen. *The Physics of Wall Street*. Boston, MA: Houghton Mifflin Harcourt Publishing, 2013.
Webb, Richard. "Primordial Broth of Life Was a Dry Martian Cup-a-soup." *New Scientist*. August 29, 2013. http//www.newscientist.com/article/dn24120-primordial-broth-of-life-was-a-dry-cupasoup.html?full=true&print=true (accessed September 3, 2013).
Weniger, Cristoph. "A Tentative Gamma-Ray Line from Dark Matter Annihilation at the Fermi Large Area Telescope." *Journal of Cosmology and Astroparticle Physics*, 2012: 1–18.
Westfahl, Gary. *The Spacesuit Film: A History, 1918–1969*. Jefferson, NC: McFarland, 2012.
Whitefield, Stephen E., and Gene Rodenberry. *The Making of Star Trek*. New York: Ballantine Books, 1968.
Wickramasinghe, Chandra. *A Journey with Fred Hoyle*. Singapore: World Scientific, 2014.
____. "Panspermia According to Hoyle." *Astrophysics and Space Science*, 2003: 255–258.
Wilson, Mark. "New Hydrogen-Isotope Measurements Refine the Picture of Water on Mars." *Physics Today*, 2015: 5:12–14.

Wood, Robert E. *Destination Moonbase Alpha: The Unofficial and Unauthorized Guide to Space: 1999*. Prestatyn, Denbighshire, UK: Telos Publishing, 2010.
Woodward, James F. *Making Starships and Stargates*. New York: Springer, 2013.
Woolf, N., and J. Roger Angel. "Astronomical Searches for Earth-Like Planets and Signs of Life." *Annual Reviews of Astronomy and Astrophysics*, 1998: 507–537.
Yahoo New Editorial Staff. "Has Global Warming Hit a Plateau?" *Yahoo News*. August 24, 2013. http:news.yahoo.com/global-warming-hit-plateau-100000352.html (accessed August 24, 2013).
Zicree, Marc Scott. *The Twilight Zone Companion*. Los Angeles, CA: Silman-James Press, 1989.
Zubrin, Robert. *The Case for Mars*. New York: Touchstone, 1996.
Zuckerman, B. "Dusty Circumstellar Disks." *Annual Reviews of Astronomy and Astroophysics*, 2001: 549–580.
Zuckerman, Ben. "The DOE Might Prefer a Living Planet." *Physics Today* (American Institute of Physics), January 2014.

Index

"AB Chrysalis" (episode of *Space: 1999*) 169
Abbott, Edwin 112
Abre Los Ojos 147
The Age of Spiritual Machines (non-fiction book by Ray Kurzweil) 142
Ahmed, S.W. 35, 119
Alfven, Hans 102
"All Good Things" (episode of *Star Trek: The Next Generation*) 125, 138, 203
"All Our Yesterdays" (episode of *Star Trek: The Original Series*) 40
"All That Glisters" (episode of *Space: 1999*) 190
"All the Troubles of the World"(short story of Isaac Asimov) 147
Allen, Paul 184
Alpha Centauri 15, 28, 58, 62, 74–76, 81–82, 88, 220
Alpha Magnetic Spectrometer (AMS) 34
"The Alternative Factor" (*Star Trek: The Original Series*) 101
amino acids 182, 202
Anderson, Poul 79, 85
android 126, 154, 155–58, 176
Angry Red Planet (film) 69, 75, 176
Another Earth (film) 105
"Another Time, Another Place" (episode of *Space: 1999*) 99
"The Anti-Matter Man" (episode of *Lost in Space*) 101, 103
"The Apple"(episode of *Star Trek: The Original Series*) 149
"Arena" (episode of *Star Trek: The Original Series*) 168
"The Ark in Space" (episode of *Doctor Who*) 88
Armageddon (film) 27
Ascension (television mini series) 79, 90, 208
Asimov, Isaac 6, 10, 12, 26, 47, 55, 57, 100, 142–43, 145, 149, 153, 154, 192, 193, 203–5
"Assignment: Earth" (episode of *Star Trek: The Original Series*) 127
Astronaut: The Last Push (film) 73

Atanasoff, John 141
"Attack of the Monster Plants" (episode of *Lost in Space*) 195
Automata (film) 153
Avatar (film) 193, 194, 199

"Back and Back and Back to the Future" (episode of *Farscape*) 137
"Back There" (episode of *Twilight Zone*) 128
Back to the Future (film) 124, 128, 137
Baker, Tom 43, 153, 155
"The Balance of Terror" (episode of *Star Trek: The Original Series*) 178
Barbarella (film) 167
Batman (television series) 176
Baumgartner, Felix 97
"The Beehive" (episode of *The Starlost*) 189
"Behold, Eck!" (episode of *The Outer Limits*) 112
"The Bellero Shield" (episode of *The Outer Limits*) 192
Big Bang 13, 29–32, 34, 103, 107, 115
Bill and Ted's Excellent Adventure (film) 127
black hole 7, 11, 24, 41–43, 86, 101, 108–9, 178, 213, 215
"Black Hole" (episode of *Ren & Stimpy*) 42
"Black Sun" (episode of *Space: 1999*) 42
"Blast Off into Space" (episode of *Lost in Space*) 28
The Blob (film) 202
"Blood Money" (episode of *Breaking Bad*) 161
Bohr, Neils 18–20
Booth, John Wilkes 128
Bradbury, Ray 69, 153, 170
Brahe, Tycho 40, 59
"The Brain Center at Whipples" (episode of *Twilight Zone*) 147
"The Brain Stealers of Mars" (short story of John Campbell) 195
"Brain Unlimited" (episode of *Science Fiction Theater*) 209
Breaking Bad (television series) 161

229

"Brian the Brain" (episode of *Space: 1999*) 147, 169
"Bringers of Wonder" (episode of *Space: 1999*) 177, 200, 204
Brooks, Rodney 144
Bush, Vannevar 141
Bussard, Robert 79
"By Any Other Name" (episode of *Star Trek:The Original Series*) 90

Calabi-Yau 115–16
Card, Orson Scott 170
Carnot, Sadi 11
Carol, Lewis 104
Carroll, Sean 22
Casimir Effect 86, 135
"Cause and Effect" (episode of *Star Trek: The Next Generation*) 131
"Cave of the Wizards" (episode of *Lost in Space*) 191
"The Chameleon" (episode of *The Outer Limits*) 163
"Change of Space" (episode of *Lost in Space*) 209
"The Changeling" (episode of *Star Trek: The Original Series*) 149, 205
"Charlie X" (episode of *Star Trek: The Original Series*) 208
"The Chase" (episode of Star Trek: The Next Generation) 203
"Chase Through Time" (episode of *The Time Tunnel*) 160
"The Circuit of Death" (episode of *The Starlost*) 215
"City of Death" (episode of *Doctor Who*) 125, 203
Clark, John 101
Clarke, Arthur C. 39, 69, 93, 95, 190
Clausius, Rudolf 12
"The Cloud" (episode of *Star Trek: Voyager*) 197
"The Cloud Minders" (episode of *Star Trek: The Original Series*) 53
cold fusion 17
"The Colonists" (episode of *Lost in Space*) 176
Colony (novel by Ben Bova) 95
comet 23, 32, 43, 48, 57–60, 82, 181, 186, 202
"The Condemned of Space" (episode of *Lost in Space*) 39
Contact (novel by Carl Sagan and film based on the novel) 86, 133, 181, 188
Copenhagen interpretation 19, 117–18
"Corpus Earthling" (episode of *The Outer Limits*) 190
cosmic microwave background 29–31, 108
"The Counterclock Incident" (*Star Trek: The Animated Series*) 106
"Counterweight" (episode of *The Outer Limits*) 98

Cramer, John 99–100, 108, 139
Crowell, Lawrence 75–76
"Cyborg"(episode of *Voyage to the Bottom of the Sea*) 158

Dark Energy 29–30, 135
Dark matter 32–33
Dark Matter (novel by S.W. Ahmed) 35, 119
"Dark Planet" (episode of *Space Patrol*) 194
"Datalore" (episode of *Star Trek: The Next Generation*) 197
Davisson, Clinton 19
The *Day the Earth Caught Fire* (film) 10
The *Day the Earth Stood Still* (film) 124, 150, 173
"Day the Sky Fell In" (episode of *The Time Tunnel*) 126
"The Death Clock" (episode of *Voyage to the Bottom of the Sea*) 112
Deathworld Trilogy (a trilogy of novels by Harry Harrison) 193
"Deja Q" (episode of *Star Trek*)
"Demon with a Glass Hand"(episode of *The Outer Limits*) 158
deuterium 16–17, 79–80, 182, 199
"Devil in the Dark" (episode of *Star Trek: The Original Series*) 172, 190, 205
"Devil's Planet" (episode of *Space: 1999*) 53, 161
Dick, Phillip K. 13, 53, 150, 161, 202
District 9 (film) 171
Do Androids Dream of Electric Sheep? (novel by Pillip K. Dick) 13
"Doctor Robot" (episode of *Science Fiction Theater*) 149
"Doomed Planet" (episode of *Fireball XL5*) 10
The *Doomsday Machine* (film) 27, 70, 170
"The Dorcons" (episode of *Space: 1999*) 161
"Dorzak" (episode of *Space: 1999*) 204
"Dragon's Domain" (episode of *Space: 1999*) 204
Drake, Frank 89, 184–85
"The Duplicates" (episode of *Tales of Tomorrow*) 105
Dyson, Freeman 78, 95

"Earthbound" (episode of *Space: 1999*) 88
Eddington, Arthur 15
Edge of Tomorrow (film) 179
Einstein, Albert 20
Einstein's Bridge (novel by John Cramer) 100, 108
electron 7, 18–20, 61, 102, 106, 215
Ellison, Harlan 146
Elysium (film) 95
"The Empath" (episode of *Star Trek: The Original Series*) 205
"The End of Eternity" (episode of *Space: 1999*) 88

Index 231

entropy 12–13
"Errand of Mercy" (episode of *Star Trek: The Original Series*) 192
Europa Report (film) 73
Everett, Hugh 117
"The Evitable Conflict" (short story of Isaac Asimov) 150
"The Exiles" (episode of *Space: 1999*) 88
"Eyes Do More Than See" (short story by Isaac Asimov) 192

Family Guy (television series) 109
Fantastic Voyage (film) 214
Farscape (television series) 100, 137, 193, 199
Feinberg, Gerald 137–38
Fermi, Enrico 169
Fermi Gamma Ray Observatory 34
Feynman, Richard 106
"Flaming Planet" (episode of *Lost in Space*) 195
Flatland (novel by Edwin Abbott) 112
"Flight into the Future" (episode of *Lost in Space*) 148
"The Flight Plan" (episode of *Land of the Giants*). 216
The Fly (film) 160
The Folk of the Fringe (short story collection by Orson Scott Card) 170
"For a Breath I Tarry"(short story by Roger Zelazny) 156
"For the World Is Hollow and I Have Touched the Sky" (episode of *Star Trek: The Original Series*) 90
Forbidden Planet (film) 87, 151, 153, 173, 177
"The Form of Things Unknown" (episode of *The Outer Limits*) 140
Forster, E.M. 149
Forward, Robert 41, 83
Foundation's Edge (novel by Isaac Asimov) 199
Frisch, Otto 169
"From Agnes—with Love" (episode of *Twilight Zone*) 148
From Earth to the Moon (novel by Jules Verne) 64–65
"From Venus with Love" (episode of *The Avengers*) 70
Frozen (film) 24

Galactic Exploration (series of novellas by Peter Cawdron) 85, 90, 187
"The Galaxy Being" (episode of *The Outer Limits*) 189
Galaxy Quest (film) 160, 191
Galileo 7, 14, 60, 189, 222
"The Gallery of Fear" (episode of *The Starlost*) 148
gauge field 8
Gell-Mann, Murray 21
"Genesis of the Daleks" (episode of *Doctor Who*) 124

"The Genesis Tub" (episode of *The Simpsons*) 213
"Genius at Work" (episode of *Land of the Giants*) 216
Goddard, Robert 64, 66
The Gods Themselves (novel by Isaac Asimov) 100
Goedel, Kurt 132
Gog (film) 87, 145, 176–77
Goldhaber, Maurice 102
Gorath (film) 62, 101, 102
Gorbachev, Mikhail 17
Gott, J. Richard 72, 136
grand unified theory (GUT) 22
Gravity (film) 6, 24, 27, 69, 91, 136
"The Great Vegetable Rebellion" (episode of *Lost in Space*) 194, 195
"The Green Death"(episode of *Doctor Who*) 147
"Green Patches" (novel by Isaac Asimov) 198
"Guardian of Piri"(episode of *Space: 1999*) 148, 161
Guardians of the Galaxy (film) 193, 196
Guth, Alan 31

habitable zone 182–83
"The Hand of Fear" (episode of *Doctor Who*) 190
Harrison, Harry 193
"He Built a Crooked House" (short story by Robert Heinlein) 112
"He Who Shrank" (short story by Henry Hasse) 214
heat death 13
"Hide and Q" (episode of *Star Trek: The Next Generation*) 216
hierarchy problem 21
Higgs boson 8, 21
Hinton, Charles 111
Hipparchus 35
"Home Soil" (episode of *Star Trek: The Next Generation*)" 191
Hubble, Edwin 29
Hubble Constant 30
"Human Circuit" (episode of *Science Fiction Theater*) 207
"The Hungry Sea" (episode of *Lost in Space*) 26
"Hypnotic Sphere" (episode of *Fireball XL5*) 205

"I Have No Mouth, and I Must Scream" (Harlan Ellison short story) 146
"I, Mudd"(episode of *Star Trek: The Original Series*) 149
"I Sing the Body Electric"(episode of the *Twilight Zone*) 153
"The Ice Warriors" (episode of *Doctor Who*) 176

"Immunity Syndrome" (episode of *Space: 1999*) 192
"Immunity Syndrome" (*Star Trek: The Original Series*) 197, 198
"In a Mirror, Darkly" (*Star Trek: Enterprise*) 99
"In His Image" (episode of *Twilight Zone*) 158
"In the Wink of an Eye" (episode of *Star Trek: The Original Series*) 140
"In Truth Is There No Beauty?" (episode of *Star Trek: The Original Series*) 192, 205
The Incredible Shrinking Man (film) 214
"The Infernal Machine" (episode of *Space: 1999*) 147
"Inferno" (episode of *Doctor Who*) 99
"The Infinite Vulcan" (episode of *Star Trek: The Animated Series*) 195
International Thermonuclear Experimental Reactor (ITER) 17
"Invaders from the 5th Dimension" (episode of *Lost in Space*) 105, 110, 113, 150, 206
Iron Man (film) 179

Jeans, James 36
"Journey to Oasis" (episode of *Buck Rogers in the 25th Century*) 208
Journey to the Far Side of the Sun (film) 104
Journey to the 7th Planet (film) 70, 205
"Journey to Where" (episode of *Space: 1999*) 52, 53, 123
"Journey with Fear" (episode of *Voyage to the Bottom of the Sea*) 70

Kaku, Michio 1, 83, 105, 111, 166, 171, 207
"Kaleidoscope" (short story by Ray Bradbury) 91
Kaluza, Theodor 113
Kanas, Nick 97
"The Kidnappers" (episode of *The Time Tunnel*) 129
"A Kind of Stopwatch"(episode of *Twilight Zone*) 139
King, Stephen 170
kipple 13
Klein, Oskar 102, 113
Krauss, Lawrence 143, 161, 178, 192, 206, 219
Kurzweil, Ray 142, 144, 157, 187

"The Lambda Factor" (episode of *Space: 1999*) 189, 208
Large Hadron Collider (LHC) 35, 42, 113
"The Last Enemy" (episode of *Space: 1999*) 104
"The Last Question" (short story by Isaac Asimov) 12, 143, 149
"The Last Sunset" (episode of *Space: 1999*) 50
"Lazarus from the Mist" (episode of *The Starlost*) 88
Lee, T.D. 105

LeGuin, Ursula 193
Leinster, Murray 193
lepton 21
"Let It Go" (song) 24
"Leviathan" (episode of *Voyage to the Bottom of the Sea*) 215
"The Lights of Zetar" (episode of *Star Trek: The Original Series*) 192
Linde, Andre 108
Lisey's Story (novel by Stephen King) 100
Little Green Men (novel by Peter Cawdron) 199
"The Little People" (episode of *Twilight Zone*) 56, 213
"The Lonely"(episode of *Twilight Zone*) 154
"The Lonesome Death of Jody Verril" (from the film *Creepshow*) 202
"The Long Morrow" (episode of *Twilight Zone*) 87
"The Long Sleep" (episode of *Science Fiction Theater*) 87
Looper (film) 131, 208
Lorenz, Edward 23
"The Loss" (episode of *Star Trek: The Next Generation*) 112
Lost in Space (television series) 10, 26–28, 39–40, 56–59, 62, 68, 80, 88, 91, 96, 101, 105, 110, 129, 142, 148, 151, 153, 154, 160, 165, 173, 178, 191, 197, 199, 204, 206, 209, 215
"The Lost Machine"(John Wyndham short story) 154
Lucky Starr and the Pirates of the Asteroids (novel by Isaac Asimov) 6

"The Machine Stops" (E.M. Forester short story) 149
Mach's Principle 84
Mallett, Ron 135
"The Man Who Evolved" (short story by Edmond Hamilton) 209
"The Man Who Was Never Born" (episode of *The Outer Limits*) 125
"The Man with the Power" (episode of *The Outer Limits*) 208
"The Mark of Archanon" (episode of *Space: 1999*) 88, 201
Mars 38–39, 50, 53–55, 58–59, 69–75, 78, 96, 98, 144, 154, 176–77, 182–83, 195, 203
Massive Compact Halo Objects (MACHO's) 33
The Matrix (film) 119
"A Matter of Balance" (episode of *Space: 1999*) 101, 106
"A Matter of Life and Death" (episode of *Space: 1999*) 101, 106
Maxwell, James 8
McKeon, Michael 147
McTaggart, John 121
"The Measure of a Man"(episode of *Star Trek: The Next Generation*) 154

Meeks, S.P. 213
Meisner Effect 124
"Menagerie" (episode of *Star Trek: The Original Series*) 26, 189, 204
"The Metamorph" (episode of *Space: 1999*) 10
"Metamorphisis" (episode of *Star Trek: The Original Series*) 197
"Midnight Sun" (episode of *Twilight Zone*) 10
"The Mighty Casey" (episode of *Twilight Zone*) 155, 156
"The Mindrobber"(episode of *Doctor Who*) 148
Minority Report (film and short story by Phillip K. Dick) 207
Minsky, Marvin 144
"Minus Planet" (short story by John Clark) 101
"Miri" (episode of *Star Trek: The Original Series*) 107
"Mirror, Mirror" (episode of *Star Trek: The Original Series*) 99, 100
"Missing Link" (episode of *Space: 1999*) 53
"Mission of the Darians" (episode of *Space: 1999*) 89
Mission to Mars (film) 69, 203
"Mr. Spaceship" (short story of Phillip K. Dick) 150, 197
Moon (film) 27
Moore, Gordon 142
Moore's Law 142–43
Moravec, Hans 152
Morgan, Jack 154
Muir, John Kenneth 99
Musk,Elon 73, 157
"The Mutant" (episode of *The Outer Limits*) 56, 190, 205

National Ignition Facility (NIF) 17
Nemesis (novel by Isaac Asimov) 47, 57, 199
Netanya (novel by Dror Burstein) 187
neutrino 33
neutron 21
"New Adam, New Eve" (episode of *Space: 1999*) 201, 216
Newton's Second Law 30
"Night Terrors" (episode of *Star Trek: The Next Generation*) 79, 205
Niven, Larry 40, 133
"No Time Like the Past" (episode of *Twilight Zone*) 128
Non-Stop (novel by Brian Aldiss) 90
"The Nth Degree" (episode of *Star Trek: The Next Generation*) 209

"Oasis" (episode of *Lost in Space*) 215
Oberth, Hermann 64
"Obsession" (episode of *Star Trek: The Original Series*) 196

"The Old Man in the Cave"(episode of *Twilight Zone*) 149
Omnes, Roland 102
"One Moment of Humanity" (episode of *Space: 1999*) 155
O'Neil, Gerard K. 93
Oort, Jan 32, 59
Ori, Amos 135
Orion 26, 222
Orphans in the Sky (novel by Robert Heinlein) 90
The Outer Limits (television series) 50, 56, 79, 112, 139–40, 158, 163, 189–90, 201, 208, 209
Overbye, Daniel 6

Pak, Chris 144
PAMELA 35, 103
"Parallels" (episode of *Star Trek: The Next Generation*) 117
Parallels (film) 117
"Penny for Your Thoughts" (episode of *Twilight Zone*) 205
Perlmutter, Saul 29
Philolaus of Croton 104
Phoenix Without Ashes (novel by Harlan Ellison) 90
Pioneer 11 24
Pioneer 10 24
Planck, Max 18, 36
Planck mass 21–22, 43, 115
Planck scale length 22
"The Planet of Evil" (episode of *Doctor Who*) 101
Planet of the Apes (film) 88, 129, 171
"Planet of the Spiders" (episode of *Doctor Who*) 160, 189
"The Plant Man" (episode of *Voyage to the Bottom of the Sea*) 195
"The Plant Man from Space" (episode of *Fireball XL-5*) 194
Poincare, Henri 23
"The Positronic Man" 154
"The Premonition" (episode of *The Outer Limits*) 139
Primer (film) 124
"Prisoners in Space" (episode of *Lost in Space*) 160
"Probe 7, Over and Out" (episode of *Twilight Zone*) 201
"Prominent Author" (short story of Phillip K. Dick) 161
proton 9, 21, 81, 103, 138, 161, 163, 172, 219
Proxima (novel by Stephen Baxter) 74–75, 79, 82, 150, 183, 188
"Proxima Centauri" (short story by Murray Leinster) 193
Ptolemy 35

"The Quality of Life" (episode of *Star Trek: The Next Generation*) 154, 166, 180

quantum gravity 21–22, 32, 108, 115
Quarantine (novel by Greg Egan) 20
quark 21
The Questor Tapes (film and novel by D.C. Fontana) 203
quintessence 31

Radio Free Albemuth (film and novel by Phillip K. Dick) 202
"Read to Me Herr Doktor"(episode of *Tales of Tomorrow*) 154
Reiss, Adam 29
"Relics" (episode of *Star Trek: The Next Generation*) 95
Rendevous with Rama (novel by Arthur C. Clarke) 95
"Requiem for Methuselah"(episode of *Star Trek: The Original Series*) 154
Resurrection (novel by Arwen Elys Dayton) 201
"Return from Outer Space" (episode of *Lost in Space*) 28, 165
"The Return of the Archons" (episode of *Star Trek: The Original Series*) 149
"Return to Tomorrow" (episode of Star Trek: The Original Series) 201
"The Revolt of the Androids" (episode of *Lost in Space*) 154
"The Ribos Operation" (episode of *Doctor Who*) 26
"Ring Around the Moon" (episode of *Space: 1999*) 189
"The Rip van Winkle Caper" (episode of *Twilight Zone*) 89
robot 70, 147, 150, 151–54, 155–58, 163, 206, 208, 211, 215
"Robot"(episode of *Doctor Who*) 153, 155
Roomba 144
Rubin, Vera 33, 133
"The Rules of Luton" (episode of *Space: 1999*) 195
Rutherford, Ernest 15, 21

Sagan, Carl 86, 133, 181, 188
Sakharov, Andrei 16
"Sally" (short story of Isaac Asimov) 145
"Sarek" (*Star Trek: The Next Generation*) 205
"The Savage Curtain" (episode of *Star Trek: The Original Series*) 191
Schmidt, Brian 29
"A Second Chance" (episode of *The Outer Limits*) 201
"Seed of Destruction" (episode of *Space: 1999*) 177
"Seeds of Doom" (episode of *Doctor Who*) 195
Serengeti (novella by Peter Cawdron) 187
Shaara, Michael 147
"Shattered Mirror" (*Star Trek: Deep Space Nine*) 99

Sheldrake, Rupert 24
"Ship in a Bottle" (episode of *Star Trek: The Next Generation*) 119
Short Circuit (film) 152
"Sideways in Time" (short story by Murray Leinster) 117
"Silicon Avatar" (episode of *Star Trek: The Next Generation*) 197
The Singularity Is Near (non-fiction by Ray Kurzweil) 144
"The Sixth Finger" (episode of *The Outer Limits*) 209
"Sky Pirate" (episode of *Lost in Space*) 28, 154, 204
Slade, Henry 111
Slaughterhouse Five (novel by Kurt Vonnegut) 136–37
Sleeper (film) 89
Slipher, Vesto 29
Smolin, Lee 108, 121
Solaris (film and novel by Stanislaw Lem) 199
"Sound That Kills" (episode of *Science Fiction Theater*) 176
"Space Brain" (episode of *Space: 1999*) 189, 197
"Space Creature" (episode of *Lost in Space*) 56, 197
"The Space Destructors"(episode of *Lost in Space*) 159
"Space Seed" (episode of *Star Trek: The Original Series*) 88
"Space Warp" (episode of *Space: 1999*) 200
"Specimen: Unknown"(episode of *The Outer Limits*) 194
"Spock's Brain" (episode of *Star Trek: The Original Series*) 77, 150, 209
"The Squire of Gothos" (episode of *Star Trek: The Original Series*) 169
The Stand (novel by Stephen King) 170
Standard Model 8, 21, 22, 21–22
Star Trek 1, 24–26, 40, 62–63, 67, 69, 79–80, 85–86, 88, 90, 93, 99, 101, 105, 110, 128, 142, 156, 158–64, 166–68, 170, 172, 175, 177, 178, 192, 195, 197, 205, 206, 209–12, 219
Star Wars (film) 28, 56, 85, 150, 173–75, 199
Steady State Universe 29
"Steel" (episode of *Twilight Zone*) 155, 156
"Strange Lodger" (episode of *Science Fiction Theater*) 160
string theory 9, 22, 111, 115, 116
"Stu and Stewies's Excellent Adventure" (episode of *Family Guy*) 127
"Submicroscopic" (short story by S.P. Meeks) 213
Suitor, Bill 96
"Sun Gold" (episode of *Science Fiction Theater*) 201
"The Sunmakers" (episode of *Doctor Who*) 70

Index

supernova 30, 39
"Survey Team" (short story by Phillip K. Dick) 53, 201

The Talisman (novel by Stephen King) 100
"A Taste of Armageddon" (episode of *Star Trek: The Original Series*) 148
Tau Zero (novel by Poul Anderson) 79, 85
Tegmark, Max 107, 118, 188
teleportation 1, 21, 139, 158–66, 173
"The Tenth Planet" (episode of *Doctor Who*) 105
Terminator (film) 125–26, 130, 157, 176
Terminator 2 (film) 126, 176
"Terror of the Vervoids" (episode of *Doctor Who*) 195
"Testament of Arkadia" (episode of *Space: 1999*) 201
"The Thaw" (episode of *Star Trek: Voyager*) 146
"There Were Giants in the Earth" (episode of *Lost in Space*) 215
thermodynamics 13–17
"This Side of Paradise" (episode of *Star Trek: The Original Series*) 177, 194
Thomson, George 19
Thomson, William 11
Thorne, Kip 86, 133–34
"The Three Doctors" (episode of *Doctor Who*) 39, 101, 108, 113
"Through the Looking Glass" (episode of *Farscape*) 100
Through the Looking Glass (novel by Lewis Caroll) 104
"Time Lock" (episode of *Voyage to the Bottom of the Sea*) 160
"Time of the Hawk" (episode of *Buck Rogers in the 25th Century*) 201
"A Time to Die" (Episode of *Voyage to the Bottom of the Sea*) 130
"Time Trap" (episode of *Star Trek: The Animated Series*) 108
time travel 1, 10, 15, 39, 42, 87, 99, 121–39, 216
The Time Traveler's Wife (novel by Audrey Niffenegger) 136
"Timelash"(episode of *UFO*) 139
Timescape (novel by Gregory Benford) 138
"Tin Man" (episode of *Star Trek: The Next Generation*) 199
Tipler, Frank 83
"Tomorrow Is Yesterday" (episode of *Star Trek: The Original Series*) 42, 127
Transcendance (film) 158
"Trial by Robot"(episode of *Fireball XL5*) 156
Tribulations (novel by Ken Shufeldt) 110
"Trip Through the Robot" (episode of *Lost in Space*) 215
tritium 16–17

"The Troubled Spirit" (episode of *Space: 1999*) 195
Tsiolkovsky, Konstantin 64, 93
"The Turnabout Intruder" (episode of *Star Trek: The Original Series*) 206
"Tuvix" (episode of *Star Trek: Voyager*) 162
"Twiki Is Missing" (episode of *Buck Rogers in the 25th Century*) 208
"Twisted" (episode of *Star Trek: Voyager*) 112
Twistor (novel by John Cramer) 99
2001: A Space Odyssey (film) 27, 147
"2066: Election Day" (short story of Michael Shaara) 147

UFO (television series) 27, 139, 200
"The Ultimate Computer" (episode of *Star Trek: The Original Series*) 71, 148, 149
"Uncle Simon"(episode of *Twilight Zone*) 157
"Unforgettable" (episode of *Star Trek: Voyager*) 80
"Uwlo of Ulm" (short story by S.P. Meeks) 213

vacuum energy 22
"Valerie 23" (episode of *Outer Limits*) 155
Van de Kamp, Peter 45
Vanilla Sky (film) 147
"Vaster Than Empires and More Slow" (short story by Ursala LeGuin) 193
"Violations" (episode of *Star Trek: The Next Generation*) 206
"Visit to a Hostile Planet" (episode of *Lost in Space*) 128
"A Visit to Hades"(episode of *Lost in Space*) 154
von Braun, Werner 65, 93
Voyage to Alpha Centuari (novel by Michael O'Brien) 183
Voyage to the Bottom of the Sea (television series) 173

"War Games" (episode of *Space: 1999*) 56, 91
War Games (film) 148
War of the Worlds (novel by H.G. Wells) 69, 171
Warwick, Kevin 157
"The Way to Eden" (episode of *Star Trek: The Original Series*) 176, 211
"Weeds" (short story by Stephen King) 202
Weinberg, Steven 116
"Welcome Stranger" (episode of *Lost in Space*) 27, 40
"We'll Always Have Paris" (episode of *Star Trek: The Next Generation*) 41
"What Are Little Girls Made Of?" (episode of *Star Trek: The Original Series*) 157
"Where No Man Has Gone Before" (episode of *Star Trek: The Original Series*) 204, 209
"Who Mourns for Adonais?" (episode of *Star Trek: The Original Series*) 216

"Whom Gods Destroy" (episode of *Star Trek: The Original Series*) 169, 211
"Wild Adventure" (episode of *Lost in Space*) 28
Wyndham, John 154, 194

Yang, C.N. 105
"Yesteryear" (episode of *Star Trek: The Animated Series*) 127
"Y.O.R.D." (episode of *The Outer Limits*) 189

"Zanti Misfits" (episode of *The Outer Limits*) 190
Zelazny, Roger 156
Zollner, Johann 111
Zubrin, Robert 50, 70
Zukerman, Ben 76
Zwicky, Fritz 33

www.ingramcontent.com/pod-product-compliance
Ingram Content Group UK Ltd.
Pitfield, Milton Keynes, MK11 3LW, UK
UKHW041942140426
5217IPUK00014B/619